REAGAN'S VICTORY

American Presidential Elections

MICHAEL NELSON

JOHN M. MCCARDELL, JR.

REAGAN'S VICTORY

THE PRESIDENTIAL
ELECTION OF 1980
AND THE RISE OF THE
RIGHT
ANDREW E. BUSCH

UNIVERSITY PRESS OF KANSAS

Published
by the
University
Press of Kansas
(Lawrence,
Kansas 66049),
which was
organized by the
Kansas Board of
Regents and is
operated and
funded by
Emporia State
University,
Fort Hays State
University,
Kansas State
University,
Pittsburg State
University,
the University
of Kansas, and
Wichita State
University

Photographs on pages 7, 38, 63, 109, 118,
and 123 courtesy of Jimmy Carter Library;
on pages 51, 85, 110, 152, and 171 courtesy of
Ronald Reagan Library;
on page 42 courtesy of
Abraham Lincoln Presidential Library

© 2005 by the University Press of Kansas
All rights reserved

Library of Congress Cataloging-in-Publication Data
    Busch, Andrew.
    Reagan's victory : the presidential election of 1980 and the
rise of the right / Andrew E. Busch.
        p.   cm. — (American presidential elections series)
    Includes bibliographical references and index.
    ISBN 0-7006-1407-9 (cloth : alk. paper) —
ISBN 0-7006-1408-7 (pbk. : alk. paper) I. Presidents—
United States—Election—1980. 2. United States—Politics and
government—1977–1981. 3. Reagan, Ronald. 4. Conservatism—
United States—History—20th century. I. Title. II. Series.
    JK5261980 .B87 2005
    324.973 926—dc22   2005020859

British Library Cataloguing-in-Publication Data is available.

Printed in the United States of America

10 9 8 7 6 5 4 3 2 1

The paper used in this publication meets the minimum
requirements of the American National Standard for
Permanence of Paper for Printed Library Materials z39.48-1984.

CONTENTS

Every election is different, but some are less different than others. Obvious differences separate the 1980 election, which brought a conservative Republican, Ronald Reagan, to the White House for the first of his two terms as president, from the elections won by Woodrow Wilson in 1912, Franklin D. Roosevelt in 1932, and Lyndon B. Johnson in 1964—liberals and Democrats all. But the similarities between what happened in 1980 and in these other landmark elections are no less strong. In each case, the winning candidate promised the voters dramatic changes in public policy rather than basic continuity. None did so with greater specificity than Reagan, who pledged to seek deep reductions in federal taxes, an easing of federal regulation of business, and steep increases in defense spending to fund a more assertive posture against the nation's Cold War rival, the Soviet Union.

In addition, the winners of all four elections achieved a substantial popular vote plurality and an electoral college landslide. (Reagan's 489–49 electoral vote victory over Jimmy Carter broke FDR's 1932 record for the most massive defeat of an incumbent president in history.) And each victor's landslide was accompanied by dramatic gains for his party in the accompanying congressional elections, sending the message to Republican and Democratic members alike that the new president's change-oriented, landslide victory was more than merely personal. In 1980, Republicans gained thirty-three new seats in the House of Representatives and twelve in the Senate, enabling the GOP to take control of the upper house for the first time in a quarter century.

What makes the 1980 election's resemblance to the elections of 1912, 1932, and 1964 significant as well as strong is what happened after the new president and Congress took office: a dramatic burst of president-inspired legislative activity that altered the role of the federal govern-ment in American society. Following Reagan, as it had followed Wilson, Roosevelt, and Johnson, Congress quickly enacted his ambitious agenda of fiscal, defense, and deregulatory policies.

Andrew Busch is renowned among election scholars for the books he has coauthored every four years since 1992 in the immediate aftermath of each recent presidential election. In this book, he seizes the advantages of hindsight and the perspective it affords, fulfilling the aim of the American Presidential Elections series to reveal how important presidential elections illuminate the history of their times. With narrative drive and analytical depth, Busch chronicles the election of 1980: the candidates (both Reagan and Carter had to fight for their party's nomination, then contend not only with each other but also with a significant independent candidate, John Anderson), the fall campaign (closely fought until the end), and the surprisingly one-sided results. He extends the story and the analysis beyond the presidential contest, treating fully the congressional and state elections that accompanied it. More than that, Busch sets the election in history, limning both the context in which it occurred and the consequences it brought for politics and public policy. Readers of *Reagan's Victory: The Presidential Election of 1980 and the Rise of the Right* can count on learning what occurred in 1980, how it happened, and why it matters.

Michael Nelson
John M. McCardell, Jr.

AUTHOR'S PREFACE

Every book has a story. In one sense, the story of this book started at a conference in Grand Rapids, Michigan, on the George W. Bush presidency. By chance, Michael Nelson and I were both participants, and during our free time we meandered into a discussion about the planned University Press of Kansas series on key presidential elections that he was coediting. He invited me to submit a proposal for a book on the 1980 presidential election, in which Ronald Reagan defeated incumbent Jimmy Carter.

In another sense, this book can be traced back to 1980 itself. That election was the first in which I took an active and sustained interest, and I vividly recall the sense at the time that it would be an election of great importance for the country. The 1979 summer of discontent, the Iranian hostage crisis, the Soviet invasion of Afghanistan, President Carter's 1980 State of the Union pronouncement that the United States was facing the gravest threat to world peace since World War II, and the moment in early 1980 when the annual inflation rate hit 18 percent came at a time when I was coming of age, and the memories remain fresh. Twenty-five years later, the 1980 election still reverberates for me in a variety of ways, as it does for the nation.

Consequently, it was a treat for me to be able to delve more deeply into the events and personalities of that election season with all the same fascination but aided by the cooler eye of distance. It was also a treat to learn many new things about events that I thought I knew well.

This book will address questions that dominate any attempt to provide a comprehensive examination of any presidential election: What was the setting of the election and what kind of world did Americans see when they looked outside the country? Who was drawn to pursue the White House, what kind of people were they, and what did they stand for? How did the parties choose their standard-bearers, and why did they choose the ones they did? How did the nation choose between the candidates? What strategies did the candidates pursue, and how much of the election's result can be explained by the circumstances of the time as opposed to the qualities and efforts of the candidates? How closely connected were the presidential and congressional campaigns and election results? And, in the end, what difference did it all make? Why should anyone care about the election of 1980?

It is my hope that this book makes some contribution toward answering those questions. If it does, the credit must be widely shared.

This book was made possible by the Social Philosophy and Policy Center at Bowling Green State University, directed by Fred Miller and Jeffrey and Ellen Paul. The Center provided me with a research fellowship in the summer of 2004, which I used to write this book. The fellowship included provision by the Center of pleasant office facilities, excellent administrative help, and the aid of a research assistant, Jonathan Miller, who was extraordinarily helpful and efficient and made my job doable. I am greatly indebted to Jonathan. I also must thank my wife, Mindy, who was willing to embark on the adventure of relocating with three small children to Bowling Green for the summer. Being the technologically proficient one of us, Mindy also created the election results tables in the appendixes for me.

A handful of key participants in the campaign of 1980 generously contributed their time in interviews designed to fill gaps in the written record. They included Richard Wirthlin, Lyn Nofziger, Gerald Carmen, and my colleague Fred Balitzer, who helped arrange the interviews.

The Jimmy Carter Presidential Library, the Ronald Reagan Presidential Library, and the Illinois State Historical Society provided invaluable assistance in procuring the photographs that are included in the book. The Gould Center for Humanistic Studies at Claremont McKenna College generously provided the funds necessary for professional indexing. Not least, I am deeply grateful to Mike Nelson and John McCardell for their detailed and helpful suggestions and to Fred Woodward and the staff at the University Press of Kansas for their professionalism. I owe particular thanks to Susan McRory, Susan Schott, and my tireless copyeditor, Kathy Delfosse.

Finally, I would like to dedicate this work to the newest member of the Busch family, Elizabeth Katerina, for whom 1980 has special importance.

January 2005

When President Jimmy Carter appeared at 9:52 P.M. eastern standard time on November 4, 1980, to concede his defeat for reelection, it was clear that something big was happening. What had seemed like a close race a week before had turned into a rout. Ronald Reagan won a 10 percentage point margin in the nationally aggregated popular vote. More to the point, Reagan won a much broader victory than expected, prevailing in forty-four states and winning 489 electoral votes. The Jimmy Carter–Walter Mondale ticket won the candidates' native Georgia and Minnesota, four other states, and the District of Columbia. The key regional battlegrounds (the South and the big industrial states) and pivotal demographic groups (blue-collar ethnics, Catholics, evangelicals) swung to Reagan.

At the same time, Republicans, under a national election theme of "Vote Republican—for a Change," gained twelve Senate seats and took control of the Senate for the first time in twenty-six years. Liberal stalwarts such as George McGovern of South Dakota, Birch Bayh of Indiana, Frank Church of Idaho, and John Culver of Iowa went down to conservative Republican challengers. In the House, Republicans gained thirty-three seats, enough to give them, in concert with conservative Democrats, a working majority on many issues. Reagan had the longest coattails of any presidential winner during the final third of the twentieth century.

Like Franklin D. Roosevelt in 1932, Reagan was elected in a time of national crisis. In his case, four interlocking national crises threatened the United States: an economic crisis of "stagflation," a foreign policy crisis symbolized by U.S. hostages in Iran and Soviet troops in Afghanistan, a crisis of public confidence, and a quietly simmering social crisis as shown in the drastic deterioration between 1960 and 1980 in numerous social indices, including crime, drug usage, and family breakdown.

After the election, many commentators declared that an electoral "revolution" had taken place, and some Republicans were quick to claim a mandate for conservative policy change. Skeptics pointed out that despite his electoral landslide Reagan had received only 51 percent of the popular vote (in a three-way race) and argued that the results should be interpreted as a simple rejection of Carter rather than a full-scale embrace of Reaganism. What could be said with certainty was that voters were willing to give Reagan and conservatism a chance and that he—like Roosevelt—had an unusual opportunity to change the face of U.S. politics. However his win was interpreted, there was no question that Reagan's victory represented a dramatic breakthrough for conservatism, which had been gaining in strength for a generation.

Reagan took advantage of his opportunity to enact controversial and far-reaching policies in the areas of taxes, domestic spending, national security, constitutional doctrine, and social life; these policies substantially changed the direction of the nation for the first time since the onset of the New Deal. In the process, Reagan promoted a new public philosophy, cemented a strong, long-term Republican coalition, and established the boundaries of political debate and action for at least the next quarter century. Reagan's 1980 victory was the first of three consecutive GOP presidential wins and set in motion the Republican capture of Congress in 1994. By the end of the 1980s, the nation had confronted and largely resolved or mitigated the crises that had helped elect Reagan. Altogether, the election of 1980 transformed U.S. politics and must be considered one of the key U.S. elections of the twentieth century.

This book tells the story of that election. The first chapter sets the stage, looking at the world at the moment President Carter delivered his "crisis of confidence" speech on July 15, 1979. Chapter 2 introduces the serious candidates, three Democrats and seven Republicans, seeking the presidency of the United States. Chapters 3 and 4 follow the presidential race as it developed, first in the primaries and then in the general election, and assess how and why these elections turned out the way they did. The congressional and state elections—perhaps nearly as important in 1980 as the presidential contest—are the focus of chapter 5. The final chapter asks what difference the elections of 1980 made. The story of this election is a compelling one, full of colorful characters, unexpected plot twists, and dramatic finales, from the February snows of New Hampshire's primary to Reagan's victory speech at the Century Plaza Hotel in Los Angeles on November 4.

It is not unreasonable to ask what more can be said about an event that was so thoroughly dissected at the time. But there are things we know now about the election of 1980 that we did not know at the time, starting with the fact that Vice President Mondale seriously considered removing himself from the Democratic ticket because of Carter's failing prospects. There are also things that we thought we knew but that were not really true, parts of the thumbnail "standard account" of 1980 that do not quite get it right. The most critical moment in Reagan's New Hampshire primary comeback was the first Republican candidates' debate, held in Manchester, not the second debate in Nashua, where he famously exclaimed, "I paid for this microphone." And, not least, it is possible with a quarter century of hindsight to see some things more clearly—such as the institutional implications of the election and its long-term effect on policy and party coalitions. Only with time has it become clear that the 1980 party conventions would be the last conventions for many years offering any significant drama. The ongoing relevance of the 1980 election was demonstrated again in 2004, when a raft of analysts tried to advance or refute an analogy between the two years. Was George W. Bush going to be another Jimmy Carter, or not?

Accounts of history often have a seductively inevitable quality to them, as if things could have happened only the way they did. The 1980 elections are particularly susceptible to such an interpretation, since the final results were exactly what one might have expected given the state of the nation at the beginning of our story. Yet the temptation to see the result as inevitable should be resisted. For 1980 was as much a year of drastic contingencies and powerful personalities as it was one of bad underlying conditions. One can only read its story in the same way that one lives through the events that shape a nation: each page as it comes, each day at a time.

1

CRISIS OF CONFIDENCE

It was July 15, 1979, and America seemed to be unraveling.

As the presidential election of 1980 approached, the nation was caught in a maelstrom of economic, social, and foreign woes that presaged not only a difficult re-election campaign for incumbent president Jimmy Carter but the potential for a broader break with the past. After sequestering himself at Camp David for ten days of contemplation, soul-searching, and meetings with hundreds of intellectuals, political leaders, and ordinary citizens, Carter returned to Washington and addressed the country in a prime-time speech in which he declared that Americans were suffering from a "crisis of confidence":

> It is a crisis that strikes at the very heart and soul and spirit of our national will. We can see this crisis in the growing doubt about the meaning of our own lives and in the loss of a unity of purpose for our nation. The erosion of confidence in the future is threatening to destroy the social and political fabric of America. . . . We've always had a faith that the days of our children would be better than our own. Our people are losing that faith.

The speech was soon dubbed the "malaise" speech by the media, although Carter never used the word "malaise." The source of the crisis was a matter of dispute. Carter implied that the American people themselves had failed. Others, in both parties, soon took up the argument that it was America's president who had failed. Carter's own advisers had been sharply divided about whether he should give the speech. Regardless, the crisis Carter described was rooted in a number of solid realities, including economic decline, foreign policy retreat, and social deterioration.

At the same time, the political ground was shifting under the president's feet. The Democratic coalition that had dominated U.S. politics since the New Deal was waning, and a conservative movement long dismissed by its detractors as hopelessly anachronistic was surging. Carter had run a winning campaign against Washington in 1976, but no one knew how long the day of the outsider would last. And the midterm elections of 1978 had altered the landscape, removing five notable liberal senators and driving congressional politics to the right.

The most tangible facet of the crisis of 1979 was the deteriorating state of the economy. In the mid-1960s, the U.S. economy had been a model of job creation, increasing wages, and low inflation (1.3 percent in 1964). As the costs of the Great Society and the Vietnam War escalated, costs paid in both taxes and deficits, inflation began to climb. The Dow Jones Industrial Average peaked in 1973 at around 1,050 and did not regain that level for the rest of the decade. The good times were over.

The nation slipped into a recession in late 1969 and 1970, and by 1970 inflation had reached 5.7 percent. In August 1971 President Richard Nixon imposed federal wage and price controls in an effort to stem the tide of rising prices. He also devalued the dollar to relieve international pressure on the U.S. currency.

Due to the distorting effects of price controls, which remained on oil even after they were ended on most goods, Americans experienced gasoline shortages in the summers of 1972 and 1973. In the fall of 1973 the energy situation took a dramatic turn for the worse. When the United States staved off the impending defeat of Israel by Egypt and Syria with an emergency airlift of supplies to Israel during the Yom Kippur War in October, the Arab oil-producing states retaliated by cutting off oil supplies to the United States. The price of oil rose almost overnight from three dollars a barrel to twelve dollars a barrel. This economic shock was followed by more shortages, a leap in inflation to 11 percent in 1974, and another, deeper recession, with unemployment averaging 8.5 percent in 1975. Although the economy had been experiencing difficulties since the late 1960s, 1973 was the point at which almost all key economic indicators, including productivity, the basis for future prosperity, headed

President Jimmy Carter delivering his July 15, 1979, address to the nation from the Oval Office. The speech was quickly dubbed the "malaise" speech by the media.

downward for the rest of the decade. The poverty rate reached a historic low in 1973 at 11.1 percent, then began climbing again.

The nation was consumed for the better part of the 1970s with two intertwined economic crises: the crisis of economic performance and the energy crisis that contributed to it. Soon after taking office, Carter made energy policy the first order of business, declaring "the moral equivalent of war" and pushing Congress to create the cabinet-level Department of Energy in 1977. Administration officials and many outside analysts predicted that energy shortages would grow and that steadily increasing prices would reverberate throughout the economy. In 1979, with another oil shortage driven by the victorious Iranian revolution in February and by a 24 percent price increase by the Organization of Petroleum Exporting Countries (OPEC) in June, inflation reached 11.3 percent. A wildcat strike by truckers protesting higher fuel costs turned violent as strikers blocked highways, shot at or stoned truckers who defied the stoppage, and kept food from reaching stores. Interest rates were climbing in order to protect lenders from anticipated future inflation. The United States was approaching yet another recession.

The statistics show only part of the economic shocks jolting the country. One after another, American icons fell on hard times. In 1975 New York City was verging on bankruptcy. By 1979 so was the Chrysler Motor Company, a warning of the gathering failures of the American automotive industry, one of the linchpins of the U.S. economy. The choices faced by U.S. policymakers—to let the giants fall or to approve costly bailouts—were miles removed from the economic choices of the sunny 1960s, when it had seemed that all government had to do was decide how to distribute an ever-increasing pie.

Throughout this period, from 1960 to 1980, the federal government continued expanding in size and scope, owing to the ethos of the New Deal and the momentum of the Great Society. Decades earlier, Franklin Roosevelt had launched a radical reconception of the role of government. His new public philosophy advocated federal action in realms long thought to be the province of state and local authorities or of private civil society. Moreover, the traditional American conception of rights had emphasized natural rights—rights such as life, liberty, and property naturally enjoyed even before the formation of government—and consequently the protection of individuals against the abuses of government. Roosevelt offered a new framework emphasizing positive economic rights. In his 1932 Commonwealth Club Address in San Francisco, Roosevelt argued that the natural rights of the Declaration of Independence found a counterpart in the new rights to secure savings and to make a comfortable living. By 1944 Roosevelt was calling in his State of the Union Address for an "Economic Bill of Rights" including a "right" to a job, housing, health care, a good education, and security from the "economic fears of old age, sickness, accident, and unemployment."

Roosevelt's use of traditional rights language and the traditional rights framework disguised the degree to which the new conception of rights might undercut the older notion. Not least, whereas the older notion required limited government and placed a high priority on property rights, the newer notion permitted a theoretically unlimited government and required a highly activist and redistributionist one.

With Roosevelt's new public philosophy as a foundation and the New Deal programs as an example, President Lyndon B. Johnson launched the next wave of federal expansion with his Great Society programs of the 1960s. Although the Great Society included new regulatory forays and broad new entitlements, such as Medicare, it featured a "War on Poverty" consisting of Medicaid, liberalized welfare, and literally dozens of smaller antipoverty programs. Johnson's successor, President Richard Nixon, demanded something of a retrenchment, calling for a more decentralized "New Federalism" and less welfare. However, in many respects, Nixon's policies are best understood as a continuation of the Great Society era, not a break with it. Along with federally imposed wage and price controls, Nixon created such major regulatory agencies as the Environmental Protection Agency (EPA) and Occupational Safety and Health Administration (OSHA), oversaw a 20 percent increase in Social Security benefits, and proposed a guaranteed-income plan and national health insurance.

Consequently, between 1960 and 1980 federal spending increased from $92 billion to $591 billion and federal revenues jumped from $92 billion to $517 billion. Even adjusted for inflation, spending essentially doubled. This growth was the result of increased domestic spending. Whereas defense spending had accounted for close to 50 percent of all federal spending in 1960, it had dropped to less than a quarter of all federal spending twenty years later. Average annual deficits rose in real terms in every administration. The annual deficits during the administrations of John F. Kennedy and Lyndon Johnson were 139 percent higher than those of Dwight D. Eisenhower's administration. Average deficits during the administrations of Richard Nixon and Gerald Ford were 111 percent higher than the Kennedy-Johnson deficits, and Jimmy Carter's were 57 percent higher than the Nixon-Ford deficits. In real terms, annual average deficits in the Carter years were eight times higher than under Eisenhower. Pages in the *Federal Register*, a rough indicator of regulatory activity, increased from 16,850 in 1966 to 87,012 in 1980.

Furthermore, in 1979 the top federal income tax rate was 70 percent, and the fourteen tax brackets were not indexed to inflation. This meant that working families were being increasingly pushed into higher tax brackets because of raises that might not even have kept up with inflation. A family making $25,000 in 1978 would have seen the tax rate on its last dollar of income increase from 19 percent in 1965 to 28 percent in 1978 if its income had exactly kept pace with inflation. For individuals caught in this squeeze—and there were millions—the federal government was increasingly unpopular.

In other respects, economists and politicians debated whether the explosion of federal taxing, spending, and regulating since 1960 had contributed to the economic meltdown or merely coincided with it. By 1979, however, it could hardly be disputed that the economy was in serious trouble and that, at the very least, the liberal economic regime had failed to either prevent or resolve that trouble. Indeed, the economic experience of the 1970s threw the dominant economic paradigm of the time into disarray.

That paradigm was Keynesianism, the economic theory that government should manipulate aggregate demand through tax and spending policies in order to speed up the economy (in recession or depression) or slow it down (during times of inflation). A Keynesian corollary, the Phillips Curve, held that there was a mathematical tradeoff between inflation and unemployment: When one went down, the other would go up. The economy of the 1970s refuted this notion, as unemployment and inflation rose in tandem. "Stagflation," the term coined to name this situation of a stagnant inflationary economy, thus called into question the validity or relevance of Keynesianism itself.

Many voices held that America's economic heyday was past and that the nation would have to learn to live with a future of little or no economic growth. Carter himself subscribed to a version of this view, holding that "limits to growth" would be a central feature of American life. The economic crisis was so severe and so disorienting that many observers across the political spectrum even questioned whether the free-market economic system would survive. The July 12, 1975, cover of the *Saturday Review* asked, "Can Capitalism Survive Another 30 Years?" Gurney Breckenfeld was pessimistic: "The way we are moving now, the private-enterprise system as we know it could well disappear in another 30 years. The problems are accumulating faster than the existing political-economic system can cope with them."[1] These sentiments were echoed by Alan Greenspan, then the chair of President Ford's Council of Economic Advisers; Greenspan told a congressional committee that the nation was rapidly approaching a "decision point" about whether a free-market economy would endure.

Time magazine likewise featured a July 15, 1975, cover story entitled "Capitalism: Can It Survive?" The answer: Probably. Robert Heilbroner, liberal economist and Nobel Prize winner, asked the same question in a *New York Times Magazine* article of August 5, 1982. His answer was that capitalism might survive, but only through a radical restructuring that would leave the public sector in control of 40–50 percent of the national economy accompanied by much greater national economic planning; permanent government controls of wages, prices, and dividends; and massive government investment in private industry.[2]

Economic pessimism could also be seen in widespread skepticism that technological innovation could provide a solution for economic woes, a skepticism unprecedented for Americans. The near-catastrophic breakdown of sophisticated technology in an accident at the Three Mile Island nuclear power plant in Pennsylvania in March 1979 reinforced this view. More generally, apocalyptic visions became commonplace, including fears of a "population bomb" (Paul Ehrlich's phrase for an explosion in population that would lead to a Malthusian future of food and natural resource shortages) and of environmental catastrophe (including, according to the theory of the moment, global freezing).

If spreading economic disaster was the most tangible cause of the "crisis of confidence," the position of the United States in the world was a close second. Ben Wattenberg, a conservative Democrat who headed the Coalition for a Democratic Majority, captured that state in a July 1979 *New York Times Magazine* article entitled "It's Time to Stop America's Retreat." After the agony of war in Southeast Asia, the United States had sought respite from the world, starting with the congressional decision in 1974 and 1975 to end all further assistance to South Vietnam. In a five-year-long moment of neo-isolationism, the United States cut its defense budget substantially, imposed severe restrictions on the Central

Intelligence Agency (CIA), and sought "détente" with the Soviet Union. In the words of scholar John Lewis Gaddis, the policy of containment, pursued by presidents of both parties since 1947, had "reached a point of crisis, if not a dead end."[3]

However, U.S. disengagement from the Cold War was not reciprocated by the Soviet Union. Between January 1, 1975, and August 1, 1979, Soviet advances began with Communist victories in South Vietnam, Cambodia, and Laos after Congress cut off aid to U.S. allies there. The former Portuguese colonies of Angola and Mozambique fell next, after Congress cut off aid to pro-Western fighters in Angola. Some 5,000 Cuban troops intervened in that country's civil war, while Cuban arms and advisers helped consolidate Communist control of Mozambique. In Ethiopia, Cuban troops and Soviet advisers intervened to aid the new government of Col. Haile Mengistu Mariam. South Yemen fell, lodged nearly 1,000 Cuban troops and advisers, and attacked North Yemen. Both Ethiopia and South Yemen gave the Soviets access to strategically vital ports and airfields with which to threaten the Persian Gulf and Indian Ocean. In Afghanistan, an April 1978 coup brought to power the Afghan communist party, promptly provoking resistance by anticommunist Afghans. By mid-1979, there were 5,000 Soviet advisers in the country.

Closer to home, Communists seized power in Grenada, a small island in the eastern Caribbean, which soon hosted hundreds of Cuban troops as well as Soviet, East German, and Bulgarian advisers. In July 1979 the Sandinista National Liberation Front (FSLN) took control of Nicaragua, whose dictator Anastasio Somoza fled. Within months, the Sandinistas were shipping arms to Communist rebels in El Salvador. Numerous other countries, such as Suriname, imported Soviet or Cuban advisers and weapons, tilting toward Moscow even when not in its orbit. Throughout this period, the specter of "Eurocommunism" hung over NATO, and Portugal almost tumbled into the Communist bloc in 1975.

In sum, in a period of less than five years, the Soviet empire had expanded by ten countries in Southwest Asia, Southeast Asia, Africa, and the Caribbean basin—all without significant interference from the United States.

Undergirding this imperial record was a substantial Soviet offensive arms buildup. From 1976 to 1980, while U.S. and allied military spending was stagnating, the Soviets built an estimated 13,500 tanks, 6,300 fighter planes, 900 submarine-launched ballistic missiles, and 1,200 land-based intercontinental ballistic missiles (ICBMs), including the first-strike-capable SS-18 and SS-19 heavy ICBMs. In 1977 they also started deploying, at the rate of one a week, triple-warhead SS-20 missiles aimed at western Europe in an attempt to tilt the strategic balance on the continent. From 1970 to 1980, when the United States was cutting military manpower by 1.4 million, the Soviets were adding 400,000 to their armed forces. As far as U.S. intelligence could determine, Soviet military spending had surpassed that of the United States in 1971, and by 1979 was 70 percent greater than that of the United States.[4] American hopes that arms control would restrain the Soviet buildup proved unfounded.

Altogether, by the end of the 1970s, despite a few setbacks (as in Egypt, where Anwar Sadat threw out Soviet advisers), the Soviets had good reason to believe—and stated with increasing confidence—that "the correlation of forces had shifted in their favor."[5] Americans faced for the first time the very real prospect of losing the Cold War. Glimpsing the abyss, Wattenberg mused, "So far, our Western freedoms have represented a mere blip in history. There is no guarantee that they will survive in any event, but the odds go down if we predicate that our children will live in a world where the Soviet Union is the most powerful military force on earth, and if we and our Western friends are perceived internationally as either 'in retreat' or impotent."[6]

In addition, the U.S. position in Iran collapsed. The shah had been a crucial U.S. ally in the Middle East. When the Iranian revolution swept the Ayatollah Ruhollah Khomeini into authority in February 1979, some Carter administration figures held out hope that the revolutionaries would prove to be more moderate than their rhetoric indicated. Andrew Young, the U.S. ambassador to the United Nations, said that Khomeini would eventually be seen as "some kind of saint." Critics charged that Carter's human rights policy had led him to undermine the shah after having earlier embraced him. At any rate, Carter clearly failed to back him at critical moments, and many held Carter at least partially responsible for Khomeini's ascendancy. Sanguine early hopes were dashed. In early February radical Iranian students attacked and briefly occupied the U.S. embassy in Teheran, giving Americans a foretaste of a later embassy takeover that would mark itself indelibly on the American memory and have a profound effect on the election of 1980.

In retrospect, the Iranian revolution can be seen as the opening phase of the long war of radical Islam against the West in general and the United States in particular. None of this was clear at the time, however.

What was profoundly clear was that the United States had lost another important ally in an important part of the world. In Iran as in Nicaragua, Grenada, Afghanistan, Ethiopia, Angola, and Indochina, "America's Retreat" was a relentless strategic reality.

Although economic and foreign policy developments drew the headlines, there were other silent crises developing through the 1970s that contributed to the "crisis of the spirit" decried by Carter in July 1979. American society had undergone a dramatic transformation since the mid-1960s. Many of the changes wrought in that era were widely acclaimed, including the expansion of civil rights for racial minorities. Other changes were much more problematic. Most notably, a radical shift in social mores had worked in tandem with legal changes to produce a variety of social problems. This trend broadened in the 1970s, as the hedonism and narcissism that had characterized the counterculture of the 1960s became mainstream. As David Frum argued in his study of the 1970s, *How We Got Here,* the decade "blew to smithereens an entire structure of sexual morality."[7]

From 1960 to 1980, a lessening of social stigmas associated with divorce and illegitimacy combined with no-fault divorce laws and more generous welfare payments to double divorce rates, triple illegitimacy rates, and massively increase the number of children raised in single-parent households. Greater social permissiveness and lax law enforcement led to a near tripling of violent crime rates. The burgeoning drug culture of the 1960s produced a significant increase in the use of illicit drugs. Even SAT scores declined. Virtually all observers considered these quantifiable declines in social well-being a crisis. A large proportion of Americans also saw a greater incidence of cohabitation, acceptance of open homosexuality, and abortion on demand (as mandated by the Supreme Court in 1973) as emblematic of a broader breakdown of the moral and familial bases of society. Out of such concerns was forged a movement of social and religious conservatives. Like economic woes, social problems were also symbolic of a broader national slide. Things were simply worse wherever one looked.

Consequently, in the political realm, Carter was right: Americans faced a deep crisis of confidence. The war in Vietnam, the failures of the War on Poverty, and the Watergate scandal severely damaged Americans' confidence in their government. Asked how often government could be trusted to "do the right thing," the percentage of voters answering "always" or "most of the time" fell from 78 percent in 1964 to 26 percent in 1980. Likewise, in 1964, only 47 percent had agreed that "people in government waste a lot of money that we pay in taxes." By 1980, 78 percent thought so. The succession of Lyndon Johnson, who chose not to run for reelection in 1968 because of his unpopularity; Richard Nixon, who was forced to resign; and Gerald Ford, who lost his one bid for election in 1976, caused many Americans to wonder if the job of presidency was too much for any one person. By 1979 those fears had been heightened by Carter's performance. Overall, surveys showed that the number of Americans expressing pessimism about the long-term future of the United States—a number that had not much exceeded 30 percent during the worst days of Watergate—stood at 48 percent in the summer of 1979.

Representing, and undoubtedly contributing to, the overall sense of disorientation was the fact that the New Deal public philosophy (and its numerous 1960s accretions) was coming apart at the seams. The dominant paradigm had finally been overcome by anomalies that it could not answer. Why was the Phillips Curve defunct? Why did a demilitarized foreign policy not achieve matching concessions from the Soviets? Why did social permissiveness not bring greater social happiness? Political figures, including Carter himself, grappled with the anomalies, to little avail. Political scientist Samuel Beer declared in a 1978 essay that Americans faced a political "equilibrium without purpose. . . . We do not enjoy a public philosophy."[8]

The New Deal electoral coalition was in an advanced stage of decay as well. That coalition had consisted of numerous disparate elements, forged together by Franklin Roosevelt around the central theme of using federal power to adjust economic conditions in favor of the lower and middle classes. Its key pillars included

- Working-class voters, to whom FDR appealed by promoting unionization and social benefits such as Social Security retirement and unemployment insurance. Many of these workers were urban Catholics.
- White southerners, who retained their long-standing loyalty to the Democratic Party. The rural South also appreciated federal farm programs and electrification projects, as did rural voters everywhere.
- Blacks, who were given access to New Deal public works jobs.

- Intellectuals, who celebrated their newfound policy influence (as seen in Roosevelt's Brains Trust) and, not incidentally, found their collectivist urges satisfied in the New Deal program.

Altogether, the Roosevelt coalition linked blacks and whites, workers and intellectuals, unions and many small businessmen, North and South, urban communities and rural areas. That is to say, it was inherently unstable and in need of constant attention and fortification.

By 1979 many of the potential cleavages within the New Deal coalition had been realized. To some extent this was a natural consequence of the passage of time since the defining event of the coalition, the Great Depression. Many observers have argued that the realization of these cleavages was also a consequence of the success of the New Deal; former Speaker of the House Thomas P. "Tip" O'Neill claimed, "We changed America. Made middle-class America."[9] By 1980 Catholics were as likely as Protestants to be middle class. In addition, the transformation of the U.S. economy away from heavy industry meant that organized labor had declined from representing about two in five workers in 1950 to representing about one in five at the end of the 1970s.

However, the New Deal coalition ultimately collapsed because of the policy decisions of the national leadership of the Democratic Party and because of the tone adopted by many Democrats after 1968. For many analysts, the handling of the civil rights issue was foremost in this category: Starting with Harry S. Truman's desegregation of the military and insistence on a civil rights plank in the 1948 Democratic platform and culminating with Johnson's embrace of the Civil Rights Act of 1964 and Voting Rights Act of 1965, the national Democratic Party staked out a position supporting federal civil rights protections for blacks. Although morally correct, Democrats paid a heavy price for this position, alienating both southern whites and white ethnic blue-collar workers.

There is no small amount of truth to this interpretation. The issue of civil rights was a major cause of disaffection of southern and working-class whites from the Democratic Party. In 1948 South Carolina governor Strom Thurmond ran as a third-party candidate on a segregationist platform and carried four Deep South states to win thirty-nine electoral votes. Alabama governor George Wallace, who gained national fame by standing in a schoolhouse door refusing access to black children, ran well in three northern Democratic primaries in 1964; when he, like Thurmond before him, ran a third-party campaign in 1968, he garnered 13 percent of the vote. Running against Johnson, Barry Goldwater, who had voted against the Civil Rights Act of 1964 on constitutional grounds, won five Deep South states for the Republicans for the first time since Reconstruction.

However, the full story is much more complicated. Although the Deep South did not vote Republican until Goldwater's campaign in 1964, much of the peripheral South had voted for Eisenhower in the 1950s (at a time when Republicans were still widely perceived as being more activist on civil rights). Six of the "outer South" states—Florida, North Carolina, Oklahoma, Tennessee, Texas, and Virginia—had voted Republican as early as 1928, when Herbert Hoover ran against the urban, Roman Catholic, and anti-Prohibition Democrat Al Smith. As a whole, southern whites may have become unmoored from the Democratic Party as a result of civil rights, but they did not shift decisively toward the Republican Party at the presidential level until the Reagan years and at the state and congressional level until the 1990s, long after the issue of basic civil rights was settled.

One must also distinguish between the catalytic effects of efforts to obtain protections for fundamental civil rights with subsequent embellishments like forced busing and racial preferences. These later policies also deeply offended southern and working-class whites, but they were peripheral to the central civil rights struggle and were of much more ambiguous moral standing. Thus, though the conventional narrative of civil rights as the primary solvent of the Democratic coalition has wide appeal due to its simplicity, there is much more to the story.

First, it is clear that Lyndon Johnson inadvertently squandered the coalition he inherited by not attending to it properly. Johnson's tilt toward the relief of urban distress and poverty alienated both the rural and the middle-class and working-class components of the original New Deal coalition. Roosevelt's grand regional and socioeconomic compromise was undone in no small part because Johnson pursued policies that allowed important segments of the alliance to feel that other segments were reaping the lion's share of benefits at their expense. Roosevelt had aimed at expanding opportunity for the great majority of Americans. Influenced by John Kenneth Galbraith's 1958 book *The Affluent Society* and by Michael Harrington's *The Other America: Poverty in the United States,* Johnson (and Kennedy before him) emphasized sacrifice by the majority on behalf of the minority.

Adding to the relatively antimajoritarian cast of Great Society liberalism was the degree to which liberals now depended on the Supreme

Court to achieve their objectives. The New Deal was built upon the supremacy of the elected branches of government and the eventual willingness of the Court to submit to the enduring preferences of the majority. By the 1970s there could no longer be any doubt that a countermajoritarian federal judiciary was central to the advancement of the liberal agenda. From imposing school desegregation and forced busing to ending school prayer to expanding the rights of criminals to limiting the death penalty to relaxing the limits on abortion, the Supreme Court had accomplished for liberals what they could not accomplish at the ballot box. In the process, the Court introduced a whole range of highly controversial social issues pitting liberals against moral traditionalists. Because the New Deal Democratic coalition was built both on a majoritarian ethos and on an accommodation between liberals and traditionalists, this development was highly destructive.

Also destructive was the sharp veering of the Democratic Party to the left on foreign policy issues after 1968. The Vietnam War effectively ended the commitment of Democratic elites to the policy of containing communism, a policy that had been enunciated by President Truman in 1947. With the nomination of George McGovern as its presidential candidate in 1972, the Democratic Party became the party of the antiwar movement and all that it implied in terms of leftish worldview and counterculture lifestyle. Democrats who had heeded the call in President Kennedy's inaugural address to "pay any price, suffer any hardship, support any friend, oppose any foe to assure the survival and success of liberty" found themselves increasingly uncomfortable in their party. The reflexive anti-anticommunism of the new Democratic establishment appealed to the intellectuals who made up one component of the New Deal coalition, but it was not at all attractive to southerners or to blue-collar workers, many of whom boasted ancestry hailing from the Soviet-occupied countries of central and eastern Europe.

More generally, many Americans could not forgive the openly anti-American and pro–North Vietnamese hue of much of the antiwar agitation, exemplified by the photos of Jane Fonda in North Vietnam during her tour of the country in 1972, and they transferred their antipathy to the party that embraced (or was embraced by) the agitators. If Republicans became the party of patriotism in the 1970s and beyond, their good fortune was traceable to the takeover of the Democratic Party in 1972 by forces that had spent the previous half decade waving Viet Cong flags and chanting "Ho, Ho, Ho Chi Minh, the NLF is gonna win."

Finally, although the New Deal program demanded an activist federal government, Roosevelt's electoral coalition was not monolithic in its support for steadily expanding federal authority. To the contrary, Roosevelt grafted his coalition onto an older Democratic Party that was heavily Jeffersonian in its orientation. That is to say, a significant portion of the voters who gave Roosevelt four terms still retained some loyalty to the older Democratic faith of limited government, states' rights, and fiscal discipline. This portion of the coalition, heavily southern and rural, supported Roosevelt out of economic desperation, appreciation for his charismatic leadership, or simple residual party loyalty. Over time, however, it became clear that liberal Democrats meant to extend the thrust of the Roosevelt program to its logical conclusion. In the 1930s the New Deal philosophy in theory left an opening for a virtually unlimited government, but New Deal programs fell far short of that point. By the 1960s and 1970s reality had moved much closer to theory, and theory itself had become more grandiose. Johnson justified the Great Society not merely on the basis that it would alleviate dire material need but also on the basis that it would expand and satisfy the human soul—an otherworldly amendment that was simultaneously ennobling and dangerously utopian. As federal spending, taxing, regulation, and deficits ballooned, as states appeared to approach the status of mere administrative units of the federal government, those Jeffersonians still in the Democratic fold gradually lost any reason to remain. Ronald Reagan himself cited the Democratic Party's rejection of Jeffersonianism as the cause of his switch from self-proclaimed New Deal Democrat to Republican in 1962.

Civil rights alienated many white southerners and working-class voters, but so did the association of the Democratic Party with the liberalism of the courts, the hedonism of the counterculture, and the anti-anticommunism of the antiwar movement. The Great Society alienated the nonurban voters, the nonintellectuals, and the nonpoor, and the growth of government in general alienated both the Jeffersonians and small business, which chafed under higher tax and regulatory burdens. Race played a part in this alienation, but, as in 1928, when religion tilted the outer South to Hoover, cultural values were critical, as were the economic bills for the New Deal and the Great Society, which were finally coming due for the middle and working classes in the form of taxes and inflation. Through this lens, even George Wallace's 1968 third-party campaign for the presidency, which served as a way station for many voters leaving the Democratic Party, was more complex than was commonly understood. Although Wallace had initially become famous for his defense of segregation, his 1968 campaign accepted most of the then recent civil rights advances as a given. Instead, his campaign emphasized cultural values, law and order, federalism, judicial overreaching, and victory in Vietnam.

Democrats hoped that Carter's 1976 victory represented a restoration of their coalition. As a moderate southerner with religious roots, Carter was able to piece the coalition back together one more time, regaining many of the southern and blue-collar votes lost in Hubert Humphrey's narrow defeat by Richard Nixon in 1968 and in George McGovern's overwhelming loss to Nixon in 1972. However, Carter barely won victory in what, conditioned by Watergate, should have been a good year for Democrats. The tensions remained, as did the fundamental sources of the coalitional breakdown. The election of 1980 would test whether Carter's restoration was a long-term phenomenon or the last hurrah of a greatly weakened New Deal coalition.

It was not the decay of the New Deal coalition alone that made 1980 a moment of maximum danger for Carter and the Democrats. After all, one cannot beat something with nothing. Their danger was exacerbated by the rise of an organized alternative in the form of the conservative movement, which had been gaining strength for over two decades. The conservative movement, like all popular movements, can be understood as a broad response to conditions that a significant number of Americans found distressing, as a loose coalition of grassroots organizations, and as an intellectual direction given voice in concrete outlets.

The conditions leading to the formation and development of the conservative movement came in three waves. First, the New Deal's expansion of federal power and threat to constitutional limits raised concerns centered on economic and constitutional issues. Perhaps the earliest organizational response came in the form of the American Liberty League, a union of businessmen and Jeffersonian Democrats who sought a mandate against the New Deal in the midterm elections of 1934. Failing spectacularly, the League was soon defunct.

However, libertarian (or classical liberal) economic views remained an important part of the coalition and gained in strength and persuasiveness. Ludwig von Mises and Friedrich Hayek restated the case for the free market in the 1940s and 1950s. Milton Friedman took up the argument in the 1960s and 1970s, writing *Capitalism and Freedom* (1962) and arguing in *A Monetary History of the United States, 1867–1960* (1963) that the Great Depression was the result of government intervention gone awry rather than of laissez-faire economics, as the liberal narrative had long portrayed it. Friedman and fellow monetarists believed that inflation was a money-supply problem and that the market was otherwise largely self-regulating. In the 1970s, Jude Wanniski's book *The Way the World Works* inspired the supply-side economic movement. Supply-siders like Wanniski and Arthur Laffer held that the way out of stagflation was to create increased incentives for production by cutting marginal tax rates. Led by the supply-siders and the monetarists, the school of neoclassical economics was enjoying a significant comeback by 1979.

The second wave in the development of the conservative movement consisted of Cold War anticommunism and an intellectual movement in favor of social traditionalism. The latter took the form of concerns about the corrosive social character of liberal modernism and was represented during the 1940s and 1950s by thinkers like Russell Kirk and Richard Weaver. It was the Cold War, however, that proved essential to the conservative movement, attracting greater popular passion than could any economic or philosophical theory. Anticommunism appealed to forces ranging from conservative intellectuals to Catholic workers in ethnic enclaves to evangelical Christians. Senator Joseph McCarthy was the most notorious symbol of this tendency, but anticommunism itself was squarely in the American mainstream, and with good cause: To most Americans, communism was politically, economically, and theologically toxic, opposed to the best and most important traditions of their country. The Cold War thus gave conservatism a new appeal to the working class and to religious believers and allowed conservatives to grasp the nettle of American nationalism.

Conservatives later declared this element to have been the glue that held the movement together. As a result, the movement itself began to take both organizational and intellectual form in the 1950s and early 1960s. Intellectually, a key moment was the 1955 founding by William F. Buckley of the *National Review,* a biweekly journal of opinion that both expounded the conservative viewpoint and served as a clearinghouse for different branches of conservatism to communicate with each other. At the grassroots level, Young Americans for Freedom was formed in 1960; it claimed 55,000 members in 1980.

As important, a grassroots organization was activated to draft conservative Arizona senator Barry Goldwater for the 1964 Republican presidential nomination. The "draft Goldwater" effort mobilized tens of thousands of conservative activists who proceeded to take over the traditional Republican Party apparatus in a host of states in the North, Midwest, and West. In many parts of the South, the "draft Goldwater" forces literally created a viable Republican Party where none had existed before. As the draft movement proceeded, Goldwater began to enjoy the prospect of a race against Kennedy, which national newsmagazines declared could be "breathtakingly close." When Goldwater's Republican rival, liberal New York governor Nelson Rockefeller, divorced and remarried, Goldwater jumped ahead in the Republican race.

Then, in November 1963, President Kennedy was assassinated, changing everything, including Goldwater's desire to run. In December 1963, despite grave misgivings, Goldwater was persuaded by the leaders of the draft committee that it was his duty to run. Columnist M. Stanton Evans would later observe that conservatives had succeeded in accomplishing one of the few genuine drafts in history: "a rare case of spontaneous ideological fervor imposing its energies on a reluctant candidate."[10] Goldwater soldiered on, but he never gained traction against Lyndon Johnson, who portrayed him as an extremist and a warmonger. Goldwater's vote against the Civil Rights Act of 1964 on constitutional grounds helped him in the Deep South but split his party and drove black voters away from the GOP for a generation or more.

Despite Goldwater's landslide defeat, the conservative movement endured, remained in control of much of what it had gained in 1964, and found a new champion in Reagan, who leaped to the forefront of the conservative movement with his nationally televised October 1964 speech on behalf of Goldwater, "A Time for Choosing." Conservatives also carried forward the strategic premise of the Goldwater campaign, that Republicans could build a presidential majority with a so-called Sunbelt strategy focused on the rapidly growing states of the South and West. Although Richard Nixon modified the strategy somewhat, it was essentially the Sunbelt strategy of 1964 that carried him to the presidency in 1968.

At the same time, a third wave was added to the conservative movement: social and cultural conservatives disturbed by the liberal social direction of the United States in the 1960s and 1970s. Intellectually, the third wave took the form of the rise of the so-called neoconservatives, often former liberals or Marxists highly concerned with such social issues as crime and family breakdown. At the popular level, the resurgence of cultural traditionalism was found in at least three overlapping organizational strands. The pro-life movement, a mixture of Catholics and evangelical Protestants, was mobilized in the wake of the 1973 Supreme Court *Roe v. Wade* decision. By 1980 the National Right to Life Committee could boast 11 million members. At the same time, a conservative women's movement (whose most notable groups were Concerned Women for America and Phyllis Schlafly's Eagle Forum) arose in opposition to ratification of the equal rights amendment. Finally, the religious Right or Christian Right coalesced in the late 1970s, becoming "a virtual labyrinth of political action committees, lobbies, educational and research foundations, publications, television programs, and churches . . . some 90 organizations."[11]

The religious Right was not monolithic, but it appealed most to the overlapping (but not synonymous) groups of evangelical, fundamentalist, and born-again conservative Christians, groups that had been politically dormant for decades. A key defining moment for the organization of Christian conservatives came in 1978, when, during Carter's administration, the Internal Revenue Service proposed rules that seemed to threaten the existence of a number of private Christian schools. In 1979 both Christian Voice and the better-known Moral Majority were formed, seeking to reverse what Christian Voice's operations director called "a downward moral spiral."[12] Baptist minister Jerry Falwell, the founder of Moral Majority, declared that "religious organizations are marching together who never worked with each other. Evangelicals, fundamentalists, conservatives, Catholics, and Mormons are all working together now."[13]

Social traditionalism, which had always held a place in the conservative movement, thus took a new and more popular form: "Whereas the traditionalists of the 1940s and 1950s had largely been academics in revolt against secularized, mass society, the New Right was a revolt by the masses against the secular virus and its aggressive carriers in the nation's elite."[14] This mobilization, Michael Barone would later write, was a development "with almost as many reverberations as the political activation of CIO union organizers and members had in the politics of the 1940s and 1950s."[15]

By 1979 the conservative movement was highly developed both intellectually and at the popular level. It had fused three basic thrusts (economic freedom, anticommunism, and social coherence) and two general orientations (libertarian and traditionalist). Holding together these disparate strands were intellectual organs like the *National Review* and, beginning in 1973, the Heritage Foundation, a conservative think tank established in Washington, D.C., for the purpose of promoting conservative policy prescriptions in the "war of ideas." Furthermore, the crisis of 1979 seemed to confirm much of the conservative critique. Conservatives argued that economic decline and energy shortages were the result of overactive government intervention in the economy, that Soviet advances were the natural consequence of U.S. military and diplomatic weakness, and that social problems were the predictable outcome of Great Society laws and counterculture morals. Whereas the New Deal–Great Society liberal paradigm could offer few answers for stagflation, Soviet expansionism, and social deterioration, the conservative movement had answers on hand: less domestic government, a more muscular United States abroad, and renewed respect for traditional moral virtues.

The growing strength of the conservative movement was both cause and consequence of a movement toward the right in public opinion generally. That such a movement took place must be asserted carefully. For one thing, Americans are not particularly self-conscious ideologically. For another, one must distinguish between the "philosophical" and "operational" aspects of ideology. Operationally, Americans remained supportive of a wide range of specific federal spending programs. Nevertheless, opinion had shifted to the right on a number of specific issues. For example, by 1979 polls were showing that a solid majority of Americans wanted the slide in defense spending reversed.

Perhaps more important, "philosophical conservatism" clearly became ascendant. In 1964 only 42 percent of the public had agreed with the statement that "the government has gone too far in regulating business and interfering with the free enterprise system" (39 percent disagreed). In 1980, 65 percent agreed. As late as 1973, Americans had disagreed with the statement that "the best government is the government that governs least" by a margin of 56 percent to 32 percent. In 1981 they agreed by a margin of 59 percent to 35 percent. By the early 1980s, 77 percent of poll respondents had come to believe that the federal government created more problems than it solved, and by a margin of 49 percent to 15 percent, respondents agreed that the federal government was too powerful. And in 1981 Americans held, by a margin of 4 to 1, that states had a better understanding than the federal government of "real people's needs," a fundamental reversal in just a decade and a half.

Election results began to reflect this movement in public opinion. In June 1978 a nationwide tax revolt was launched by the overwhelming passage in California of its Proposition 13, a measure to cut property taxes. In the midterm elections of November 1978, twelve of sixteen states with measures on the ballot to limit or reduce taxes also saw them pass.

At the same time, there was substantial movement to the right in Congress. Republicans gained only fifteen seats in the House and three in the Senate, but the relatively small numbers masked a much greater qualitative shift. This was especially true in the Senate, where five prominent liberal Democrats went down to defeat, including New Hampshire's Thomas McIntyre and Iowa's Dick Clark, who was beaten with the help of pro-life volunteers who leafleted church parking lots the Sunday before the election. Wendell Anderson of Minnesota, Floyd Haskell of Colorado, and William Hathaway of Maine rounded out the list. In total, ten new senators were deemed more conservative than their predecessors; only four new senators were considered more liberal. Liberals of both parties who survived were chastened. Senator Charles Percy (R-Ill.), who barely survived reelection, asked voters to forgive his liberal indiscretions. Democrat Bill Bradley won an unexpectedly tough Senate race in New Jersey only by proposing a $25 billion tax cut of his own against a tax-cutting novice opponent.

The House too turned to the right. Seventy-seven House freshmen arrived, and almost all were committed to federal retrenchment, regardless of party. *Newsweek* opined that "the real message of the election returns was the ratification of a new and no longer partisan agenda for the nation—a consensus on inflation as the priority target and tax-and-spend government as the primary villain. . . . [Republicans'] real triumph was philosophic and often vicarious—the pride of authorship in a new politics in which Democrats talk like Republicans to survive."[16] Shortly after the election, Congressman Jack Kemp (R-N.Y.) proclaimed, "We've changed the focus of politics in America from their ground to our ground. We've shifted from the defensive to the offensive. They're now arguing on our turf."[17]

At the state level, Republicans also fared well, gaining about three hundred state legislative seats and tripling the number of states where they controlled both legislative chambers (from five to fourteen). They made a net gain of seven governorships, none more important than that of Texas, where William Clements became the first GOP governor in that state since Reconstruction.

The changed electoral dynamic translated into a changed political dynamic in Washington. Even before the 1978 elections, the Democratic Congress had passed the Steiger Amendment cutting capital gains taxes. The Senate passed a modified version of the 30 percent across-the-board Kemp-Roth personal income tax cut, though the bill died in conference committee, a victim of Carter administration pressure. After the election, one White House staffer foresaw that congressional liberals "are going to start looking at what happened to Dick Clark and start casting votes for their political futures instead of for what they think is right. And you can hardly blame them. How would you like to be Frank Church or George McGovern in 1980?"[18] Thus, Democrats remained the numerical majority in Congress (as they had been since 1954), but they were in a weakened position politically, and in many respects they had entirely lost control of the agenda. Unified Democratic control of government in these circumstances was at least as much a liability as a benefit. Unambiguous party responsibility was a necessary precondition for a major partisan shake-up if one was going to occur.

The final ingredient in the cauldron of 1980 was the prominence of the archetype of the political outsider. The outsider was a figure whose political appeal rested largely on his ability to distance himself from—or even to run against—the normal workings and institutions of national politics. The outsider was almost always for "reform" and against the "establishment" and sought to present himself as an alternative to "politics as usual." This archetype is deeply grounded in Anglo-Saxon history. In England, the "country party" regularly contrasted its virtue and connection to the people with the alleged corruption, incompetence, and abuse of the "court party." In the modern U.S. version, "outsiders" would run against the corruption, incompetence, and abuse of "Washington insiders," and sometimes against the media or cultural elites who gave them succor.

During the long and perilous years of the Great Depression and the Cold War, the nation had little use for outsiders in the White House.[19] Confidence in federal authority remained high, as did regard for experience in national affairs. However, the consensus of the 1950s gave way to competing critiques from left and right. Catastrophes at home and abroad, suffered with old Washington hands like Johnson or Nixon at the helm, caused many citizens to reassess the benefits of having candidates with experience. Many argued that the appeal of the outsider was fueled by detrimental features of modern public life, though there was no agreement on what those features were. Some cited the loss of substance in an age of media-driven politics and sound bites. Others, primarily on the left, argued that corporate influence on government left average citizens powerless and alienated. Observers on the right pointed to the growing insulation of national government from the people because of the growth of bureaucracy, the centralization of government in Washington, and the enhanced power of the unelected and unaccountable judicial branch. Outsiders also filled an institutional vacuum left by the decline of parties, and they took full advantage of the opportunities presented by the megaphone of the modern media.

The movement of U.S. politics toward the outsider was gradual. It began in 1964, when Barry Goldwater was carried to the Republican nomination on the strength of an outside movement seeking to overturn the entrenched elites of the Republican Party. The next major party explosion of outsider influence came in 1972, when George McGovern won the Democratic nomination with the significant aid of the new politics movement, which also sought to overturn the party's traditional power base with a rhetoric of renewal. However, neither Goldwater nor McGovern, both of whom hailed from the U.S. Senate, represented the phenomenon of the outsider to its fullest extent. That task was left to George Wallace. Wallace was a governor, far removed from the inner sanctum of national politics, and his populist (and often demagogic) appeal disdained all organized political forces. Drifting in and out of the Democratic Party, Wallace won surprising success in three 1964 primaries, ran a strong third-party campaign in 1968, and was in serious competition for the 1972 Democratic nomination until a would-be assassin's bullet ended his campaign just prior to the Michigan primary.

In 1976, in the wake of Watergate and the Nixon pardon, Jimmy Carter became the outsider candidate. As a governor, he could rail against Washington and promise the United States "a government as good as its people." For Carter, not being part of the "Washington mess" was a strength, not a weakness. He was the first outside candidate of the postwar period to win a presidential election. However, in 1980 Carter was the incumbent, and the fires that he had stoked were still burning. Carter faced the prospect of having to defeat other outsiders in both the Democratic primaries and in the general election. The Republican frontrunner, Ronald Reagan, promised to run a strong outsider campaign, as a former governor and as the standard-bearer of the conservative movement. Thus, although every election since 1964 had featured an outsider of some sort, 1980 had the potential of being the first election in modern times pitting two outsiders against each other in a general election. Congressional incumbents—especially those of the majority party—were also looking over their shoulders at the approaching horsemen of the country party.

What all of this meant was that Democrats were in a precarious position as they faced the 1980 elections. Indeed, in May 1979 Vice President Mondale considered Carter's political situation so grim that he seriously considered resigning or removing himself from the 1980 Democratic ticket.[20] Economic, foreign, and social conditions were bad and getting worse, with no end in sight. The Democratic coalition was severely frayed and was about to face a test that no one could guarantee it would survive. The conservative movement posed an increasingly powerful challenge both intellectually and organizationally. The voters were restless and increasingly ill-disposed toward the liberal status quo. Democrats controlled the government, with the responsibility that that power implied. And Carter, running for reelection as an incumbent in an era of outsiders, had to find a way to be "in Washington" without being "of Washington."

2

THE CANDIDATES A CROWDED FIELD

The president who warned the nation of the crisis of confidence had, in his own words, "always intended to seek reelection."[1] He reached an agreement in November 1978 with Vice President Walter Mondale to run again as a team. As a one-term governor of a medium-sized southern state, James Earl Carter Jr. was not a likely chief executive in the broad sweep of U.S. presidents. Born on October 1, 1924, Carter was the son of a peanut farmer from the small town of Plains in southwest Georgia. The first Carter to finish high school, Jimmy went on to graduate in the top 10 percent of his class from the U.S. Naval Academy in 1946. After seven years in the Navy, some of them served on a nuclear submarine, he returned home upon the death of his father to run the family farm.

Carter entered politics in 1962 when he lost a race for a seat in the Georgia State Senate but successfully challenged the results on grounds of fraud. He ran for governor of Georgia in 1966 but finished third in the Democratic primary. He spent the next four years running for the same position. According to political correspondent Jules Witcover, "For four years he worked the state like a migrant worker hustling for harvest work, putting in a regular day at the family's peanut plant, then driving to all corners of Georgia to speak and meet voters."[2] When he ran again in 1970, he won by a margin of 49 percent to 38 percent in the Democratic primary against popular former Democratic governor Carl Sanders, and by a margin of 59 percent to 41 percent in the general election against Republican Hal Suit. Throughout his early career, he hewed to the segregationist line, cozying up to such segrega-tionists as George Wallace and former Georgia governor Lester Maddox.

As governor, however, Carter gained a reputation as one of the first of the new breed of southern Democrats who focused on economic de-velopment and governmental efficiency and eschewed racial politics. An austere, religious, hardworking, sincere, and utterly tenacious man, Carter was also known for his striking ambition, a hard edge that showed itself in cold calculation, bouts of deviousness, and a mean streak toward opponents. Carter's January 1971 inaugural address as governor was no-table for his declaration that "the time for racial discrimination is over." He appointed numerous blacks to state positions and placed a portrait of Martin Luther King Jr. in the state capitol. As governor, Carter also oversaw a dramatic increase in state spending and imposed regulations protecting Georgia's wild rivers.

At the same time, Carter reorganized state government to improve effi-ciency and introduced "zero-based budgeting," a concept requiring that government programs be reevaluated each year. He also pushed for re-introduction of the death penalty and more-stringent sentences for drug violations. Carter was one of the last Democrats to abandon the Vietnam War, and when Lt. William L. Calley Jr. was convicted of war crimes at My Lai, Carter proclaimed "American Fighting Man's Day," replete with a call for citizens to display the flag and drive with their headlights on. At the 1972 Democratic national convention, Carter seconded the nomination of Henry Jackson, a moderate Democrat from Washington state. He was in Georgia politics what he would later become in national politics: some-one who could appeal to (or alienate) both conservatives and liberals.

At the Democratic national 1972 convention, his supporters ran an unsuccessful campaign to put his name into contention for the Demo-cratic vice presidential slot. Carter aides Gerald Rafshoon and Hamilton Jordan, in charge of the vice presidential foray, walked back to their ho-tel the night George McGovern was nominated and asked, "Why can't Jimmy run for President?"[3] It was, it turned out, a question that Carter had already asked himself. Shortly after the 1972 Democratic conven-tion, Peter Bourne (head of Georgia's drug-abuse program) wrote Carter a memo urging him to run. In the fall, Rafshoon and Jordan outlined for Carter his (positive) prospects and a tentative strategy. Carter spent the next two years preparing for the campaign, including a fruitful stint heading the Democratic National Committee's 1974 election effort. In late 1974, as his legally mandated single gubernatorial term drew to a close, he announced his candidacy for president of the United States. No one took him seriously.

In the 1976 primaries Carter won by taking a surprise plurality among voters who specified a selection among the candidates (that is, excluding those who preferred "uncommitted" delegates, who were actually a plurality) in the Iowa caucuses, by driving George Wallace from the race early by beating him in the crucial Florida primary, and by taking advantage of the fact that multiple liberal aspirants split the vote on the left. Thematically, he succeeded in turning his weaknesses into strengths. "Jimmy Who?," an ex-governor with no foreign policy experience, became the perfect candidate to focus on domestic problems: a morally upright outsider untainted by the recent failures and scandals of Washington. He famously promised a government "as honest and truthful and decent and fair and idealistic and compassionate and as full of love as are the American people." In his nomination quest Carter was aided tremendously by the post-1968 reform of the Democratic nominating process, which substantially reduced the role of party regulars. After winning the Democratic nomination, Carter held on against an onrushing incumbent Gerald Ford to squeak out a bare victory in November 1976, thanks to Watergate, a debate gaffe by Ford when he seemed to say that Poland was not under Soviet domination, and—at least in Ford's view—the damage done to the incumbent by Ronald Reagan's primary challenge. The time of the outsider had fully arrived.

Carter brought numerous strengths to the presidency, including great raw intelligence, self-discipline, personal integrity, and a folksy charm that many Americans saw as a welcome respite from the "imperial presidency" of the recent past. However, over time many of these characteristics began to work against him. His intelligence allowed him to grasp large quantities of data, but he was often unable to discover a coherent thread. His work habits included a compulsive concern with detail that obscured broader messages. Folksiness, which included a remarkable reduction of formality in the office of the presidency, wore thin as Americans looked for authoritative leadership. By training Carter thought like an engineer, and he often failed to grasp why a policy that he had systematically examined and deemed superior needed to be "sold" to Congress or the American people. In this respect he resembled Herbert Hoover, the engineer and technocrat who was undoubtedly one of the most intelligent men to be president in the twentieth century.

Perhaps most ominously for the president, Carter found himself in an uncomfortable political environment. The political coalition on which he depended for success was unraveling. Political scientist Stephen Skowronek identifies such moments as "disjunctions": The old regime or the previously dominant coalition has splintered but remains, for a moment, nominally responsible for governing. The disjunction during Carter's administration manifested itself in at least three ways.

First, Carter's outsider approach was itself an indication of the degree to which the old Democratic power structure had shattered. He governed as he had campaigned, as a man apart. Contemporary observers often attributed this feature of his presidency to Carter's natural aloofness or to his reliance on a relatively small and insular circle of Georgians, the so-called Georgia Mafia, including Hamilton Jordan, Jody Powell, and Gerald Rafshoon. However, something deeper was at work: a more general fragmentation of Democratic power.

Second, as he had during his governorship, Carter focused a great deal of his presidential rhetoric and energy on governmental efficiency, the time-honored position of those who cherish the programmatic record of their party but lack the political resources to extend it. Carter's technocratic emphasis echoed not only Hoover but also other similarly situated presidents, such as Franklin Pierce and John Quincy Adams.

Finally, when he did attend to substantive policy, Carter defied easy ideological categorization. As Stephen Skowronek argued in *The Politics Presidents Make,*

> [Carter] challenged the liberal regime to take the test that circumstances had thrust upon it and candidly acknowledge that its old solutions were now part of the problem. He insisted that changes in the economic and international climate had shifted the task of liberal political leadership categorically and that a simple, straightforward articulation of received premises would no longer do. . . . Carter was a nominal affiliate of a vulnerable regime projecting a place in history in which liberalism would prove its vitality through hard-nosed readjustments of its operating assumptions.[4]

Carter drew from the liberal well when it came to race (he supported affirmative action and busing), education (promoting an expanded federal role through the creation of the federal Department of Education), and jobs (endorsing the Humphrey-Hawkins full employment bill). Though he artfully dodged the abortion issue during the 1976 campaign, his administration was generally pro-choice, and he was a vocal supporter of the equal rights amendment. When it came to energy policy—Carter's "moral equivalent of war"—his answers were largely in the tradition of the New Deal, calling for more national planning and a comprehensive federal policy. Carter's foreign policy was grounded in McGovernism—eschewing force, accommodating the nation's enemies, and chastising its friends—until circumstances brought about a reversal in late 1979.

At the same time, though, Carter came to office having run a campaign against the Washington establishment, much of which was liberal. His open embrace of evangelical Christianity ran against the grain of the increasing secularization of U.S. liberalism. He attacked the tax code—the product of a quarter century of unbroken Democratic control of Congress—as "a disgrace to the human race." Carter was the first Democratic president of the twentieth century not to ask Congress for a slew of major new federal programs. Woodrow Wilson had had the New Freedom, Franklin Roosevelt the New Deal, Truman the Fair Deal, Kennedy the New Frontier, and Johnson the Great Society. Carter had a call for restraint. He rarely tried to fashion a moniker for his agenda, and when he did—the New Foundation—it fell flat. Indeed, some of Jimmy Carter's presidential addresses read like the rhetoric of another ex-governor who wanted to be president, Ronald Reagan—though Carter's delivery was never as crisp as Reagan's. In his 1978 State of the Union address, for example, Carter warned that

> there is a limit to the role and the function of government. Government cannot solve our problems, it can't set our goals, it cannot define our vision. Government cannot eliminate poverty or reduce inflation or save our cities or cure illiteracy or provide energy. And government cannot mandate goodness. Only a true partnership between government and the people can ever hope to reach those goals. Those of us who govern can sometimes inspire, and we can identify needs and marshal resources, but we simply cannot be the managers of everything and everybody.

Carter sought but never achieved a balanced budget. When it came to regulation, Carter sent mixed messages. On the one hand, the overall regulatory apparatus of the U.S. government exploded in size and power during his presidency. The annual *Federal Register* of new federal regulations ballooned by 30,000 pages from 1976 to 1980, and Carter promoted more-stringent environmental and consumer regulations, including a new Consumer Protection Agency. On the other hand, Carter supported deregulation of certain transportation industries, most notably airlines, on the grounds that deregulation would increase efficiency and benefit the consumer. He also came to favor partial decontrol of the oil and natural gas industries, though decontrol was coupled with a so-called windfall-profits tax, a combination that seemed to satisfy no one.

Despite notable diplomatic successes with China and in the Middle East, as the broker of the Camp David Accords between Israel and Egypt, Carter quickly acquired a reputation for waffling and weakness in foreign affairs. In 1977, in his first major foreign policy address, Carter disdained the "inordinate fear of communism" that he said had dominated U.S. foreign policy for three decades. In its place Carter offered a foreign policy focused on global North-South issues, nuclear arms control, and the promotion of human rights. No picture captured the pacific nature (or naïveté) of Carter's foreign policy better than the June 1979 scene of Carter embracing Soviet dictator Leonid Brezhnev at the signing of the second Strategic Arms Limitation Treaty (SALT II). He came to office promising to cut defense spending, and he promptly canceled the B-1 bomber and delayed a decision on the MX missile, a mobile ICBM. Acceding to pressure from the antinuclear movement, he also canceled the neutron bomb, a tactical nuclear device designed to stop a Soviet tank advance in Europe, after several NATO leaders took the politically risky step of endorsing it.

Carter abruptly called for a withdrawal of U.S. military forces from South Korea, then reversed course. Better relations with Beijing came at the price of reneging on the U.S.-Taiwan Mutual Defense Treaty. On human rights grounds, Carter refrained from supporting the shah of Iran in his moment of maximum peril, only to see him replaced by the Ayatollah Khomeini; he pressured Somoza out of Nicaragua, only to face the Communist Sandinistas; and he tried to pressure the Soviets to give freedom to dissidents, such as Anatoly Sharansky, Andrei Sakharov, Alexander Ginsburg, and George Vins, who were imprisoned, facing internal exile, or prohibited from emigrating, only to ease off when it seemed that arms control negotiations would be jeopardized. He proposed a dramatic reduction in nuclear arsenals, then backed off at the first sign of Soviet disapproval. In 1978, confronted with an increasingly aggressive Soviet thrust, he tentatively began to reverse course, calling for a modest increase in defense spending. In 1979 this reversal would accelerate.

If Carter was a transitional figure in presidential politics, the question remained: a transition to what? Was Carter the prototype of the new president? Or was he just a stop on the road to something different? His pollster, Patrick Caddell, urged him to forge a "fundamentally new ideology," a "synthesis" that was neither "stew" nor "patch-up job" nor "bits and pieces of old policies." Carter endorsed the notion of developing such an ideology, but Caddell admitted that the task was beyond his own abilities, and Carter never devoted himself to the project.[5] Consequently, as one White House correspondent put it, "There was a kind of hollowness about Jimmy Carter's administration, from beginning to end. He seldom seemed to articulate a clear idea of just what he wanted to do and how he planned to do it. Although he often communicated goodness and compassion, he didn't communicate purpose."[6]

In the hands of a very skilled politician, the situation might have yielded the new synthesis that Caddell advocated, though its contradictions would have made it inherently unstable. As it was, with his limitations of vision and persuasive ability, Carter appeared hopelessly inconsistent to many Americans and came under increasing attack from both left and right for being a phony, a hedger, or even a betrayer. Carter speechwriter James Fallows left the White House and wrote a scathing indictment of Carter in the May 1979 issue of *Atlantic Monthly,* calling his the "Passionless Presidency." By July 1979 Carter's approval rating in the Gallup poll had sunk to 29 percent, lower than Nixon's had been in the midst of Watergate. An image had become nearly fixed in the minds of Americans: Carter was honest, but he was no leader.

Carter's rightward drift, his appearance of incompetence, and above all his political weakness invited a challenge from leading figures in his party. As early as December 1978, former New York City Council president Paul O'Dwyer began organizing a "dump Carter" movement, complaining that "Jimmy Carter's whole pitch now is to the conservatives, increasing the military budget and cutting back on social programs— that's the antithesis of what you'd expect from a reasonably progressive Democrat."[7] Foremost among the "progressive" Democrats was Senator Edward M. "Ted" Kennedy of Massachusetts, younger brother of President John F. Kennedy and of former attorney general, New York senator, and 1968 presidential aspirant Robert F. Kennedy. Edward Kennedy had crossed Carter's presidential path in 1976 as a potential opponent whose surprising decision to avoid the race opened the doors to Carter's victory. As the Carter presidency wore on, what Carter saw as a hard-nosed readjustment of liberalism, Kennedy and other liberals saw as heresy to the faith. Carter's view that "There is a limit to the role and the function of government" was, to the left wing of the Democratic Party, nothing less than a betrayal of FDR and JFK.

Edward Kennedy, forty-seven years old in 1979, was the senior Democratic senator from Massachusetts, having been first elected in 1962. The sole surviving Kennedy brother—and the sole surviving son of patriarch Joseph P. Kennedy—Edward was assumed after 1968 to be equipped for the presidency and ambitious for it, the heir apparent to Camelot. He shared his brothers' ability to stir the party faithful, but in 1969 the heir apparent lost some of his shine when, after a party on Chappaquiddick island in Massachusetts, he drove off a bridge with a young woman named Mary Jo Kopechne, left her to drown, and failed to report to the police until the next day. Indeed, the lingering political fallout from the Chappaquiddick incident was the most plausible explanation for Kennedy's failure to enter the 1972 and 1976 races.

In the meantime, Kennedy continued as a voice for unabashed liberalism in the Senate. He was chosen as Senate majority whip by the Democratic caucus in 1969, then was defeated for the post by Robert Byrd of West Virginia in 1971. Kennedy played an instrumental role in the cutoff of U.S. aid to South Vietnam, pushed for national health care, argued for greater federal controls to handle the energy crisis, and criticized Carter's move toward restraint in domestic spending. At the Democratic Party's midterm convention in Memphis in December 1978—a dress rehearsal for the 1980 Democratic nomination scuffle—Kennedy made an emotional speech calling for national health insurance and arguing that the party must sometimes "sail against the wind."

Although in a White House meeting in March 1979 Kennedy assured Carter of his support for a second term, pressure grew on him to enter the Democratic primaries against the president. There followed an intricate dance between senator and president. Despite Kennedy's mantra—"I expect the President to be renominated and I expect him to be reelected and I intend to support him"—Democrats around the country began announcing their desire to draft Kennedy. Hardly a week passed in the first half of 1979 that did not bring news of further Democratic disenchantment with Carter. Representative Cardiss Collins (D-Ill.), head of the Congressional Black Caucus, declared that she was leaning toward Kennedy. A group of prominent California Democrats took out a full-page advertisement in the *Los Angeles Times* accusing Carter of a "crisis of leadership" and calling on Kennedy or other party leaders to enter the fray. A group of Iowa Democrats organized to support a Kennedy candidacy, New Hampshire was host to a nascent Kennedy write-in campaign, and top leaders of Handgun Control, Inc., indicated they were disappointed in Carter and would look to Kennedy. The Cuyahoga County, Ohio, Democratic committee took up a resolution to draft Kennedy, draft movements were organized in Illinois and Florida, the New York Democratic state committee approved a resolution criticizing Carter, and on May 7, 1979, Representative Richard M. Nolan (D-Minn.) announced he would lead a nationwide effort to draft Kennedy because Carter had "abandoned" the Democratic Party.

In the spring and summer of 1979 Kennedy grew more forceful in his denunciations of the president. In a speech to newspaper editors, Kennedy demanded "vision for the longer run" and "action and inspiration," calling Carter's windfall-profits tax proposal a "transparent fig leaf" covering Carter's surrender to oil industry "intimidation"—an accusation that Carter promptly called "just a lot of baloney." In national polls in early 1979 Kennedy held a 2-to-1 lead over Carter among Democrats nationally and in key primary states, such as New Hampshire.

In June 1979 the president held a pre-campaign meeting at which he boasted that if Kennedy ran, he, Carter, would "whip his ass." Kennedy later told political correspondent Theodore White that Carter's July 15 "malaise" speech was crucial in causing him to seriously consider running. He had, however, been preparing since at least 1978, when he had hired a political organizer familiar with Iowa. At the inauguration of Washington, D.C., mayor Marion Barry on January 2, 1979, Kennedy had reportedly taken down inaugural chairman Theodore Hagans's phone number, "just in case I ever have to put on an inauguration of my own."[8] Finally, on September 7, the potential foes met at the White House. Carter hoped for a firm public statement from Kennedy repudiating a presidential bid. What he got instead was Kennedy's private repudiation of his mantra of the spring.

In the end, Kennedy ran, offering a full-throated liberalism in place of Carter's more complex ideological whisper. Perhaps just as important, he also rejected Carter's outsider approach. In the view of White, it was Kennedy's "infinite love of government . . . that comes closest, I think, to being the genesis of the Kennedy campaign of 1980." Kennedy

*President Carter and Senator Kennedy
eyeing each other warily in the Oval Office
in mid-1978.*

harbored a deep disdain for Carter's leadership, "the contempt of a master machinist for a plumber's helper," and complained to White that "this outsider can't solve our problems. . . . Even on issues we agree on, he doesn't know how to do it."[9]

Kennedy, like most contemporary observers, undoubtedly thought he would win. He may have also perceived that his chances were running out. He would no longer be taken seriously if he was too many times only a near-candidate. His duty to honor the family legacy and his duty to rescue Democrats and the nation from what he considered Carter's incompetence combined to drive him into the race.

Like Carter—and any other candidate—he brought to the campaign both strengths and weaknesses. Among his strengths was, first and foremost, the Kennedy name, which had been golden in Democratic politics (and at least fine silver in much of the nation at large) since President Kennedy's death in 1963. Indeed, he was the only Democratic politician of the time who could immediately leap in front of an incumbent Democratic president in the polls just by throwing his hat into the ring. Kennedy also enjoyed a position of high visibility as an experienced member of the Senate majority. And not least, he brought a passion for liberal causes that excited the party's base, those activists and voters who seemed most likely to participate in the upcoming primaries and caucuses.

Chappaquiddick and the character issues it raised—including drinking, marital conflict, and unwillingness to take responsibility—were not Kennedy's only weaknesses. In addition, he affirmed most of the positions that had broken asunder the Democratic coalition: He was pro-busing, pro-racial preferences, pro-abortion, pro–judicial liberalism, pro-welfare, pro–War on Poverty, and anti-anticommunist. It was not at all clear whether the Ted Kennedy of 1979 would have supported the John Kennedy of 1962 on Cuba or tax cuts. Consequently, it was difficult to see how Kennedy would be more successful at restoring the party coalition than Carter had been. Furthermore, in his disdain for outsiders and the outsider approach, Kennedy was swimming upstream, though he could hope that Carter's problems had reminded voters of the importance of experience. And, of course, he would have to defeat an incumbent, never an easy thing to do even when circumstances are otherwise propitious. Whatever Carter's other shortcomings, he and the people around him were skilled at the political use of his office.

Carter the president and Kennedy the heir apparent were not alone in their quest for the Democratic nomination. While Kennedy considered, Governor Edmund G. "Jerry" Brown Jr. of California eased into the race. Like Kennedy, Brown had also crossed Carter's path in 1976, but as an actual rather than merely a potential candidate. A latecomer to the 1976 race, Brown—who had then served little more than a year as governor—won primaries in Maryland, Nevada, Rhode Island, and California. His theme was a culturally liberal variation of Carter's anti-Washington populism, and "many were convinced that if Brown had started in New Hampshire with everyone else, the nomination would have been his, not Carter's."[10]

Like Kennedy, Brown was the scion of a political family, the son of former California governor Edmund G. "Pat" Brown. In 1966 the elder Brown had, after two terms, lost his reelection bid to Ronald Reagan. After his 1976 nomination defeat, Jerry returned to California and "presented himself successfully as a leading advocate of tax cuts and governmental economy."[11] He proposed limitations on welfare payments and advocated calling a convention to write a federal constitutional amendment requiring a balanced budget. At the same time, he fought the death penalty and nuclear power, and he named Jane Fonda to the State Arts Council (an appointment that was rejected by the legislature). In 1978 he won a crushing reelection victory in California, winning by a margin of 1.3 million votes.

Brown was young and energetic and came from the biggest state, but he was also regarded as slightly flaky by many experienced observers. In some circles, the moniker "Governor Moonbeam" stuck. Trained as a Jesuit, Brown now dabbled in Eastern thought, and his campaign slogan emitted more than a touch of Zen: "Protect the earth, serve the people, explore the universe." More economically conservative than his father but also more socially daring, the unmarried Brown raised eyebrows in 1979 when he went on a trip to Africa with singer Linda Ronstadt.

At age forty-one, Brown's youth was both an asset and a liability—at one point in the pre-primary jostling, Carter joked that Brown's campaign was "California's way of celebrating the year of the child."[12] With a strong sense that the United States was caught in a transitional moment, Brown was, if anything, both more ideologically eclectic and more of an outsider than Carter had been. Like Carter, he touted an impending "era of limits." Political reporter Adam Clymer observed that the Californian had "almost no professional political support" but was "a formidable campaigner [who] might pull off an upset."[13] Sensing Carter's weakness, and perhaps ruing his late entry in 1976, it was clear by the summer of 1979 that Brown intended to run. This development helped push Kennedy into the race. As Theodore White put it, "If the presidency of Jimmy Carter was collapsing, it seemed as silly for Kennedy to let Brown claim the nomination as it had been unwise, in retrospect, for Robert Kennedy to let Eugene McCarthy claim the nomination in 1968, when Johnson's presidency was collapsing."[14] When Kennedy did enter, Brown's task became much more difficult.

Taken together, Carter, Kennedy, and Brown were a powerful trio, and no other serious Democratic candidate emerged. Some potential contenders, such as New York governor Hugh Carey, were briefly mentioned as possibilities but did not choose to run. And, of course, there were the standard collection of oddballs, led by Lyndon LaRouche, who believed that Queen Elizabeth II of England directed the international drug trade. It was a testament to Carter's vulnerability that he attracted two high-profile challengers. Despite all his problems, though, Carter possessed an underlying advantage, beyond the obvious one of incumbency: He was firmly in the center on both the left-right scale and the insider-outsider scale. Kennedy flanked him to the inside and to the left. Brown flanked him to the outside and both to his left (socially) and his right (economically). However low Carter's approval ratings would plummet in the summer of 1979, he could still hope that the race would pivot around his centrist position.

Just as Carter's problems had attracted primary competition, they also inflated the size of the Republican field. Perennial candidate Harold Stassen, who had already run for the Republican nomination five times since 1948, and little-known California businessman Benjamin Fernandez threw their hats into the ring. Former NATO commander General Alexander Haig ran a short, unannounced minicampaign. Illinois governor James Thompson flirted with running, as did New York Representative Jack Kemp (cosponsor of the Kemp-Roth income tax proposal in Congress), who made the speaking rounds in the early stages of the race but declined to enter. Liberal Republican senator Lowell Weicker of Connecticut actually announced his candidacy and then withdrew, as did first-term senator Larry Pressler of South Dakota.

More-serious candidates also abounded. Two Illinois congressmen— Philip Crane and John Anderson—ran, hoping to defy the conventional

John Anderson had served in Congress since 1961, gradually moving left while his party was moving right.

wisdom that held that House members could not win the presidency. Though from the same state, Crane and Anderson hailed from two opposite ends of the Republican Party. Crane, a former history professor, was elected to the House in 1969 to fill a vacancy created when Congressman Donald Rumsfeld joined the Nixon administration. He was closely connected with the conservative movement, serving as chairman of the American Conservative Union, and he hoped to win support from that wing of the party. An energetic forty-eight years old, Crane announced first, in August 1978, and enlisted the aid of the conservative direct-mail wizard Richard Viguerie, who had pioneered and mastered the tactic for causes on the right. However, by mid-1979 Crane was suffering from a financial shortfall and high staff turnover.

Anderson, for his part, was the sole voice of what was once known as "Rockefeller Republicanism." He started his House service in 1961 as a conservative. Deeply religious, he had three times sponsored a constitutional amendment proclaiming the United States to be a Christian nation. By 1978 he had drifted far enough to the left—and the GOP had moved far enough to the right—that he was nearly defeated in a primary by a little-known conservative challenger. Anderson's conversion process centered around urban issues and civil rights. His first move toward liberalism came over the Fair Housing Act of 1968, which he supported in the wake of the assassination of Martin Luther King Jr. and the subsequent riots in Washington, D.C., and dozens of other cities. His first big break with the GOP occurred when he became one of the first Republicans in the House to openly turn against Nixon in the Watergate scandal. Facing a backlash from longtime friends, he found himself increasingly disaffected from his home of Rockport, Illinois. In 1980 he chose not to seek reelection to the House from his northwest Illinois district and ran for president instead.

With a shock of white hair, Anderson, then fifty-seven, had a distinguished appearance. He sought to convey the image of a deep thinker offering "new coalitions" and holding off the gathering hordes of the New Right. He was also known for being a loner with a strong streak of sanctimony, and he echoed Carter's pessimistic outlook, arguing in a 1975 book that "our political system suffers from a crisis in its soul."[15] By far the most liberal of the plausible Republican contenders, Anderson opposed the MX missile and attended pro-choice candlelight vigils. He obtained the help of direct-mail guru Tom Mathews—the Richard Viguerie of the left—whose client list included the Sierra Club, the American

Civil Liberties Union, the National Organization for Women, Common Cause, the Democratic National Committee, and Ted Kennedy. Aiming at the "alienated middle," Anderson's appeal was built around "the Anderson difference." He had his greatest appeal in college towns and other places where his sort of Republican was an acceptable alternative for liberals who had soured on Carter. His advisers expected to earn free publicity from sympathetic media and hoped for success in the eighteen states that allowed crossover voting in their primaries, where he hoped to attract non-Republicans.

From the Senate hailed Bob Dole of Kansas and Howard Baker of Tennessee. Dole had pulled the Republican National Committee through difficult times as its chairman during Watergate and had compiled a solid record in two terms in the Senate. A dry midwestern conservative, he had been Gerald Ford's vice presidential running mate in 1976. In that campaign, he had acquired a reputation as a partisan attack dog, not least for his claim in the vice presidential debate that "every war of this century has been a Democrat war." A war hero himself, Dole had a strong biography but no clear rationale for his campaign, a problem that would vex his pursuit of the presidency for the next two decades. He promised to find positive solutions for problems (in contrast to the GOP's image of only being against things) and had a more complicated record than his reputation allowed (supporting, for example, expanded eligibility for Food Stamps). He hoped to build a coalition of veterans, farmers, and the handicapped. However, those groups hardly added up to a majority. Throughout 1979 Dole was bogged down in Senate work, and like Crane, he found fund-raising difficult.

Of the two senators, Baker was the stronger political force. He was the son-in-law of the famed Republican Senate leader Everett Dirksen, and both his father and mother had themselves served in Congress. In fourteen years in the Senate, he had made a name for himself as a moderate, nonpartisan broker between Senate factions. His turn against Nixon during the Watergate hearings was legendary, and as Senate minority leader in 1978 his backing for ratification of President Carter's Panama Canal treaties had been critical to the administration's success.

This record gave Baker a favorable audience in the press corps, but it also made him a suspicious figure to many Republican voters, whose support he would need for the nomination. The backlash to his treaty stand forced him to bypass the early southern primaries. He also supported the equal rights amendment, opposed a constitutional amendment banning abortion, and backed most environmental legislation. He had expertise in foreign affairs, which was likely to be a big issue in 1980, and he hoped to capitalize on his visibility in the pending battle over SALT II. Baker had been considered and passed over for the vice presidency three times—by Nixon in 1968, by Nixon in 1973 when Vice President Spiro Agnew resigned, and again by Ford in 1976. He was a Washington politician, and not afraid to tout his experience and knowledge.

Also in contention were John Connally of Texas and George H. W. Bush, whose home was Connecticut, Maine, Massachusetts, Texas, or Washington, D.C., depending upon how one looked at it. Connally, the son of a tenant farmer, was a former Democrat who had served as John F. Kennedy's secretary of the navy and had then served three terms as governor of Texas. Sitting in the front seat of Kennedy's car in Dallas, Connally had been severely wounded by one of the bullets fired in the president's assassination. Seeking to attract southerners away from the Democratic coalition, Nixon had named him secretary of the treasury in 1971. In 1973, he had formally switched parties and become a Republican. Acquitted of a milk industry bribery charge in 1975, Connally could never fully escape the taint of Nixon-era corruption, nor was he ever fully trusted by Republicans as one of their own. He was conservative, but in the pro-big-business style rather than in the more populist style of the conservative movement.

As he began his presidential bid, he could claim the support of many CEOs and a few eastern establishment Republicans such as former attorney general Herbert Brownell and former Republican National Committee chairman W. Leonard Hall. Well-financed, brash, and noted as a stirring speaker with a commanding presence, Connally promised to restore national confidence through vigorous leadership. Carter, he charged, had "little sense of the use of power on a global scale." He chose to forgo federal matching funds, and the spending limits that came with them, in order to take full advantage of his fund-raising capacity. No candidate repeated this tactic until George W. Bush in 2000. Throughout early 1979, if any candidate had media "buzz," it was Connally.

Of the entire group, George H. W. Bush had the broadest résumé. Born in Massachusetts into a New England patrician family, Bush had grown up in Connecticut, where his father became a U.S. senator. He had attended Andover, then enlisted at the age of eighteen to become the youngest fighter pilot in the U.S. Navy during World War II. He had been shot down by the Japanese and been rescued by a U.S. submarine, and had gone on to graduate from Yale after the war. In the 1950s he had moved his family to Midland, Texas, and become an oilman, eventually starting Zapata Oil, a major offshore drilling company.

In the 1960s he had entered Texas politics, winning a U.S. House seat in Houston in between losing tries for the U.S. Senate in 1964 and 1970. Bush was then named to a succession of executive appointments and political posts, including U.S. ambassador to the United Nations, head of the Republican National Committee, U.S. envoy to China, and, in the last months of the Ford administration, director of the CIA. Like Baker, he had been considered for the vice presidency by Nixon when Agnew left. Bush was an enthusiastic campaigner and was almost uniformly praised as decent, honest, and capable. On the other hand, he was widely considered "bland," was not a notably good speaker, and was poorly known outside Washington.

Bush was unimpressed by Jimmy Carter when he met the president-elect to brief him about intelligence matters, and he had begun tentatively exploring the possibility of a presidential run almost four years before the election of 1980. In 1978 he had formed a political action committee, the Fund for Limited Government, and traveled 96,000 miles speechifying, meeting bigwigs, and campaigning for Republican candidates. In 1979 he traveled another 246,000 miles. Bush was meticulous about sending personal notes to the people he met. His politics were described as "somewhat to the center of center,"[16] and he appealed most strongly to Republican moderates. He went out of his way to cultivate the Ford wing of the party. His higher staff was largely inherited from Ford, and his lower staff was dominated by New England Republicans who were not comfortable with the more conservative direction of the party since Goldwater's nomination (though his lower staff included a sprinkling of 1976 Reagan workers). Bush was also aided by Susan Morrison, the Democratic National Committee's former director of communications, and by about twenty-five former CIA people, "Spooks for Bush," who took a variety of organizational posts in the campaign.

Bush was in many ways the preferred candidate of the so-called Eastern establishment that had dominated Republican nomination politics before 1964. Early on, he had acquired the support of such figures as former senator and ambassador Henry Cabot Lodge, publisher Clare Booth Luce, former governor and presidential also-ran George Romney, former Senate minority leader Hugh Scott, and U.S. Representatives Millicent Fenwick and Barber Conable, most of them notable moderate-to-liberal

Republicans (although Luce had supported Goldwater in 1964). These would later be joined by Elliot Richardson, Nixon's attorney general who resigned in protest during Watergate. Bush advocated standard Republican economic prescriptions, but supported the equal rights amendment, opposed a constitutional amendment banning abortion, and had once supported gun registration, though he had recanted.

Bush and Baker would compete for much the same constituency; indeed, one of Bush's key strategic aims was to knock Baker out of the race early. At the same time, he had to peel some conservative support away from Reagan. Consequently, Bush eschewed labels and when pushed would settle for "moderately conservative." Nor was this fuzziness merely a tactic. In many ways it revealed the essence of Bush; his nephew John Ellis once said, "[he] has no political ideology. His ideology is friendship."[17] Promising "a president we don't have to train," Bush was the consummate insider in a time that seemed to favor outsiders. In any event the Republican Party of 1980 was not the Republican Party of 1960. Bush had to convince a Sunbelt party that he was not really a preppie New Englander. He started his campaign by pointing out that, unlike either Connally or Reagan, he had been a "lifelong Republican."

Standing above this field was the front-runner, Ronald Reagan. Reagan had run for the presidency twice before. In 1968 a late-blooming and halfhearted effort had nevertheless come close to denying Nixon a first-ballot victory in Miami. Only the intervention of Strom Thurmond on Nixon's behalf kept a pro-Reagan tide in the South from putting Reagan into contention in a multiballot convention.

In 1976 Reagan had made a more serious run, this time against incumbent Ford. His stance was pro-defense, antidétente, and pro-federalism, and his themes included a balanced budget and opposition to the Panama Canal treaties then under negotiation ("We built it, we paid for it, and we're going to keep it"). After barely losing the first primary in New Hampshire, Reagan lost another four in a row to Ford. With the press baying at his heels in expectation of a withdrawal, Reagan confounded them: Although behind in the North Carolina polls by 15 percentage points, he announced that he was in the race all the way to the convention. When results arrived from the Tarheel State, Reagan had upset Ford and regained credibility and momentum.

He went on to win Indiana, Texas, California, and several other states, benefiting tremendously from crossover votes in states with open primaries. Reagan won a total of 46 percent of all primary votes cast, excluding

Alabama, New York, and Texas, which had only delegate primaries without a presidential preference poll (of those, he took Texas and Alabama handily). He did better than that in the nonprimary states, where the organization and intensity of his supporters were crucial. Throughout the country, Reagan gained support, built organization, and developed contributor lists that would prove crucial four years later.

When Republicans arrived for their convention in Kansas City in August 1976, no one could be certain who was going to win the nomination. Ford exercised the full influence of his office and pulled out the nomination in the end, winning 1,187 delegates to Reagan's 1,070. The next day, Reagan told the California delegation and his aides, "The cause goes on." On the last night of the convention, Reagan was asked to address his fellow Republicans. His reception from the delegates shook the Kemper Arena. In the words of Reagan's campaign chairman, Senator Paul Laxalt of Nevada, "Though we lost we really won."[18] The campaign of 1980 had begun.

Reagan was born into an Illinois family of modest means in 1911. His father, a shoe salesman, suffered from alcoholism. His mother infused in him a strong religious sense that he maintained through adulthood and that became an integral part of his approach to policy issues. He majored in economics at Eureka College, learning classical economics before the rise of Keynesianism. He then became a radio sportscaster, and ultimately went on to a successful career in Hollywood. He appeared in over fifty films, including *King's Row, Bedtime for Bonzo,* and *Knute Rockne—All American,* in which he played dying football star George Gipp (for which role he was ever after nicknamed "the Gipper"). During World War II he joined the army and made training films. Active in the effort to keep the Screen Actors Guild out of the hands of communists, Reagan became president of the guild in 1947 and served six one-year terms. Altogether, his Hollywood experience made two profound impressions on the self-described New Deal Democrat: Taxes were too high (he found himself in the 91 percent income tax bracket in the years before the Kennedy tax cut scaled back the top rate to 70 percent), and communists were a real and determined threat to liberty.

As his movie career ebbed, Reagan took work as the host of General Electric Theater, one of the most-watched television shows of the 1950s. He also traveled around the country for General Electric, giving inspirational speeches to 250,000 employees in 139 plants. These speeches and others focused on the benefits of the free-enterprise system. Reagan would later say that his experience on the speaking circuit was "almost a postgraduate course in political science for me" as he heard hundreds of complaints and stories about "how the ever-expanding federal government was encroaching on liberties we'd always taken for granted."[19] These convictions steadily led him away from his Democratic loyalties. He campaigned for Nixon in 1960 as a "Democrat for Nixon," and then, citing his former party's abandonment of Jeffersonianism, he changed his party affiliation to Republican in 1962. In 1964 Reagan became a national figure in the conservative movement when he worked hard on behalf of Goldwater. Most important, he delivered an address that was nationally televised on October 27, 1964, that put him on the national political map. In "A Time for Choosing," or what became known to his supporters simply as "The Speech," Reagan told Americans,

I have spent most of my life as a Democrat. I recently have seen fit to follow another course. . . .

No nation in history has survived a tax burden that reached a third of its national income. Today, thirty-seven cents out of every dollar earned in this country is the tax collector's share, and yet our government continues to spend seventeen million dollars a day more than the government takes in. . . .

This idea that government is beholden to the people, that it has no other source of power except the sovereign people, is still the newest and the most unique idea in all the long history of man's relation to man. This is the issue of this election: whether we believe in our capacity for self-government or whether we abandon the American revolution and confess that a little intellectual elite in a far-distant capital can plan our lives for us better than we can plan them ourselves.

You and I are told increasingly that we have to choose between a left or right. There is only an up or down: up to man's age-old dream—the ultimate in individual freedom consistent with law and order—or down to the ant heap of totalitarianism. And regardless of their sincerity, their humanitarian motives, those who would trade our freedom for security have embarked on this downward course. . . .

You and I have a rendezvous with destiny. We will preserve for our children this, the last best hope of man on earth, or we will sentence them to take the last step into a thousand years of darkness.[20]

"The Speech" ultimately brought in over $1 million for the Goldwater campaign. It also brought Reagan to the attention of a group of California Republican businessmen, who persuaded him to run for governor in 1966 against incumbent Pat Brown.

Reagan first had to face the moderate Republican mayor of San Francisco, George Christopher, in a bitter primary election. Discounted by Christopher as a mere actor, Reagan won by better than 2 to 1. Then, discounted by Brown too as a mere actor, he beat the incumbent by a million votes. As Reagan closed in on him at the end of the 1966 campaign, Brown ran a commercial in which he told a group of schoolchildren, "I'm running against an actor, and you know who killed Abraham Lincoln, don't you?" (This combination of intellectual snobbishness and meanness afflicted many of Reagan's subsequent foes.) Reagan, for his part, ran against California's burgeoning crime, welfare, taxes, and regulation, as well as the student disorder on its college campuses. In 1966 Reagan's win was only one of many Republican victories, but it would turn out to be the most significant of any of them. In the words of analyst Michael Barone, "Reagan showed, in a state that contained one out of every ten Americans, that the old rule that conservative Republicans could not win in large industrial states was obsolete." As Barone noted, there was a demand in the political marketplace for politicians offering limited government and a culturally conservative response to the turmoils of the day.[21] Almost immediately, Reagan became the favorite of conservatives in the upper tier of Republican presidential prospects.

After a tumultuous four years filled with confrontations both with Democrats in the California legislature and with student radicals—in 1969 he called out the National Guard to restore order at the University of California, Berkeley—Reagan won reelection by a narrower but still solid margin of half a million votes. During his governorship, he scaled back the welfare rolls, cracked down on campus unrest, and balanced the budget, but he also signed some tax increases and what was at that time the most liberal abortion law in the country. He later said that he had not fully understand the implications of the abortion legislation. In 1973 he led the campaign for Proposition 1, a tax-cutting initiative that failed at the polls but succeeded in laying the groundwork for Proposition 13 five years later. For this, Reagan was called by some "the father of the tax revolt." In the process he deepened his contacts with a network of conservative economists who would play a role in his 1980 campaign and in his presidency.

When he won the 1966 California gubernatorial race, Ronald Reagan quickly became the conservatives' favorite for the White House.

After leaving Sacramento in January 1975, Reagan began writing syndicated newspaper columns and giving short radio messages on stations around the country. At one point his column was printed in 226 newspapers and his broadcasts were heard on 286 radio stations.[22] Briefly suspended during his 1976 campaign, these radio and newspaper presentations were resumed after the convention and continued until October 1979. At the same time Reagan used $1.5 million of leftover campaign money to form Citizens for the Republic, which built a grassroots organization and kept his supporters connected. Altogether, Reagan reached millions of Americans on a regular basis with his political message.

What was that message? Remarkably consistent through the years, it started with the proposition that freedom was the essence of the United States. As early as 1952 Reagan had delivered a commencement address in which he had declared that the nation was defined by "nothing but the inherent love of freedom. . . . deep within the heart of each of us is something so God-like and precious that no individual or group has a right to impose his or its will upon the people, that no group can decide for the people as well as they can decide for themselves."[23] The freedom Reagan extolled was not the one promised by the positive rights doctrine of the New Deal or by the social nihilists of the counterculture. It was the old freedom, more or less as understood by the Founders: the freedom found in limited government, constitutionalism, individual rights (including the right to property) against the abuses of the state, and a moral social order of self-restraint in which ordered liberty could thrive.

Reagan's opponents labeled him reactionary as he continued to insist on the importance of things like enumeration of powers, property rights, individual responsibility, and religion, concepts that self-styled progressive thinkers had long discarded. However, to the average citizen it was far from clear that Reagan was wrong. In any case, Reagan's boldness made the progressives uncomfortable, bringing into the daylight as it did the contradictions between the liberal regime and the founding faith that it claimed to be improving.

Every great innovation in public affairs depends for its popular success on a story about how the world works, what is important and what is not, and how things got to be the way they are. The progressive narrative, which had dominated U.S. public life for decades, was based on the propositions that the Founders were mistaken about crucial features of a good polity and that movement away from the founding principles—including the redefinition (and perhaps subordination) of liberty—was hence inevitable progress. Reagan's argument cut to the heart of these propositions by saying, in so many words, that the progressives were wrong. The nation's movement away from founding principles was not progress. It was a mistake, a moment of temporary amnesia when Americans forgot who and what they were, that had led them into the disasters that by 1979 were rapidly accumulating. True progress depended on remembrance. Since FDR, only Goldwater had dared to challenge not just the mechanics of liberal programs but the intellectual essence of the liberal regime. And as Theodore H. White would say, as a politician Reagan had "all the Goldwater virtues and none of his flaws."[24]

Reagan also had some unique virtues of his own, including a sunny demeanor, a self-deprecating sense of humor, and a winning way on the campaign trail. Democratic strategist Tom Quinn, who served as Jerry Brown's presidential campaign manager, asserted that "Ronald Reagan was one of the most effective campaigners in the country."[25] As Reagan's longtime California associate and future U.S. attorney general Edwin Meese III observed, Reagan "enjoyed campaigning, enjoyed the crowds, and enjoyed delivering his message to them, not simply on television, where he excelled, but in person. Reagan drew emotional sustenance from his audience and their responses.... Campaigning was a forum, not simply for stating his ideas, but for informing and energizing those who shared them."[26]

Even if Reagan did not share Goldwater's flaws—except for a penchant for occasional ill-advised comments—Reagan had some of his own. Although firmly in grasp of the big picture, he delegated details to an extent that was sometimes imprudent. In this he was the direct opposite of Carter, who harbored an obsession with detail at the expense of the big picture. Despite Reagan's success in California politics, he had never fully overcome the skepticism of the Washington- and New York–based national media about an actor seeking the presidency. Many Republicans still remembered the fate of Goldwater and hesitated to join another ideological crusade for someone who would be portrayed as an "extremist" by his foes. At the same time, Reagan had angered some conservative activists by declining their entreaties to form a conservative third party. And despite the enormous affection of most movement conservatives for Reagan, it appeared in 1979 that he had not yet wrapped them up. By some estimates, he had a solid base of 30–40 percent of the party, but no more. Indeed, some national commentators in the spring of 1979 claimed they detected slippage by Reagan and a real opening for rivals such as Connally, Baker, Bush, or even Crane.

Above all, many analysts and activists were concerned by Reagan's age. Then sixty-eight, Reagan would turn seventy shortly after inauguration day 1981. Was he up to the rigors of the campaign, not to mention the presidency? In early 1979 Baker's spokesman referred to a Reagan-Baker meeting as a "father-son talk." Crane hoped to capitalize on the question of Reagan's age by serving as the alternative for movement conservatives worried about the issue, and Dole claimed, "I'm the younger Ronald Reagan." Bush made a point of his jogging routine. Reagan's team understood that there was no antidote for these fears but to engage in the hurly-burly of campaigning, to prevail in early primaries, and thus to prove Reagan's mettle on the field of battle.

In the meantime, national polls showed Reagan leading the announced Republican field by big margins. He also possessed a key structural advantage: The race would largely be fought on his terrain. In the view of *Washington Post* correspondent Mark Shields, writing on the morning of Reagan's November 13, 1979, announcement, "In one very important sense, former California Gov. Ronald Reagan has already won the campaign that he enters tonight. For, in fact, Mr. Reagan, more than any other national figure, has determined the public agenda for the presidential campaign of 1980."[27] Reagan's apparent dominance of the field allowed him to pursue what political scientist Charles O. Jones called a "trifocal" strategy, aiming simultaneously (rather than sequentially) for an advance toward winning the Republican nomination, for unification of the party, and for winning the general election.[28] The rest of the field faced a two-step challenge: First to become the clear alternative to Reagan by defeating his rivals, then to somehow defeat Reagan himself.

In mid-1979 only one other Republican could match Reagan's stature: Gerald R. Ford, former president of the United States, in 1976 the narrowest of victors over Reagan and the narrowest of losers to Carter. Though Reaganites were bitter at his use of incumbency in the Kansas City convention, Ford retained the admiration of many Republicans for his service in the difficult post-Watergate time. They also respected him for his hard-charging campaign against Carter in which he came within a hair's breadth of erasing a 23 point deficit. But Ford continued to carry the burden of having pardoned Nixon and of having been an "accidental president." In the Republican primaries he would carry the additional burden, as did Baker, of having publicly supported the Panama Canal treaties. Nevertheless, polls in the late 1970s consistently tested Ford's name against Reagan and Carter and found him competitive. Carter's pollster Patrick Caddell later said that the Carter camp most feared Ford.

Although solidly conservative as a Republican congressional leader from Grand Rapids, Michigan, in the 1960s, Ford did not like Reagan. He blamed Reagan's 1976 challenge for undermining his reelection bid. Admitting in his memoirs that Reagan was "far more knowledgeable about a wide range of issues than many people thought," Ford also decried the Californian for "his penchant for offering simplistic solutions to hideously complex problems."[29] Ford distrusted the new social conservatives and Reagan's populism. Analysts anticipated that Ford would draw his greatest strength among moderate Republicans, as he had done in the 1976 GOP primaries. Consequently, though Ford posed a threat to Reagan by virtue of his stature, he posed a mortal danger to candidates like Bush and Baker by virtue of his ideological position in the Republican field.

If Ford were to run, he would be running without the benefit of incumbency, and it was not clear whether he (or his wife Betty) had the stomach for another grueling campaign. In April 1979 the former president said he "would not duck the responsibility" of becoming the GOP nominee if Republicans were deadlocked. After saying "I'm not a candidate. . . . I have no plans to be a candidate," Ford added "I learned a long time ago in politics, never say never."[30] Ford remained a question mark for months. Bush was said to have Ford's blessing and had clearly inherited a large part of his national organization, while Ford wrote a fund-raising letter for Dole's concurrent Senate campaign. All the time, the thirty-eighth president remained a "statesman-in-waiting."[31]

Analysts have held widely varying views on how to assess the field of serious Republican candidates. To Theodore H. White they were the "most impressive group of aspirants that the old party had offered the nation since primaries first let people pick candidates."[32] Michael Barone less charitably declared that "by standard criteria the Republican field was not awesome."[33] Whatever their capacities, they collectively represented the degree to which the Republican Party and national sentiment had shifted to the right. Of the whole batch, only Anderson carried the standard once held by mighty contenders like Nelson Rockefeller and Thomas Dewey. Even the moderates like Bush and Baker brought to their campaigns themes of less government, balanced budgets, and a tougher line against the Soviets. If the Republicans were largely united on the message, they were also unusually optimistic about their chances.

THE RACE FOR THE NOMINATIONS
THE DEFEAT OF THE LIBERALS,
THE VICTORY OF THE SUNBELT

President Carter's "crisis of confidence" speech brought a momentary rise of about 10 percentage points in Carter's approval ratings. Within days the bounce was gone amid concerns about his leadership abilities. When he followed up by asking his entire cabinet to resign and then accepted only three of the resignations, his request was widely seen as a cynical gimmick. Then gasoline shortages resumed in August 1979. Buffeted by a nearly unending stream of bad domestic news, Carter was suddenly whipsawed by more bad news from abroad. Over the Labor Day weekend, American intelligence reports were published confirming the existence of a 2,000-man Soviet combat brigade on Cuba, leading to a firestorm in Congress. Senate Foreign Relations Committee chairman Frank Church (D.-Idaho), lambasted the administration. Church, one of the most liberal members of the Senate, was facing a tough reelection fight in 1980. Carter was forced to attend to the matter on national television and attempted to reassure the nation on September 7 (coincidentally, the day Kennedy told him that he was reconsidering his noncandidacy statement). Trying to look strong, he declared that "this status quo is not acceptable." When it became clear within a short time that the status quo was indeed going to be accepted, he became Teddy Roosevelt in reverse, speaking loudly and carrying a twig. An increasing majority of Americans thought Carter too small for the job. He even became the object of ridicule when he claimed to have been attacked by a large rabbit while fishing in Georgia, and his collapse during a 10-kilometer run added to a perception of weakness.

In early September 1979 Henry Ford II was asked if he supported Carter as strongly as he had in 1976, when he had been a big backer. "We all make mistakes," was Ford's reply. It was a reply that captured what seemed to be on most Americans' minds. More troubling to Carter, it was a sentiment shared by many of his erstwhile supporters. Figures such as 1976 Carter fund-raiser Morris Dees fled to the Kennedy camp, as did Peter F. Flaherty, who had engineered Carter's big win in the 1976 Pennsylvania primary. Carter appeared to be more vulnerable to intraparty challenge than had been any but a handful of elected incumbent presidents—perhaps Johnson in 1968, Truman in 1952, or William Howard Taft in 1912. Kennedy was set to announce his formal entry into the race on November 7.

Carter, despite his troubles, was not going to lie down. The Carter camp had been preparing for a serious challenge for months, during which time they had built a strong organization and had succeeded in shifting a few key primary dates to their liking (unfriendly Connecticut moved later; friendly Florida, Georgia, and Missouri moved earlier). Not least, the president and his men had honed their strategy. They would make Kennedy the issue, focusing first on character and then, if necessary, on ideology. They would do their best to foreclose a protest vote by framing the choice not as a primary election ("who suits you best?") but as a general election ("who do you want to be president?"). In October Carter prevailed in a Florida caucus test vote and by all accounts became more disciplined and more aggressive. As Kennedy's candidacy became less of an abstraction, Democratic politicians and activists began to examine his flaws more closely. An internal White House survey of Democratic state chairmen showed that Carter had pulled in front. On October 20 Carter ventured into the lion's den, giving well-received remarks at the opening of the John F. Kennedy Presidential Library in Boston. Some national polls of Democratic voters also showed the race narrowing, though Kennedy retained a healthy lead.

Then, on November 4, the world turned upside down. A nationally televised CBS documentary on Kennedy, featuring interviews with Kennedy by family friend Roger Mudd, turned ugly when Mudd pressed the Massachusetts senator on Chappaquiddick, his faltering marriage, and other difficult issues. Kennedy was also unable to explain cogently why he wanted to be president:

Well, I'm—were I to—to make the—announcement . . . is because I have a great belief in this country, that it is—has more natural resources than any nation in the world . . . the greatest technology of any country in the world . . . the greatest political system in the world. . . . And the energies and resourcefulness of this nation, I think, should be focused on these problems in a way that brings a sense of restoration in this country by its people to. . . . And I would basically feel that—that it's imperative for this country to move forward, that it can't stand still, or otherwise it moves back.[1]

The interview aired against the television premier of *Jaws,* but it was Kennedy who was flailing in deep water.

As catastrophic as it was, the Mudd interview did not hurt Kennedy as much as did the other big news of November 4, 1979: the capture of the U.S. Embassy in Tehran, the capital of Iran, by Islamic radicals. Since the victory of the Islamic revolution in Iran, revolutionary violence and anti-American rhetoric had become ascendant. In February the embassy had been seized and held for a few hours. The twenty-man crew of a U.S. Air Force listening post in northern Iran had also been held captive for several days. When the former shah, who had been diagnosed with cancer, appealed for entry to the United States for medical treatment, Carter had faced a difficult decision: Should he show compassion to a former ally, even at the risk of provoking further violence against Americans still in Iran? On October 20, he had approved the entry.

The seizure of sixty-six Americans by the revolutionary mob demanding that the United States send the shah and his fortune back to Iran changed the face of U.S. politics almost immediately. The shah's entry may have been the reason for the attack, or it may only have been the pretext. Either way, Americans were treated to nightly pictures of blindfolded hostages being paraded by their captors and of hate-filled crowds chanting "Death to America" and "Death to Carter." Burned indelibly into their minds was the picture of two Iranian radicals using a U.S. flag to carry out garbage. While the Ayatollah Khomeini, the supreme governing authority in revolutionary Iran, sought to maintain the façade that "students" had taken and were keeping the hostages, it was quite clear that they remained hostages with his blessing. Although a handful were released, ultimately bringing the number held to fifty-two, it also quickly became clear that this crisis was more significant and more difficult than the short-lived disturbance of the previous February. ABC started a nightly news program, which became *Nightline,* to track the crisis. After about two months, CBS evening news anchor Walter Cronkite started a practice of ending each broadcast by stating how many days the hostages had been in captivity.

In theory Carter might have been blamed for the crisis—either because he had let the shah into the United States or because he had let Khomeini into Iran—but the short-term response of Americans was to rally around their flag and their president. Within a month Carter's approval rating had jumped to 61 percent (he had been at 32 percent just before the crisis began), and he led Kennedy among Democrats nationally by a margin of 48 percent to 40 percent (he had been behind 54 percent to 32 percent in early November). Both Kennedy and Brown had the misfortune of formally announcing their candidacies the week after the hostage crisis broke, and they saw their announcements overshadowed. Carter was also able to adopt a new strategic position: the Rose Garden strategy, in which he emphasized his presidential duties and allowed direct campaigning to be done by surrogates like First Lady Rosalynn, Vice President Mondale, and cabinet secretaries. Henceforth, for the next six months, Carter would remain "above the fray," refusing to directly engage his opponents.

The crisis not only changed the political balance; it also fundamentally changed the political climate in the country. Almost overnight, there was a revival of American patriotism unseen in the decade of the 1970s. It was as if Americans, humiliated in Vietnam, regularly scorned in the United Nations by a motley collection of Third World tyrants, and in retreat around the world for the better part of the decade, had simply decided that enough was enough. As historian David Farber recounts,

> Americans demonstrated both a sometimes fierce, even xenophobic nationalism and emotional bond to their fellow Americans held captive in Iran. . . . Longshoremen spontaneously decided not to load any cargo bound for Iran. . . . millions of people kept their car headlights on during the day to show their solidarity. Church bells rang at midday to honor the captives. . . . hundreds of thousands of Americans wrote letters to the Iranian embassy and the Iranian U.N. delegation. Dozens of popular songs about the crisis played on the airwaves.[2]

Flag sales ballooned, rallies extolled the blessings of the United States, and sporting stores began carrying shooting targets centered on Khomeini's all-too-familiar face.

Yet November 4 drew only the threat of a military response. President Carter ordered two aircraft carriers and their support ships into the Persian Gulf, a deployment featured by newsmagazines that declared "U.S. Builds for a Showdown." The administration rejected Iranian demands for the return of the shah and his money and secretly drew up plans for a rescue mission, a naval blockade, or the mining of Iranian harbors. While Carter tried desperately to negotiate, operating as if Iran had a viable and rational government, he left little doubt that the United States would retaliate with force if the hostages were harmed. On the other hand, he refused to use force to respond to the seizure itself, a violation of international law that could by itself have justified war.

Carter's decision not to use force in November or December 1979 must be considered one of the key decisions of his presidency, though it is impossible to know whether it was for good or ill. Carter aides later held that the president's restraint may have prevented a confrontation with the Soviet Union over Iran, and it may well have saved the lives of the hostages. On the other hand, a more forceful response—or the threat of one—might have resolved the issue much sooner, before it could turn against Carter as 1980 wore on. Such a development may or may not have saved the presidency for Carter. It was, after all, the onset of the hostage crisis that had restored his political fortunes, and Republicans and Democrats alike agreed that Carter would be subjected to some severe questioning about Iran once the crisis was over.

Treating the act of war as an act of war might also have turned aside the swiftly gathering tide of Islamic extremism that flowed from the Iranian revolution. In a certain sense, Iran was the opening salvo of what has now, by the early twenty-first century, been a quarter century of jihad against the United States, and the United States held its fire. When commentators later remarked upon the unprecedented brazenness of the September 11 hijackers attacking U.S. soil, they forgot that the U.S. Embassy in Tehran had also been U.S. soil. In retrospect, it is difficult to avoid the conclusion that the humiliation the United States suffered and the utter lack of punishment of those who inflicted it had an invigorating effect on jihadists everywhere.

Finally, it is conceivable that rather than bringing confrontation with the Soviets, early U.S. military action against Iran might have deterred the Soviet invasion of Afghanistan. Instead, with no fear of a U.S. response and a great deal of fear that their Afghan clients were on the verge of collapse, Soviet troops took Kabul, the capital of Afghanistan, on Christmas Day, 1979. The hostage crisis brought Americans' blood to a boil, but Afghanistan was also crucial in rallying the public to a new patriotism and a harder foreign policy line. The Soviets had crossed an important threshold. Before, the Kremlin had always considered it necessary to cover Third World interventions with the use of proxies, such as Cubans in Angola. It was an ominous sign when the Soviets no longer felt such a fig leaf important. The geography of their thrust was also particularly troublesome. In combination with their control of Ethiopia and South Yemen, Soviet control of Afghanistan was drawing a noose around the Persian Gulf.

"Détente" seemed, more than ever, to have been a mere tactical device by the Soviets to lull the West while seeking a decisive advantage in the "correlation of forces" in contests around the globe. The Cold War, which had never really ended in the Kremlin, was back on in Washington. In short order, Carter withdrew SALT II from Senate consideration, announced an embargo on grain sales to the Soviet Union, and declared a U.S. boycott of the 1980 summer Olympics to be held in Moscow, fearing a reprise of the 1936 Nazi propaganda extravaganza in Berlin. Carter admitted in an interview that "the action of the Soviets has made a more dramatic change in my opinion of what the Soviets' ultimate goals are than anything they've done in the previous time that I've been in office." The newsmagazines declared "détente" to be dead; their covers featured illustrations of doves crushed under the treads of Soviet tanks.

When Carter delivered his State of the Union address on January 23, 1980, the vast majority of it was devoted to foreign policy. He called the Soviet invasion "a radical and an aggressive new step" whose implications "could pose the most serious threat to the peace since the Second World War." He then drew a line in the sand: "An attempt by any outside force to gain control of the Persian Gulf region will be regarded as an assault on the vital interests of the United States of America, and such an assault will be repelled by any means necessary, including military force."

This "Carter Doctrine," as it immediately came to be called, would be backed up with loosened restrictions on intelligence agencies, resumption of selective service registration, a bigger defense buildup, and the bolstering of the newly formed Rapid Deployment Force for use in the Middle East. Carter had already come to support a modest defense increase. In 1979 he had dispatched an aircraft carrier to discourage a Cuban-backed assault on North Yemen and had endorsed a NATO plan to counter Soviet SS-20s with a deployment of "Euromissiles." His transformation from proponent of McGovernism to Cold Warrior was now complete.

In the long run, the reentry of the United States into the Cold War posed political difficulties for Carter. It was too easy to ask: If a tougher policy was needed, why not go with a candidate who had known that all along? And how exactly was it that the president, in a decade filled with Soviet advances, had noticed nothing amiss until Afghanistan? For the time being, however, the main effect was to showcase Carter as a national leader and Kennedy as the chief spokesman of the party's anti-anticommunists.

It was in this atmosphere that the Iowa caucuses had been held two days earlier, on January 21. In the spring of 1979, before the Mudd interview, before Iran, before Afghanistan, observers in Iowa had held Carter to be in serious trouble. A *Des Moines Register* poll showed Carter trailing Kennedy by 40–17 among Democrats. Carter, of all people, had to take Iowa seriously; he had put it on the political map in 1976 when his early "win" there helped propel him to the Democratic nomination. Now almost every candidate in both parties saw Iowa and the early primaries as the gateway to the nomination. If 1976 had shown the way to the new dynamic in nomination politics, 1980 codified it.

Kennedy had called Iowa the first real test of the campaign and had set a goal of keeping Carter below 50 percent in what was essentially a four-way race (Carter, Kennedy, Brown, and uncommitted). When the caucus votes were tallied on the night of January 21, Jimmy Carter had beaten Kennedy by nearly a 2-to-1 margin (59 percent to 31 percent, with Brown around 10 percent). Carter had beaten Kennedy's self-declared 50 percent threshold with room to spare, carrying all but one of Iowa's ninety-nine counties. Iowa's heavy union population and reputation for dovishness did not avail the challenger. It was the first time that Ted Kennedy had ever lost an election.

Carter had effectively translated his constitutional position into an unassailable political position. Just as the public seemed to be growing a bit weary of the Rose Garden strategy, Afghanistan revived it, allowing Carter to cancel the one scheduled debate in Iowa. For his part, Kennedy suffered one misfortune after another, many of them self-inflicted. Because of the hostage crisis, the challenger received not one mention on national television news for two weeks after his announcement. When the media began paying attention again, Kennedy invited a deluge of criticism by attacking the shah, inadvertently placing himself on the side of the Ayatollah; crowds in Tehran cheered his name, a distinctly unhelpful development. After the Soviet invasion of Afghanistan, he criti-

Carter's 1980 State of the Union Address was
a call to arms against Soviet expansionism.

cized Carter for the grain embargo and Olympic boycott, leading Vice President Mondale to implicitly question his patriotism.

Carter out-organized Kennedy in Iowa—a result that had already been hinted at in his sweep of the state's Democratic straw poll in December—and almost everywhere else. The national Kennedy headquarters in Washington, D.C., did not have phone service until several days after it had opened. Kennedy's syntax was notoriously poor, and once the challenger referred to a "farmily fam," he was set upon by the press every time he flubbed a line. In response, Kennedy's staff imposed on him written speeches; as a result, his delivery was forced.

Then came the inevitable media probing of Chappaquiddick, including highly damaging stories in *Reader's Digest* and the *Washington Star*. Carter capitalized on Kennedy's problems by running ads in Iowa highlighting the president as a family man: "Husband. Father. President. He's done all three jobs with distinction." Feminists, a potential source of energy for the Kennedy campaign, were turned off by accounts of his womanizing and dissembling. His campaign also faced money problems. By January 21, 1980, the Kennedy campaign had raised $4.1 million. Only $160,000 was left. Crippled by the campaign finance law of 1974, which limited individual contributions to $1,000, Ted (unlike his brothers) was unable to rely on the family fortune or the beneficence of a few dedicated rich supporters. Thus, the Kennedy campaign in twenty-seven states was "self-financing," meaning the state organizations had to raise their own budgets.

Kennedy suffered from endless comparisons with his brothers, none of them flattering. Above all, though, was the problem of his message. Theodore White argued that Kennedy had struggled to find a theme beyond a nonideological promise of "leadership": "No message had come clear enough to remove a sitting President from leadership. The rest of the Kennedy campaign was an exercise in personality."[3] Kennedy attacked the Carter diagnosis of "malaise." His signal phrase during the Iowa campaign—"The issue that is really before us as a people is whether we are going to continue a policy of drift here at home and a policy of lurching from crisis to crisis overseas"—neatly captured the fears of many Americans. Yet Kennedy failed to follow up with a coherent vision of what would stop the drifting and lurching.

Perhaps, as Pat Caddell argued, Democratic voters had shifted to the right; perhaps the weight of events abroad had not only bolstered the president but made Kennedy's foreign policy positions implausible. At any rate, Kennedy seemed to think that was the case. In Iowa he called for a balanced budget, supported a defense increase, blamed the hostage crisis on a loss of world respect for the United States, and chastised Carter for allowing "Cubans in Angola, Soviets in Cuba, and Soviets in Afghanistan." He was largely constrained by Iran and Afghanistan from attacking the president personally, though, and he had clearly lost the one issue he had hoped would catapult him to the nomination: Perceptions of Carter as unpresidential and unelectable disappeared, at least for the moment.

Like the Democratic contestants, the Republicans knew how important it was to win Iowa. No one understood better than George Bush, whose campaign had consciously copied Carter's intensive and early focus on the state four years earlier. Bush had built an excellent organization in Iowa, and he won all six straw polls that were held there in 1979. (He also won a straw poll in Maine, grievously wounding Howard Baker, and placed a close third in a Florida straw poll, breathing down John Connally's neck in that crucial southern state.) Altogether, Bush had spent 329 days campaigning in 1979, a large portion of them in Iowa. As Carter had in 1976, the little-known Bush staked everything on gaining national exposure from an early win in 1980.

The front-runner, Reagan, also understood the importance of Iowa but was led to believe by his campaign manager, John Sears, that victory was well in hand. Indeed, Reagan considered Iowa—where he had started his broadcasting career—as his "adopted home state."[4] Consequently, he campaigned little there, making only eight perfunctory appearances, and declined to enter the January 5 debate sponsored by the *Des Moines Register and Tribune*. This was a mistake, and not only because Bush was outworking him there. It also gave Reagan little opportunity to reassure voters concerned by his age. According to polls, Reagan's support in Iowa fell from 50 percent to 26 percent after the debate.

Except for Reagan (who still appealed to conservatives) and Bush (whose foreign policy experience suddenly seemed much more relevant), no other candidates were catching fire, in Iowa or elsewhere. Crane was too obscure, Dole too wooden, and Baker and Connally too disorganized, though Connally had raised millions of dollars. Baker also suffered from the withdrawal of the SALT II treaty from Senate consideration; he had built his strategy around playing a pivotal role in the deliberations. Aware of the danger from Bush, Baker launched a last-minute ad blitz against him. Anderson received media plaudits for his debate performance on January 5, when he alone declared himself in support of the grain embargo. Iowa Republicans were not so sure about the embargo. But in any case, Anderson was focusing on New Hampshire.

Bush came in ahead of Reagan, 31.5 percent to 29.4 percent, despite an unprecedented mobilization of pro-life voters for Reagan. The rest of the Republican field ran far behind. Commentators began writing Reagan's political obituary and declared Bush the new front-runner. Bush proclaimed himself the owner of "Big Mo"—a Don Meredith phrase from *Monday Night Football* transported to the world of politics to describe the intangible momentum that every primary candidate covets.

As in 1976, five weeks separated the Iowa caucuses from the New Hampshire primaries. Then, Carter had used the interval to great effect to build on his unexpected success. Now, in 1980, Bush hoped to do the same and was actually in a better position than Carter had been to do so: He was already organized in forty states. Reagan and Kennedy knew that February 26, 1980, could be the expiration date on their realistic presidential aspirations. On the Republican side, polls put Bush suddenly ahead in New Hampshire. Heady with success, Bush seemed unsure what to do next and could talk only of his "momentum." Two days before the Iowa caucuses, Bush had decided to avoid taking the campaign to a new level of issue specificity.[5] In the words of his political director, David Keene, "Phase two wasn't ready."[6]

Reagan, for his part, made a radical shift in strategy after the Iowa caucuses. He shucked the above-the-fray front-runner approach in favor of a much more active and engaged campaign. As he later described it, "Day after day, we traveled in the snow-splattered highways of the state from early in the morning to late at night; I'd speak to anyone who was willing to listen to me, then we'd get back in our convoy of cars and buses and drive someplace else and seldom got to bed before midnight."[7] Reagan's organization on the ground in New Hampshire also redoubled its efforts. Gerald Carmen, running the campaign in the Granite State, showed up for work at 5:30 the morning after Iowa, and he later acknowledged that "we couldn't lose it" in New Hampshire without being driven from the race.[8]

Unlike in Iowa, Reagan also participated in two debates. Both were important, though only the second is famous. The *Nashua Telegraph* sponsored that second debate but wanted to limit it to the two leaders, Reagan and Bush. When the Federal Election Commission ruled in favor of a Dole complaint that this arrangement constituted an illegal campaign contribution by the *Telegraph* to Reagan and Bush, Reagan agreed to pick up the cost from the newspaper and then invited the other five major candidates, Anderson, Baker, Connally, Crane, and Dole. On the evening of the debate, four of the five others appeared; only Connally was absent. Bush was flummoxed and speechless, preferring a return to the original arrangement, though he had agreed with his staff ahead of time to let other candidates in if such a situation were to develop. When Reagan tried to address the restless crowd, *Nashua Telegraph* editor Jon Breen tried to shut off his microphone. Without missing a beat, Reagan retorted, "I'm paying for this microphone, Mr. Green" (almost getting the name right). The crowd cheered.

When all was said and done, Bush looked stiff and petty, Reagan looked generous and firm, and the rest of the field looked like props in a play larger than themselves. Reagan's staff would tell him that "the gymnasium parking lot was littered with Bush-for-President badges."[9] The next night, the networks spent 20 percent of their news segments covering the confrontation in Nashua. Bush compounded his errors by running radio ads trying to explain what had happened and by leaving for Houston forty-eight hours before the voting began.

Most commentators then and since have considered this moment a key turning point. In reality, Reagan's comeback had much more to do with his antitax message, which resonated well in a state whose residents had long resisted the imposition of an income tax. Bush, more skeptical of big tax cuts, paid a price for his skepticism. (Remembering the lesson, Bush took pains to sign the "no new taxes" pledge in New Hampshire when he ran for president again in 1988.) Reagan also benefited from a well-organized campaign run on his behalf by the National Rifle Association (NRA), one of that organization's first major forays into presidential politics. (Anderson, for his part, burnished his contrarian credentials by telling a meeting of the Gun Owners of New Hampshire that they should support gun registration.) Before the Nashua debate, polls showed that Reagan had already regained the lead—starting with the first debate in Manchester, New Hampshire, where he had scored with his humor and his eloquent closing statement. In the view of Reagan's pollster Richard Wirthlin, the Manchester debate was the turning point of the New Hampshire primary. To Wirthlin, Manchester established Reagan's credibility and was "one of those defining moments when he was able to reach the right audience with the right message."[10]

Meanwhile, tension built to a boil in the Reagan camp between John Sears, who had also managed Reagan's 1976 campaign, and the Californians who had advised and befriended Reagan since his earliest days on the gubernatorial campaign trail. Gerald Carmen later said that 1980 in New Hampshire was "the only election I've ever been in where the campaign manager was more of an issue than the candidate," and the resulting disruption extended "all up and down the chain."[11] Part of the tension was personal. In November Sears had pushed for the resignation of Reagan's longtime family friend Michael Deaver. He had also driven out press aide Lyn Nofziger and policy adviser Martin Anderson, and he had his sights set on Ed Meese, the last of the Californians. Disagreements over strategy also played a role. Sears had brought the campaign credibility in the eyes of the Eastern press corps, but his strategic blunder in Iowa was, to the mind of the Californians, of a piece with his more general tendency to keep Reagan under wraps as much as possible. Not least, Sears had allowed the campaign's finances to spin out of control. On February 26, the very day of the New Hampshire primary, Reagan fired Sears and replaced him with William Casey; the exiled Californians returned. Intending to let Sears go in any event, Reagan did so before the primary results were known. He would not be accused of scapegoating if the results showed a Bush win.

He need not have worried: The results were Reagan 49.6 percent, Bush 22.7 percent. No one else was close. Baker came in third with a scant 12 percent, Anderson won a fraction under 10 percent, Crane and Connally tallied under 2 percent each. Bob Dole finished with 587 votes. (It would not be the last time that New Hampshire would bedevil Dole, who lost primaries there to George H. W. Bush in 1988 and to Patrick Buchanan in 1996.) Bush's campaign had missed its moment of opportunity. Reagan was again the undisputed front-runner.

On the Democratic side, the campaign was not as dramatic, nor was the victor's margin as decisive, but the effect was ultimately as profound. Carter used the presidency quite blatantly in New Hampshire, announcing funds for a new four-lane highway, a Small Business Administration loan to struggling ski resorts, and a special commuter train from Concord to Boston. The day before the primary, the president publicly welcomed to the White House the U.S. Olympic hockey team, which had won an emotional victory against the supposedly "invincible" Soviet team and then gone on to win the gold medal in the 1980 winter Olympics. Just as in the Republican race, the NRA campaigned, in this case against Kennedy.

After his tack rightward in Iowa, Kennedy returned to the left in New Hampshire, staking out his familiar ideological position, to which he adhered for the rest of the campaign. In a major address at Georgetown University on January 28, Kennedy declared, "I have not yet begun to fight," reiterated his demand for national health insurance, and called for new wage and price controls and gasoline rationing. He opposed sanctions against Iran, supported a U.N. tribunal to examine the "crimes of the Shah," and warned against Carter's "helter-skelter militarism," including draft registration. Kennedy's address won an estimated 20 percent of the airtime available on the evening news.

The force of the speech halted Kennedy's slide in the Granite State but did not revive his standing nationally. Kennedy refocused on economics, telling the New Hampshire United Auto Workers that the United States faced "the greatest economic crisis since the Depression." The challenger was increasingly frustrated by the president's insulation from the campaign, once "debating" a tape recording of remarks Carter had made in 1978. Kennedy was out of money and bereft of professional polling, but Carter's New Hampshire polling revealed growing concern among voters about the danger of war. Kennedy had already won a "moral victory" by coming within 4 points of the president in the Maine caucuses, largely with the aid of student volunteers upset about draft registration. Carter reoriented his message, stressing the Camp David Accords and other evidence that he was a "peacemaker." When the votes were counted, Carter had replayed his 1976 win, outdistancing Kennedy by 47 percent to 37 percent.

Jerry Brown, whose campaign was lost in the drama and increasing animosity of the Carter-Kennedy contest, received only one in ten votes, the same proportion as in Iowa. Brown, like Carter and Kennedy, had staked much on early success. Now he retreated, declaring that he would make a last stand in Wisconsin on April 1.

Reagan's first task after New Hampshire was to put his financial house in order. He had already expended two-thirds of his federally allowed spending, and William Casey put the campaign on a sounder footing by reining in expenses. The remaining key Republican primaries included

Massachusetts and Vermont (March 4), South Carolina (March 8), Illinois (March 18), Wisconsin (April 1), Pennsylvania (April 22), Texas (May 3), and Michigan (May 20). Reagan was not expected to win the New England pair, but he had to show credibly. Bush was reeling from defeat in New Hampshire, but he saw an opportunity in Massachusetts and Vermont to consolidate a position as the moderate alternative to Reagan. Anderson hoped to build on his respectable finish. The New England primaries were very tight. Reagan won narrowly in Vermont and finished a close third in Massachusetts. Bush narrowly won Massachusetts and placed third in Vermont. Anderson finished a close second in both. Strategically, the winner was Reagan. He had held his own, and Bush had failed to break out as the sole alternative. Despite winning no primaries, Anderson—who posed much less of a real threat to Reagan than Bush did—became a media cause célèbre because of his unexpected surge.

South Carolina's Republicans had decided for the first time to hold an open primary as a party-building measure designed to attract attention and draw some Democratic voters into the GOP. John Connally chose to make a last-ditch stand against Reagan in that primary. By then, he had been hurt badly by an October speech he had made on Middle East peace in which he suggested the creation of a Palestinian state and Israel's return to the 1967 borders, safeguarded by U.S. troops. He had also been hurt by his loss to Reagan in the Florida straw poll. As a result of the New Hampshire primary, Bush had already supplanted Connally as the main alternative to Reagan. In the end, despite being endorsed by Senator Strom Thurmond and former governor James Edwards, the gulf between Connally's fund-raising prowess and his popular appeal was demonstrated: He won only 30 percent to Reagan's 55 percent.

Reagan was propelled into big wins in three following southern primaries. Connally was propelled into a statement ending his campaign on March 9. He had spent $12.6 million and could claim one delegate. South Carolina Republicans, in disposing of Connally, began a long tradition of sorting out their party's competitors, a role they would play again in 1988, 1996, and 2000.

A hidden victory in this period was also crucial to Reagan's nomination. Since declaring "never say never" in April 1979, Gerald Ford had dabbled with the prospect of entering the race. Wirthlin called this possibility "the Damocles' sword, if you will, hanging over our head."[12] At first Ford had described his availability as a contingency in case of a deadlock among the other Republican candidates, but in early 1980 the possibility began to take on the flavor of a "stop Reagan" effort. The day after the New Hampshire primary, Ford flatly asserted in a *New York Times* interview that Reagan could not be elected because he was too conservative. Some moderates in the party then implored him to take up the mantle, pressure that increased after Baker left the race on March 5. Reagan's campaign manager, William Casey, later remarked that he was "scared to death" by Ford's ruminations.[13]

A Draft Ford Committee was established. But the nominating system of 1980 was not the nominating system of 1952, when party leaders could draft a reluctant Adlai Stevenson to stop a hard-charging Estes Kefauver. Reagan's delegates were pledged, and he was rapidly accumulating enough of them to make such Byzantine maneuvering moot. At least as important, the popular legitimacy conferred by his victories in the primaries counted for more in 1980 than it would have in 1952, before the McGovern-Fraser Commission's demand in 1970 for "full, meaningful, and timely participation" served as the basis for reform in both parties. Ford was reluctant to split the party, Bush made it clear he would not roll over for the former president, and Republican governors discouraged Ford from entering.

On March 12 Ford met with his advisers and was not given a promising prognosis. On March 15 he declared definitively, "I will not become a candidate. I will support the nominee of my party with all the energy I have. America is in deep, deep trouble and needs the help of all of us." It is far from clear that Ford could have stopped Reagan had he entered—Wirthlin thought not—but the road to Reagan's nomination was now a much smoother one.

In Illinois on March 18 Reagan (himself an Illinois native) had to face not one but two other favorite sons: John Anderson and Philip Crane. Crane was fading. Anderson came out of New England strong, and in Illinois he was running in a state with a moderate Republican governor, James Thompson. Over the previous two months he had also been "discovered" by American liberals, aided by the support of General Motors heir Stewart Mott (who had given George McGovern $400,000 in 1972) and by being favorably featured in the cartoon *Doonesbury*. Bush was running out of time to consolidate his position, and he launched an attack on Anderson.

As in New Hampshire, a debate was important to the outcome. In the Chicago forum, Reagan teasingly confronted Anderson about the latter's comment in a *Playboy* interview that he would rather have Ted Kennedy as president than Reagan. Then Crane pulled from his pocket a fund-raising letter that Anderson had signed for Senators George McGovern, John Culver, Birch Bayh, and Frank Church—four of the most liberal Democrats in the upper chamber, all engaged in tough reelection fights. Polling showed that Anderson, who had led slightly before the debate, began to trail. His fund-raising dropped off as some Republicans began to realize how liberal he was, and Reagan succeeded in using the debate to humanize himself in the eyes of moderate suburban voters.

After a hard-fought campaign, Reagan prevailed over Anderson, 48 percent to 37 percent. Anderson won a majority of crossover votes from Democrats and independents, but Reagan won a solid 30 percent of them too. On the other hand, Anderson only won 26 percent of the Republicans who cast a ballot. Anderson fought on, but he was irreparably wounded within the GOP. Bush was a distant third. Crane was an even more distant fourth, and was finished.

Wisconsin's open primary, held two weeks later, had significantly affected numerous nomination races over the years. Lyndon Johnson had been driven from the Democratic race in 1968 by the prospect of losing Wisconsin, and George McGovern had become a plausible front-runner by winning there four years later. Because of its history, journalists automatically assigned Wisconsin importance. Bush and Anderson each looked to its progressive pedigree, dating back to former governor and U.S. senator Fighting Bob LaFollette shortly after the turn of the century, and saw the Wisconsin primary as a crucial opportunity for them to regain their footing. (Of course, Wisconsin's tradition was hardly monolithic—the state had also been the home of Senator Joseph McCarthy on the right.) That did not happen. Relying on a strong appeal to culturally conservative and anticommunist ethnic voters, including Democrats who could vote in the open primary, Reagan won Wisconsin on April 1 by a solid margin of 40 percent to Bush's second-place 30 percent and with Anderson bringing up the rear with 27 percent.

In Pennsylvania, which voted on April 22, Bush sharpened his own proposals and focused his attacks on Reagan's economic program, which he famously called "voodoo economics" (a phrase Democrats would still be using years later). "Phase two" of Bush's issue development had finally arrived, but too late to save the nomination for Bush. Bush also spent $800,000 in Pennsylvania to Reagan's $30,000. By winning a modest victory in the presidential preference poll, Bush kept his campaign alive for another month. However, the superior Reagan organization actually won more delegates than Bush did in the separate delegate selection portion of the Pennsylvania primary. Unlike Bush, Anderson had not been entered in Pennsylvania due to a staff error (as a write-in candidate, he still got 2.1 percent of the vote). Two days after the Pennsylvania primary that momentarily saved George Bush's bid for the Republican nomination, Anderson's ended.

Anderson's withdrawal set up a May 3 Texas showdown between the top two contenders, Reagan and Bush. At long last, Bush had achieved his strategic goal. Texas was, in a way, Bush's home field, and Connally's withdrawal gave him a clean shot, though it was never clear whether Connally would have taken more votes from Bush the fellow Texan or from Reagan the fellow conservative. Bush's New England roots had always kept many Texans from seeing him as one of their own, and he had failed in two statewide campaigns for U.S. Senate, though he had won the Republican nomination. Reagan campaigned as the true conservative, as he had in his wipeout victory over Ford in 1976. Bush spent $500,000, Reagan almost nothing; after having wildly overspent in the early months of the race, his campaign was nearly broke. Bush had been charging on the campaign trail that Reagan was behind the distribution of fliers tying him to the Trilateral Commission, a group of prominent individuals accused by some ultraconservatives of promoting "one world government." When Bush meekly backed away from his allegations in an impromptu televised confrontation, he was hurt.[14] On primary day, Bush came close, but not close enough. Reagan won, 51 percent to 47 percent.

Bush kept fighting, but Reagan racked up another five primary wins. In Michigan on May 20, Bush won a wide victory, gaining a 58-to-32 margin with the active help of Governor William Milliken. Nevertheless, Bush's "victory" in Michigan and Reagan's in Oregon the same day put Reagan over the minimum number of delegates needed for the nomination. Although one last round of primaries remained, Bush withdrew from the race on May 26, releasing his delegates to Reagan in hopes of retaining goodwill that might be translated into a vice presidential selection.

In total, after the Iowa caucuses, Reagan lost only two primaries in Bush's New England home (Massachusetts and Connecticut) and two large states with substantial moderate Republican strength (Pennsylvania and Michigan). Reagan won 61 percent of the total primary vote and twenty-nine of thirty-three state primaries (excluding Puerto Rico and the District of Columbia, where he did not appear on the ballot). He did even better in the caucus states, winning 83 percent of delegates at stake there because of the premium placed on organization and intensity of support in caucus settings. Bush, trailing far behind, won one-fourth of the primary vote, and Anderson one-eighth. Reagan did best in the West and South, but he compiled impressive majorities in every region.

After spending the three weeks following the Wisconsin primary in personal reflection, Anderson not only left the race, he left the party. Anderson had won not a single primary, but by one academic estimate, he had received the best press in the Republican field from January through April 1980.[15] At the urging of his direct-mail consultant Tom Mathews, liberal Democratic fund-raiser Stanley Shinebaum of Los Angeles, and a host of others, he chose to carry on his fight as an independent candidate for president. It had long been clear that he was more popular outside the Republican Party than he had been inside it, a fact brought home to him in Illinois. Indeed, some observers thought that Anderson's success had contributed to Kennedy's slide by siphoning away some of Teddy's support.[16]

In this endeavor, Anderson exemplified a growing trend. In the nineteenth and early twentieth centuries, non–major party candidates were third-party candidates. Typically, an issue would arise that neither major party wanted to address. A third party would grow from the bottom up, running candidates at the local, state, and congressional levels first. Only after a groundswell of support would it hold a convention, write a platform, and nominate a presidential candidate to carry its banner. As in the major parties, the candidate was a representative of and was subordinate to the party. In the 1900s this model was gradually replaced by one in which a third party was sometimes built around the candidate (Theodore Roosevelt in 1912, Henry Wallace and Strom Thurmond in 1948). By 1968 George Wallace's American Independent Party was little more than a creature of the candidate, who wrote its platform and forbade it from running candidates for lower office.

Anderson took the personalization of alternative politics to the next logical step. He simply ran as an individual, issuing statements and naming a running mate without a pretense of party. Eugene McCarthy had experimented with a truly independent run in 1976; though he was not on all fifty ballots and won only 757,000 votes (0.9 percent), he may have cost Carter between one and four close states.[17] It was Anderson's much stronger run in 1980, though, that presaged H. Ross Perot's anti-party independent campaign of 1992.

Anderson had an ill-concealed contempt for Carter, but he was originally driven above all by a desire to prevent Reagan (whom he sometimes referred to as "this guy, Reagan") from becoming president and to punish his party for having embraced conservatism. It was Reagan's ascent that fueled Anderson's drive, and his first calculations were predicated on how not to inadvertently throw the election to the presumptive Republican nominee.

By Memorial Day Anderson stood at around 25 percent in the polls—only about 10 points behind the major party leaders—and he became a factor that neither major party nominee could ignore. By June 1 Anderson was either on the ballot or engaged in court contests to get on the ballot in every state. Carter feared him as a rival for the liberal vote. And the Reagan campaign produced an internal memo detailing which U.S. House seats Republicans would have to pick up in order to control a majority of state House delegations in the event Anderson's candidacy produced an Electoral College deadlock, which would throw the presidential race into the House for the first time since 1824.[18]

Carter's post–New Hampshire ride was rockier than Reagan's. He never trailed in delegates or in the national polls. He would, however, forge out in front, seemingly on the verge of decisive triumph, then suffer a surprise defeat that kept his rival alive and hoping.

As in the GOP contest, the Illinois primary held the potential to shake up the Democratic race. Kennedy had not yet won a single contest except in Massachusetts, a win that surprised no one and was counterbalanced by a Carter win in Vermont the same day. In the meantime, Carter had breezed through the South. Illinois was a large, urban, industrial, and heavily unionized state with high unemployment and big minority and Catholic populations. On paper, it should have been fertile ground for Kennedy's insurgency. Yet Carter's organization was superb, and the unpopular and abrasive mayor of Chicago, Jane Byrne, had endorsed Kennedy. (Transportation secretary Neil Goldschmidt subsequently declared that he had "lost confidence" in her and would look for other places to spend federal transportation dollars.) Byrne and Kennedy were jeered as they walked together in the Chicago St. Patrick's Day parade. The president won Illinois by more than a 2-to-1 margin, and he accumulated a 155-to-14 advantage in delegates. Overall, after the Illinois slaughter, Carter's delegates outnumbered Kennedy's by 615 to 192. At this point, it became clear even to Kennedy's delegate counter that little hope remained of Kennedy catching Carter before the convention.

A week later, Carter looked to New York, where polls had recently shown him with a 20 point lead. He outspent the challenger by 2 to 1, hoping to deliver the coup de grâce. Kennedy himself considered withdrawing from the race and may well have if the president's lead had held up. Instead, things fell apart for Carter. More bad economic news led to a 6 percent drop in the stock market in the ten days before the New York primary election. Carter's emergency budget and credit controls program came under increased criticism, though it had been announced just before the Illinois primary. Worst, the United States cast a vote for a U.N. resolution calling for an Israeli pullout from Gaza, the West Bank, and Jerusalem. Carter repudiated the vote, claiming miscommunication with the U.N. mission. Then, days before the primary, Secretary of State Cyrus Vance testified before a congressional committee and appeared to endorse the original resolution.

All in all, the vote and Vance's testimony enraged New York's large Jewish community, and the episode as a whole reinforced the impression that no one, including the president, was in charge of foreign policy. Kennedy won going away, 59 percent to 41 percent, and simultaneously picked up another, closer win in Connecticut. Kennedy regained the Catholic vote he had lost in Illinois. He benefited from a rash of news stories praising the "gallantry" he was demonstrating in his steep uphill fight. The protest vote, long held at bay by Carter's strategy of encouraging a "general election" vote, had appeared in all its wrath. Interestingly, one of Kennedy's close aides also pointed out that "the less he thought he could win, the better candidate he was."[19]

On April 1 came the primary in Wisconsin, with its progressive lineage. Could Kennedy build on the momentum of New York? Could Brown salvage his flailing campaign by stepping into a vacuum caused by Carter's stumble? The answers were no and no. The day before the primary, the Carter administration announced it was canceling planned cuts in dairy price supports. The day of the primary, Carter held a 7:15 A.M. press conference to announce what turned out to be an illusory breakthrough in the hostage crisis. The incumbent defeated Kennedy by nearly as great a margin as in Illinois, 56 percent to 30 percent.

Brown had outspent everyone and finished his campaign with a garish televised rally directed by Francis Ford Coppola. When Brown won a total of 12 percent of the votes, it was over for him. He announced his withdrawal from the race that evening. There never had been room for three in the race; Kennedy's entry had doomed Brown. Wisconsin, which Carter would have skipped if not for the advice of Walter Mondale, was a big win for the president, but it came at a big price. Carter's early-morning press conference came back to haunt him, as voters for the first time concluded that Carter was manipulating the hostage crisis for political gain. Carter beat Kennedy badly in Kansas the same day and in Louisiana four days later.

After this defeat, Pennsylvania loomed as a do-or-die state for Kennedy, as it did for Bush on the Republican side. Kennedy, like Bush, squeaked through by the skin of his teeth: 45.7 percent to 45.4 percent, or a difference of 4,522 votes out of 1.5 million cast. In Pennsylvania the bitter rivalry between Carter and Kennedy reached full expression. Kennedy became more aggressive, attacking Carter's economic policies as equivalent to those of Nixon and Herbert Hoover. Down by 12 points in his own polls, Carter came back to the character issue with scathing person-on-the-street ads assailing Kennedy's trustworthiness, as well as his stands on defense, welfare, and spending. Analysts widely agreed that neither candidate left Pennsylvania as strong as he had entered. Both were bloodied. Kennedy had not been knocked out, but neither had he won a decisive victory, an impression underscored by Carter's big same-day win in the Missouri caucuses. Taking Missouri into account, Carter actually won forty more delegates on April 22 than had his rival.

After Kennedy's narrow and muddled escape from elimination, Carter came back with eleven wins in the next twelve primaries, losing only D.C. and winning Texas, Indiana, Maryland, and Oregon, among others. At the finish line, though, Kennedy revived. Despite trailing badly in delegates, Kennedy claimed to believe that the party simply would not nominate Carter if he could not win at least one of the "big three" states up for grabs on the final primary day: California, New Jersey, and Ohio. Declaring that foreign policy was now "manageable," Carter left the sanctuary of the Rose Garden. Frustrated by Carter's continued unwillingness to debate even after he had rejoined the campaign trail, Kennedy offered the president a deal: Debate me face-to-face, and I will withdraw from the race if I do not win a majority of all the votes cast on June 3. The White House refused. Kennedy grew more bellicose, predicting that Carter would finish third in November and calling the incumbent a "pale carbon copy" of Reagan. Carter took a positive tack, campaigning on an upbeat theme of accomplishment in Ohio, an industrial state much like Illinois and the biggest of the contested states next to California.

Out of the last round of eight primaries on June 3, Kennedy won five, including California and New Jersey, and outpolled Carter by 230,000 votes nationwide. Carter salvaged the day by winning West Virginia, Montana, and, crucially, Ohio. The day, which many commentators called "super Tuesday," was filled with irony. Carter's West Virginia had been the site of John F. Kennedy's most important 1960 primary win. More important, Ted Kennedy's day of greatest triumph was also his day of doom, for Carter collected enough delegates in defeat to put him over the mathematical requirement for nomination. Carter made a conciliatory victory statement, to which Kennedy responded by declaring, "Today Democrats from coast to coast were unwilling to concede the nomination to Jimmy Carter. And neither am I. . . . We are determined to move on to victory at the Convention." Whether the day should be seen as a Pyrrhic victory for Kennedy, who won the day but lost the nomination, or for Carter, who won the nomination but lost the election, is hard to say.

After the New Hampshire primary, and especially by late March, there could be little question that Kennedy was overmatched. Carter won twenty-four of thirty-three primaries, attaining 51 percent of the total primary vote to Kennedy's 37 percent and Brown's 3 percent. Carter also won 64 percent of delegates from the caucus states. Only in his native East did Kennedy gain more delegates than Carter. Yet Kennedy remained in the race, inflicting consistent rhetorical punishment and occasional electoral punishment on Carter. Like a powerful football team facing a fired-up rival, Carter always led but could never quite put the game away.

Kennedy's moments of revival came only when voters seemed to have good reason to believe that he would not actually be nominated. In Iowa and New Hampshire, Democrats decided they did not want Kennedy to win. In New York and then Pennsylvania and then California, Carter's immediately preceding strings of successes had convinced them there was little danger of that. A vote for Kennedy became a protest vote against Carter rather than a vote for a viable contestant for the presidency of the United States. Whenever Kennedy's viability seemed to return, victory departed.

As the primary season wore on, the urgency of the protest grew greater. With the hostage crisis dragging on interminably, the luster of Carter's Rose Garden strategy wore off. The rally of public opinion for Carter was gone. On April 26, two days after the Pennsylvania primary, Americans learned that a rescue mission to free the hostages had been attempted—and had failed miserably. The complicated mission, which called for eight helicopters and eight C-130 and C-141 transport planes, had gone awry at a desert staging area. Carter had been forced to cancel the mission when three of the helicopters malfunctioned; a minimum of six were required. Attempting to leave the area, one of the helicopters had collided with a C-130, leaving eight U.S. servicemen dead. Americans soon saw a new set of pictures from Iran: the charred bodies of the U.S. soldiers displayed in the streets of Tehran, the burned-out hulks of military aircraft littering the Iranian desert.

Carter received some credit for acting and for manfully accepting full responsibility for the failure, and the polls temporarily rewarded him. The net effect, though, was to remind Americans that the hostages were still there and that the United States—or at least its president—seemed as impotent as ever. U.S. military readiness, already an issue, was further called into question. And the long-standing conflict between the secretary of state, Cyrus Vance, and the more conservative national security adviser, Zbigniew Brzezinski, came to a head. Vance, who had opposed military action in Iran, resigned in protest.

As if Iran were not troublesome enough, Fidel Castro abruptly opened the port at Mariel, Cuba, for anyone wishing to leave. Ultimately, 120,000 Cubans headed for the United States, including a large contingent released from Castro's jails. Carter reversed the nation's position from welcoming the refugees to trying to stop them with Coast Guard cutters. Never did he appear to be in control of the situation or of the borders of the United States. Throughout the spring, tensions with U.S. allies grew more severe, with Germany and France, fearing repercussions with the Soviets, objecting to the firm U.S. response to Afghanistan. In May Carter was infuriated when French president Valéry Giscard d'Estaing cozied up to Leonid Brezhnev in a secret meeting in Warsaw.

Domestically, the economy took another downward turn. Consumer inflation, the cost of finished goods, had reached an annualized rate of 18.2 percent in February, shocking the nation. Producer inflation, the cost of production, was worse. If there had been any doubt, from that moment on runaway inflation was the number one economic issue in the United States. Americans began to wonder if their economy would come to resemble that of Weimar Germany in 1923. Throughout the primary season and the general election, inflation remained a dominant issue. Interest rates climbed some more: The prime rate went from 15.75 percent in February to 20 percent on April 2.

From April to June, corporate profits fell 18 percent, the third-steepest decline on record. Carter's emergency balanced-budget plan further inflamed liberals. When Congress spurned it, Americans saw the old Carter again, who seemed as toothless at home as abroad. When the president went back on the campaign trail in May, he told an Ohio audience that America had "turned the corner" on its economic problems; the next day, his Council of Economic Advisers announced that leading economic indicators showed the probability of a severe recession. Unemployment continued rising, from 6.2 percent in February to 7.5 percent in June. Median family income deteriorated more sharply in 1980 than in any other year in the post–World War II era.

Racial disturbances broke out in Boston, Wichita, and then Miami, where riots left sixteen dead, more than four hundred injured, and $100 million in property damage. By the time Kennedy won California on June 3, Carter seemed to have sewn up the nomination, but in terms of the nation's problems and his own strategic situation, he was back where he was in July 1979, with one exception: There were now fifty-two Americans trapped in Iran, with no end to their captivity in sight.

As late as the 1960s the national party nominating conventions were still regularly the decisive moment in the nominating process. Delegates were ambassadors from their state and local parties, and they retained discretion over the convention's choice. Most conventions required more than one ballot to come to a conclusion; the Democratic convention of 1924 had taken 103 ballots to nominate a candidate. Unexpected dark-horse nominees sometimes emerged, created by the combination of deadlock among the major candidates and the unrelenting search for electability. Today, because of the rise and front-loading of primaries and the binding of delegates, the delegates have lost their discretion, and the conventions have lost their drama. Not only are the presidential nominees known long before the convention opens, but their vice presidential selections are usually announced and the party's platform ironed out well in advance. The year 1980, the last time the conventions mattered, was the end of the long transition to the present form of the conventions.

The Republicans held their convention first, July 13–16 in Detroit, Michigan, a city selected by Republicans to show that they intended to reach out for black and urban voters. Although the Republican nominee was known in advance, his vice presidential selection was not. There were also innovations in the Republican platform that provided moments of passion and uncertainty. The platform called for repeal of the fifty-five-mile-an-hour speed limit, a popular position in the wide-open West, and demanded that the United States achieve military superiority over the Soviet Union. But the greatest controversy swirled around the hot social issues that had come to the fore in the 1970s, most notably the equal rights amendment (ERA) and abortion.

Republican platforms dating back to 1940 had supported the concept of an equal rights amendment to the Constitution. However, social conservatives saw the ERA less as a call for fairness than as a mandate for radical feminism. Conservatives such as Beverly LaHaye and Phyllis Schlafly organized a women's countermovement that was linked to the broader movement of the religious Right. In 1980 they gained a major voice in the Republican Party and insisted that unequivocal support for the amendment be stripped from the platform. Amid much controversy, they won new language in the platform that declared,

> We acknowledge the legitimate efforts of those who support or oppose ratification of the Equal Rights Amendment. We reaffirm our Party's historic commitment to equal rights and equality for women. We support equal rights and equal opportunities for women, without taking away traditional rights of women such as exemption from the military draft. . . . We oppose any move which would give the federal government more power over families. . . . We reaffirm our belief in the traditional role and values of the family in our society.

The pro-life movement had also gained much ground. In 1976—only three years after *Roe v. Wade*—the Republican platform was ambivalent. It emphasized the disagreement among Republicans, calling the issue of abortion "one of the most difficult and controversial of our time," before rather tepidly declaring that the party "supports the efforts" of those seeking a constitutional amendment. In 1980 pro-life forces packed the platform committee's subcommittee on human resources and secured passage of an unwavering plank, shorn of doubts, in which the GOP "affirm[ed] our support of a constitutional amendment to restore protection of the right to life for unborn children." From 1980 on, unambiguous support for such an amendment has remained a part of the Republican platform.

Liberal Republican women objected to the abortion and ERA planks, and some donned the white dresses of suffragettes to parade in Detroit. The platform passed by voice vote. To the relief of the Reagan team, platform opponents were unable to get a majority in five state delega-tions, which was required to call for a floor debate and roll-call vote. At the same time, social conservatives forced out liberal Mary Crisp as Republican National Committee cochair (Crisp went to work for Ander-son's independent campaign). Journalists covering the convention made much of the brouhaha, and they were right to see events in Detroit as a watershed. Both the abortion plank and the ERA plank demonstrated the degree to which the new Republican coalition revolved around the sudden power of the cultural Right.

The greater drama at the Republican convention surrounded the ques-tion of whom Ronald Reagan was going to select as his vice presidential running mate. This was a key public test of Reagan's decision-making skills, a chance for Reagan to cement party unity, and an opportunity to add balance and appeal to the ticket for the general election campaign. Reagan came to Detroit without having announced—or made—a choice. The campaign collected information on twenty-one potential running mates, including Howard Baker and George Bush, Representatives Jack Kemp and Guy Vander Jagt, Senators Paul Laxalt and Richard Lugar, and former cabinet officers Donald Rumsfeld and William Simon. Senator Jesse Helms of North Carolina, a favorite of the New Right, threatened to put his own name forward to the convention to ensure the ideologi-cal purity of the ticket. Baker removed himself from the list two weeks before the convention. Bush was a logical choice, since he could bal-ance the ticket both ideologically and geographically, whether he was from Texas or from New England. Polls of delegates also showed Bush as the clear plurality favorite. But Reagan was wary of Bush, whose per-formance at Nashua and in the Texas confrontation led Reagan to fear he might melt under pressure.

Reagan turned to another possibility, that Gerald Ford might be lured into a "dream ticket." Reagan first broached the idea with Ford on June 5, at the behest of party leaders and some campaign insiders. Reagan's poll-ster Richard Wirthlin concluded that only Ford among potential veeps would add serious strength to the ticket. Ford helped his cause with a stem-winding address on the first evening of the convention. Rumors of negotiations between Ford and the Reagan camp electrified the assem-bly, but a snag developed when it became clear that Ford (or his advisers, including Henry Kissinger and Alan Greenspan) hoped for something resembling a "copresidency" in which Ford would hold special responsi-bility over budget and national security issues. Reagan could not accept such an arrangement, a point driven home to him when he watched Ford discussing it in an interview with Walter Cronkite. When Ford himself concluded it was unworkable, he went to Reagan's hotel suite and removed himself from consideration.

Reagan, who had thought for days that talks with Ford might work out, suddenly had to choose someone else. He turned immediately to Bush as the second-strongest candidate in the Republican primary field, and Bush immediately accepted, assuring Reagan he could support the platform. To quell the rumors on the floor of the convention, Reagan took the extraordinary step of traveling to Joe Louis Arena and personally addressing the delegates to inform them of his decision. The crowd, relieved to have an answer, cheered raucously. Some angry conservatives talked of drafting Helms, but the effort fizzled as he received only fifty-four votes in the vice presidential roll-call vote. Bush was the only vice presidential nominee between Lyndon Johnson in 1960 and John Edwards in 2004 to have been an active rival for the presidential nomination.

Reagan had dodged a bullet. The sort of arrangement that seemed to be unfolding with Ford was a sure prescription for conflict and confusion and would have appeared to many as a sign of the nominee's weakness. It would also have raised important constitutional questions and may have become a lightning rod for criticism once commentators had had a chance to reflect on it more thoroughly. Had the two men gone through with it, the "copresidency" itself might have become the biggest issue of the campaign. "I can't tell you with what anticipation we began to look forward to the idea that this was really going to happen," Pat Caddell later said.[20] That Reagan had considered such an arrangement at all was disquieting. That in the end he had firmly rejected it was reassuring.

The next night, Reagan was nominated, with 1,939 delegates. Holding out for candidates long lost, 37 delegates insisted on voting for Anderson and 13 for Bush. The night after that, Reagan delivered his nomination acceptance speech. It was vintage Reagan. The nominee called for "a new consensus with all those across the land who share a community of values embodied in these words: family, work, neighborhood, peace and freedom. . . . I want my candidacy to unify our country; to renew the American spirit and sense of purpose." He made a conciliatory statement about equal rights for women, then called attention to three "grave threats": a "disintegrating economy, a weakened defense, and an energy policy based on the sharing of scarcity." It took him little time to go for the jugular. Understanding that elections against incumbents are elections about incumbents, Reagan identified "the major issue of this campaign": "the direct political, personal, and moral responsibility of Democratic Party leadership—in the White House and in Congress—for this unprecedented calamity which has befallen us."

> They tell us they have done the most that humanly could be done. They say that the United States has had its day in the sun; that our nation has passed its zenith. They expect you to tell your children that the American people no longer have the will to cope with their problems; that the future will be one of sacrifice and few opportunities. My fellow citizens, I utterly reject that view. . . . I will not stand by and watch this great country destroy itself under mediocre leadership that drifts from one crisis to the next, eroding our national will and purpose.

Reagan went on to pledge to "restore to the federal government the capacity to do the people's work without dominating their lives." Claiming that "our federal government is overgrown and overweight," Reagan promised to put it on a diet by freezing federal hiring, cutting taxes and wasteful spending, and turning functions over to state and local governments. "The federal government exists to serve the American people. On January 20th, we are going to re-establish that truth." Then came a litany of recent foreign policy disasters, a critique of Carter mismanagement in that area, and the encapsulation of Reagan's prescription for the world: "We know only too well that war comes not when the forces of freedom are strong, but when they are weak. It is then that tyrants are tempted." Throughout the speech, Reagan anticipated the knockout punch he would throw in front of a different national audience on October 28: "Can anyone compare the state of our economy when the Carter Administration took office with where we are today and say, 'Keep up the good work'? . . . Is the United States stronger and more respected now than it was three-and-a-half years ago? Is the world today a safer place in which to live?"

Reagan concluded by returning to his political roots. Quoting from Franklin D. Roosevelt's 1932 acceptance speech, Reagan deftly identified himself with the New Deal icon while pointing out the degree to which modern liberalism had deviated from Roosevelt's first promise, which was to cut expenditures, balance the budget, and eliminate useless offices. After a moment of silent prayer to begin "our crusade," Reagan and Bush linked arms, the convention exploded in cheers, and whatever

Reagan accepting the Republican National Convention's nomination for president of the United States, July 16, 1980.

divisions had resulted from the primaries or the platform controversies were healed. As Reagan left Detroit, he led Carter in the polls by around 30 percentage points.

The steady decline in Carter's standing since the early spring and the strength of the Reagan challenge gave Kennedy one last, slender thread on which to hang his presidential hopes. Beaten in the primaries but seeing that Carter's leadership and electability were once again very much in doubt, Kennedy took the offensive. Shortly after the last round of primaries on June 3, he again demanded a debate with Carter. The president seriously considered the proposal for about thirty-six hours, decided to go ahead with the debate, and then reversed himself. Kennedy's camp also began a long public relations campaign aimed at producing an "open convention" by defeating a party rule binding delegates to their pledged choice through at least the first ballot. Their hope was that Carter's plummeting standing might persuade a large number of Carter delegates that they should abandon ship.

Through 1968, delegates could exercise such discretion at any time. The post-1968 reformers, though, saw such maneuverings as undemocratic, inasmuch as they might produce a delegate count that bore little or no relation to the preferences the voters had expressed in the primaries. After the 1976 election the Democratic National Committee (at the behest of the White House) adopted rule F3(c), the binding rule, for the 1980 primaries and caucuses. It still had to be confirmed as a convention rule by the convention itself, and Kennedy's campaign realized that if they were to have hope, rule F3(c) would have to be knocked down.

Events continued moving against Carter. The hostage crisis dragged on, the twin evils of recession and inflation hung on, and Carter announced his third economic recovery program of the year. Not least, "Billygate" came and would not go away. Carter's ne'er-do-well brother Billy had long amused the nation with his buffoonery and his marketing of "Billy Beer." In the midst of the Republican convention, the story broke that Billy had registered as a foreign agent for Mu'ammar Gadhafi's Libyan government, which had paid him $220,000. Questions were immediately raised: Did the President know? Did he approve? And what, if anything, did Libya get for its money? With the media in hot pursuit, the president grappled with these questions for weeks. In late July Carter's Gallup approval rating slipped to 21 percent, the lowest figure ever recorded in the poll's forty-five-year history. Both campaigns detected significant movement among delegates against F3(c).

As this summer of discontent dragged on, support for an open convention broadened considerably. Governor Hugh Carey of New York had been mentioned as a possible alternative to Carter in early 1979, but he had refrained from entering the race. In the summer of 1980 he resurfaced as a supporter of the open convention, inviting speculation that he hoped the rules change would aid not Kennedy, who was already discredited by his poor primary showing, but a new, third candidate who could unify the party—perhaps himself. Supporters of other would-be candidates hoping to fill the vacuum caused by Carter's collapsing position took up the cause. These included Senator Henry Jackson and Edmund Muskie, who was in a particularly awkward position as Carter's secretary of state. Even Vice President Mondale's name was whispered, though he gave supporters no encouragement. Speaking on behalf of a number of jittery Democratic senators, Senate majority leader Robert Byrd called for an open convention. So did a caucus of 67 Democratic House members, who had seen poll results showing Carter in third place, behind both Reagan and Anderson, in a number of key congressional districts.

The only good news for Carter came when Democratic governors, hoping to preserve party unity, declined to endorse the open convention. (This was the second year in a row the governors had come to Carter's aid: In July 1979, when other Democrats were flocking to the Kennedy banner, they passed a resolution endorsing the president's renomination.) The biggest problem for the proponents of an open convention, despite growing concern within the party about Carter's prospects, was that they were allied in only a narrow tactical sense. What they wanted out of the open convention—Kennedy, Jackson, Muskie, or anybody but Carter—was a source of division.

Carter saved his position with both an effective defense and a counteroffensive. The defense came at the last possible moment, when Carter seemed to quiet the Billygate storm by turning in a masterful performance in an August 4 press conference. A *New York Times* survey that straddled the press conference showed Democratic voters split evenly—43 percent to 43 percent—between Carter and Kennedy before the event; Carter won 57 to 32 after it.[21]

Carter's counterattack relied on three things. First, as journalist Elizabeth Drew pointed out, "The Jackson, Muskie, and Open Convention people, to the extent that they are distinguishable, say that the game is hopeless unless Kennedy gets out; they say they are finding too many people unwilling to try for an 'open Convention' if it means that Kennedy might be nominated—and Kennedy is not about to get out."[22] Indeed, hoping to broaden his appeal, Kennedy secretly invited Senator Byrd to be his running mate at the convention. The West Virginian declined.[23] Carter and his people homed in on the argument that Kennedy and his supporters were the instigators of the open convention idea, a point the president made in his August 4 press conference.

Second, Carter appealed to the reformist sentiments of Democrats when he portrayed the proposed rule as a throwback to the "old brokered-type Convention."

Finally, Carter relied on a massive campaign of personal contact with wavering delegates—and on the fact that the delegates themselves had often obtained their position precisely because of their personal loyalty or connection to the president. For example, the largest single organized bloc—464 delegates by one count—were the members of the National Education Association. They were attending the convention out of loyalty to the union and to the president who had given them the federal Department of Education in 1980. It was in the end not the binding rule that posed the greatest obstacle to the "dump Carter" forces. The new nominating system had already transformed the role of the delegate from a representative of the party to a representative of the candidate.

Nevertheless, when the Democratic convention finally opened in New York City on August 11, Carter's renomination was not certain. This makes 1980 the last year that any convention opened with its central task—the nomination of the party's candidate for president—in any doubt whatsoever. Carter had the delegates he needed for a majority: 1,666 were required, 1,982 were pledged to him. The question was whether he could keep them. On top of everything else, liberals were angered yet again: In what some analysts felt was a move to protect Carter's right flank on defense, National Security Adviser Zbigniew Brzezinski had worked with the Defense Department to draft a new strategic doctrine, found in Presidential Decision Directive 59, committed to limited nuclear war-fighting—without the agreement or knowledge of Secretary of State Muskie.

The rules battle was tough, intense, and not entirely predictable. Three delegations in particular—Illinois, Michigan, and Pennsylvania—were deemed by both the Kennedy and Carter camps to be key battlegrounds, and they received enormous attention. Individual delegates were targeted and hounded relentlessly. A young woman in the Illinois delegation was offered a city job by the mayor's office if she would support the Kennedy rule change. Cabinet officials and other heavy hitters were dispatched to buttonhole delegates, singly or in groups. In special cases, presidential phone calls were used as a weapon.

The key moment came on the first day of the convention. Kennedy supporters carried signs saying the binding rule reduced delegates to robots. Open convention supporter Edward Bennett Williams told the convention that "for the first time in 150 years, delegates to the national convention are being asked to deliver their final freedom of choice, and to vote themselves into bondage to a candidate."[24] Carter supporters pointed out that Kennedy had had no problem with the rule until it became clear that he was the one trailing in the delegate count. Atlanta mayor Maynard Jackson, a Carter supporter, retorted that Kennedy wanted to change the rules in the middle of the game to allow a "fifth ball, a fourth out, or a tenth inning."[25] Then came the last momentous convention roll-call vote of a twentieth century that had earlier been filled with them. State by state, the delegations announced their votes. The Kennedy motion—arcanely known as Minority Rule no. 5—fell 276 delegates short of acceptance. Carter had lost only about fifty votes compared with his previously known delegate strength. Shortly after the vote Kennedy announced that his name would not be put into nomination.

The next day, despite having removed himself from the presidential race, Kennedy pushed to a floor vote a number of alternate platform planks opposed by Carter. That Kennedy pursued this line of action was a testament to both Kennedy's commitment to liberal ideology and his bitterness at Carter. Carter's position prevailed in opposition to a single, comprehensive national health insurance plank. However, most of Kennedy's alternatives won. These included planks supporting Medicaid funding for abortions, opposing Democratic Party campaign assistance to any candidates who did not endorse the equal rights amendment, supporting a $12 billion public works program and additional spending on mass transit and public housing, and calling jobs the party's "single highest domestic priority." Another Kennedy plank that passed, opposing an anti-inflation policy of high interest rates and unemployment, received the president's concurrence.

Careful not to allow the platform debate to give Kennedy a "test vote" with which to demonstrate Carter's weakness, the president's campaign did not take a hard stand against most of the alternatives. It also succeeded in turning most of the popular Kennedy planks into voice votes rather than roll-call votes, which could yield numbers showing just how little control Carter had over his convention. (The use of voice votes also facilitated some deal making with the help of the convention chair: Tip O'Neill declared that Kennedy's wage and price freeze had lost on a voice vote "in clear contradiction of the sound in the hall," in a prearranged plan that allowed the president to save face on the economic planks.)[26]

All of the economic planks were voted on after Kennedy was allowed to make a prime-time speech on their behalf to the convention. In a hall painted blue with Kennedy signs, the Massachusetts senator addressed the party and the nation "not to argue for a candidacy but to affirm a cause. . . . I am asking you to renew the commitment of the Democratic Party to economic justice." In proposing the alternative planks, he was raising not just economic issues but "also a moral issue":

> The commitment I seek is not to outworn views but to old values that will never wear out. Programs may sometimes become obsolete, but the ideal of fairness always endures. . . . It is surely correct that we cannot solve problems by throwing money at them, but it is also correct that we dare not throw our national problems on a scrap heap of inattention and indifference. The poor may be out of political fashion, but they are not without human needs. The middle class may be angry, but they have not lost the dream that all Americans can advance together. . . . For all those whose cares have been our concern, the work goes on, the cause endures, the hope still lives, and the dream shall never die.[27]

An emotional demonstration ensued for the next forty minutes. After a while, O'Neill stopped even trying to gavel the convention back to order. Kennedy's speech had produced what would be the only moment of genuine passion during the four days of the assembly. Carter had been upstaged, his convention hijacked, before he even made an appearance.

Nor was Kennedy finished. His camp had succeeded in inserting into the rules a provision requiring those seeking the nomination to respond in writing to the platform at least two hours before the start of nominating speeches Wednesday night, the third day of the convention. Carter and his advisers spent the better part of the day determining how to finesse the Kennedy planks so that the president neither angered Kennedy nor appeared too accommodating. Later that evening, despite the lack of a formal nomination, Kennedy still received 1,150 votes in the presidential roll call.

Finally, Thursday arrived—Carter's day—and none too soon for him.

As Reagan had in July, Carter sought to use his acceptance speech to outline the themes that would guide his general election campaign. He began by reviewing the pantheon of Democratic heroes: FDR, Truman, John F. Kennedy, Johnson, and Hubert Humphrey (whom he called "Hubert Horatio Hornblower," before correcting himself). Virtually pleading for Kennedy's help ("I need you, Ted"), he praised Kennedy as a "tough competitor and a superb campaigner" whose Tuesday-evening speech had been "a magnificent statement of what the Democratic Party is and what it means to the people of this country and why a Democratic victory is so important this year."

Carter proceeded to set up one of his themes against Reagan:

I've learned that only the most complex and difficult task comes before me in the Oval Office. No easy answers are found there, because no easy questions come there. I've learned that for a President, experience is the best guide to the right decisions. . . . The life of every human being on earth can depend on the experience and judgment and vigilance of the person in the Oval Office. . . .

Some have said that it makes no difference who wins this election. They are wrong. This election is a stark choice between two men, two parties, two sharply different pictures of what America is and what the world is, but it's more than that—it's a choice between two futures.

To Carter, those futures were one of economic security, justice, and peace or one of despair, surrender to special interests, and risk of war. Reagan offered a "make believe world" in which the poor and minorities did not exist and women were to be seen but not heard: "In their fantasy world, all problems have simple solutions—simple and wrong." He then went on to attack the Republican platform on arms control, defense spending, human rights, energy, and tax cuts. Taking a page out Johnson's 1964 playbook, Carter took the Republicans to task for extremism and for "repudiating the best traditions of their own party." Altogether, he said, the Republicans had proposed

an attack on everything that we've done in the achievement of social justice and decency that we've won in the last 50 years, ever since Franklin Delano Roosevelt's first term. . . . The choice between the two futures could not be more clear. If we succumb to a dream world then we'll wake up to a nightmare. But if we start with reality and fight to make our dreams a reality, then Americans will have a good life, a life of meaning and purpose in a nation that's strong and secure.[28]

At the end of his speech, Carter, Mondale, their families, and a host of Democratic officials crowded the dais in a show of unity. Long missing, though, was the one man whom Carter most needed there. When Kennedy finally reached the scene, he acknowledged the Massachusetts delegation, briefly shook Carter's hand, and quickly left to chants of "We want Ted," which continued reverberating through the hall. He had spent all of two minutes, sixteen seconds on the platform. The traditional gesture of unity—victor and vanquished hand in hand, arms raised—never happened, even though Kennedy had earlier practiced it with an aide. Looking to the ceiling, Carter could see that the celebratory balloons, also traditional, were caught and would not fall.

The balloons that did not drop and the handclasp that did not happen were fitting metaphors for the previous eighteen months of the Carter presidency. Yet the president had reason for hope. Despite everything, the unnaturally large Reagan edge ebbed. Carter received a bounce from his convention of around 10 percentage points, putting him within 7–10 percentage points of the challenger.

The 1980 nomination contests revealed a great deal about the parties, the candidates, and the machinery for presidential nominations. Not least, 1980 demonstrated both the advantages and the serious flaws of the reformed nominating system itself. On one hand, the outcome accurately reflected the preferences of each party's voters—at least the preferences they had held on the day that they voted. On the other hand, numerous shortcomings of the system were displayed. The problematic tendencies of the new campaign finance limits of 1974 became clearer. Insurgents like Kennedy were hurt and incumbents were helped by restricting the flow of campaign resources—a paradoxical outcome, given the populist rhetoric surrounding those limits. More generally, by making it more difficult to raise large sums of money from a small group of dedicated supporters, the Federal Election Campaign Act (FECA) made it less likely that candidates would be able to stay in the race after a few early defeats. The early departures of top-tier candidates such as Baker (March 5), Connally (March 9), and Dole (March 15) anticipated the races of the early twenty-first century, when most candidates are gone within a couple of weeks of the Iowa caucuses, and many do not even survive until the voting begins.

The rule "Run early and run everywhere," penciled on paper by Carter in 1976, was carved in stone in 1980. Almost every candidate took

Carter's success four years earlier as a model. Those who took it most seriously—Carter himself, and Bush—were the candidates who most exceeded the expectations of the summer of 1979. When Reagan ignored it by downplaying Iowa, that error nearly cost him the nomination. When Connally ignored it by waiting until the South Carolina primaries to take his stand, he was swept away. When Kennedy was forced to ignore it by tight finances, he paid a heavy price. What might have been important victories for Kennedy in Massachusetts and Pennsylvania were largely negated by the Carter camp's decision and capacity to enter contests and win in Vermont and Missouri the same days.

Once the media had declared an early winner, momentum became a factor with which one had to reckon. This was not entirely a new phenomenon. Indeed, momentum had been a feature of nominations a hundred years before, when it took the form of "bandwagons" for darkhorse candidates at the national convention. What 1976 demonstrated and 1980 confirmed was that this momentum could flow from early contests. In 1976 momentum carried Carter to the nomination; in 1980 Bush had the "Big Mo," even if he subsequently lost it. The most that could be said was that the potential for early primary momentum offered a glimmer of hope to little-known candidates.

The 1980 nominating races also demonstrated a troubling lack of flexibility in the system. By March 15 it was too late for Gerald Ford to enter the race; too many delegates were already wrapped up. The open convention drive was not merely a self-serving tactic promoted by a failing Kennedy; it was also an attempt to correct what many outside the Kennedy camp saw as a flaw in the process. The system had become so candidate centered and so plebiscitary that the party had no way to protect itself from the impending disaster of a Carter renomination. A candidate who might have been a good choice in February or March 1980 was not looking as good in July and August. Yet the course was set, the delegates bound by both formal rule and by informal but no less crucial ties of political loyalty. This was largely a consequence of the post-1968 Democratic reforms, which consciously sought to end the independence of the delegates from the candidates and thus end the importance of party power brokers.

The inability of the 1980 nominating system to respond to changed circumstances was worsened by the Democratic rule requiring the use of proportional representation in delegate allocation. Generally, proportional representation—another post-1968 reform tenet—meant that even losing candidates could gain a large number of delegates in state contests. In the context of 1980, proportional representation meant that once Kennedy fell behind, he would have a very difficult time catching up, even when Carter's stock was falling rapidly. For example, in California 306 delegates were at stake. Kennedy won the primary by a solid margin, 45 percent to 38 percent. Yet when the delegates were allocated, Kennedy outdistanced Carter by only 166 to 140—a net gain of 26 delegates from the most populous state. He was not going to overcome Carter's early lead that way. In contrast, in 1972, when California still had a winner-take-all rule, George McGovern beat Hubert Humphrey by a similar margin of 44 percent to 39 percent and took home all 271 delegates.

More to the point in August 1980, the nomination fight had demonstrated the degree to which Jimmy Carter was in significant trouble. That Kennedy's strength was largely the result of voters' protest against Carter was obvious by the fact that his chief primary victories came only after he seemed to have lost any real chance to win. That Kennedy's biggest set of wins came on the last day of the primaries, despite Carter's heavy efforts, was also a warning sign for the president. Polling showed Carter's support actually dropping in Ohio after he visited the state. Likewise, when Carter lost key platform votes in his own convention, when Kennedy's speech brought the only moment of exuberance to an otherwise gloomy gathering, and when over 1,000 delegates voted for Kennedy in the convention roll call despite his retirement from the race two days earlier, it was clear that Carter was in trouble.

Nevertheless, Carter won. He did not precisely administer a thrashing to his opponent's posterior, but his prophecy (or defiant bluster) of mid-1979 was closer to the truth than anyone could have predicted at the time. Kennedy, despite the glitter of Camelot, was highly flawed. Both his ideas (McGovern redux) and his style (more suited to union-hall stumping than to the cool medium of television) were retrograde. His character problems were a burden greater than he or his advisers had anticipated, his campaign was not well organized, and for long and critical periods he seemed to have little to say.

Carter, on the other hand, was perceived as steady, was well-organized, grasped better than Kennedy the shape and style of the politics of the future, and for long and critical periods did not need to campaign as long as it appeared that he was tending the nation's business. He also outspent Kennedy by a 3-to-2 ratio. In a time of increased conservatism and skepticism about Washington, Carter was blessed with an opponent who was an insider to his left. Ironically, he may have been blessed as well by the fact that that opponent was of sufficient stature to freeze out of the race most other potential foes, though it is not entirely clear who might have done better than Kennedy.

The president and his people knew well how to use the power and prestige of the presidency. The most vulgar form of that power—an unending cascade of federal dollars and patronage, including distribution of 275,000 temporary census jobs—may not have gained Carter as much as many at the time thought. Primary voting analysis showed little effect in areas that received aid, and after a while a backlash developed. It was the symbolism of the presidency in time of crisis that undercut Kennedy's chief rationale. Events, then, were another item that worked for Carter, at least during the decisive months of November 1979 through February 1980. Carter's pollster Pat Caddell contended that Carter would have beaten Kennedy even without Iran and Afghanistan—on the basis of character—but this cannot be known. It would, at any rate, have been a very different race, closer and even more bitter.

Reagan could also credit his own strengths, his opponents' weaknesses, and events for his nomination. One of the chief weaknesses of his opponents was that they were divided. Indeed, Bush's advisers largely blamed Anderson for their coming up short, as Bush and Anderson split the moderate/liberal vote in the early primaries. The Bush strategy of knocking Baker out early succeeded, only to be foiled by Anderson's unexpected rise. Of course, Reagan also had to share the early conservative vote with Connally, Crane, and Bush himself, who angled hard for it. When conservatives rallied around Reagan, after concluding that Bush was not one of them, Bush was probably finished, Anderson or no Anderson.

Except for Anderson, the Republican field was divided into candidates who had little to say (including Bush) and candidates who had conservative things to say, and Reagan was the master of the latter. His message, honed for a quarter century, was given greater force by the same events that helped Carter in the short run. His answers—a deadline and ultimatum in Iran, a blockade of Cuba in response to Afghanistan—struck some as too belligerent but sounded the right notes for many who were weary of the United States in retreat. His support for the Kemp-Roth tax cut and his call to "set the oil industry loose" fit his party's growing concern with "big government."

Reagan showed a sound tactical sense, the confidence to change advisers when things were not working well, and the intangible but crucial ability to reach the voters—a skill he would soon apply in the general election. He won the nomination despite getting more bad press from January through July than anyone else in the Republican field.[29] With a deft touch, Reagan campaigned for the Republican nomination while rarely running against other Republicans, thus observing the "Eleventh Commandment" for which he was famous ("Never speak ill of a fellow Republican"). By campaigning hard after Iowa, he dispelled the age issue. Indeed, by September, Reagan was described as "vigorous" by more voters than either Carter or Anderson. Although he outspent Bush by $20 million to $17 million, this advantage was not very meaningful. Under the management of John Sears, the Reagan campaign spent too much money early and actually found itself outspent by Bush in several key contests later. Overall, Bush outspent Reagan by 4 to 3 on media. In the Republican Party in 1980 Reagan was the right man at the right time.

More broadly, the nomination struggles showed how the parties (and the country) had changed. Both parties nominated men from their conservative wings. Both nominees were men of the outside. Both had won their nominations in the Sunbelt. Indeed, there was a striking overlap in the places where their rivals, Bush and Kennedy, won: Three of Bush's four wins after Iowa were in Kennedy states (Massachusetts, Connecticut, and Pennsylvania). West of the Mississippi, neither loser won a single state between Bush's win in Iowa in the very first contest and Kennedy's in California and New Mexico on the very last day of the primaries. Not only were Bush and Kennedy shut out of the southern states, but Reagan and Carter dominated them there utterly. Reagan beat Bush in Alabama 70 percent to 26 percent, where Carter beat Kennedy 82 percent to 13 percent; Reagan won Louisiana 75 percent to 19 percent, while Carter won 56 percent to 23 percent; Reagan held North Carolina 74 percent to 16 percent, Carter did the same 70 percent to 17 percent; Tennessee went for Reagan 74 percent to 18 percent and for Carter 75 percent to 18 percent.

Carter was the first Democratic candidate since William Jennings Bryan in 1896 to win his nomination without the support of either Pennsylvania or New York.[30] It would be a mistake to make too much of the rightward movement of the Democrats—Kennedy's platform victories among the activists belie it—but the center of gravity among the party's voters had nevertheless shifted. On the Republican side, the change in the Republican platform reflected the new power of the social conservatives. Iowa, New Hampshire, and many other states also saw the grassroots effectiveness of single-issue groups opposing abortion and gun control. The moderate governors, who had helped nominate Eisenhower and had tried to block Goldwater, were largely unheard in 1980. This loss of influence confirmed a change in the party that had taken place in 1964, but in 1980 (except for Milliken of Michigan) the governors were not just impotent, they were docile. The conservative shift in the GOP had even made its way, most improbably, to New York, where Reagan swept the delegate selection primary on March 25.

And one of the most important but least noticed features of Reagan's win over Bush was the degree to which Reagan's Republicans—that is to say, the winning Republicans—were more middle and working class, more ethnic, more Catholic, more entrepreneurial, and more "new money" than Bush's Republicans were. In New Hampshire, Reagan led Bush decisively among Republican voters with annual incomes under $10,000. Although he lost statewide in Connecticut, he whipped Bush in blue-collar, industrial Bridgeport. In Florida the Cuban elite supported Bush; the Cuban working class, Reagan. So it went across the United States. What this would mean in November, time would tell.

THE GENERAL ELECTION
THE GIPPER WINS ONE

There was no clear starting point for the 1980 general election campaign. As correspondent Elizabeth Drew pointed out, from April on "the fall campaign had backed into the primary campaign, presenting at times the picture of a free-for-all": Carter running against Kennedy, Reagan, and Anderson; Reagan running against Carter; Anderson running against Carter and Reagan, all at the same time.[1] The most that could be said was that by mid-August, only the three major contenders remained.

Carter struggled with the conundrum of his office. As in the primaries, he hoped to capitalize on the benefits of incumbency and would emphasize the dangers of selecting an untested president who would require four years of on-the-job training. Yet he was also burdened with a national situation that bordered on the catastrophic. As the incumbent, he was a prime target of blame for these conditions, as his low approval ratings and the tough challenge from Kennedy demonstrated. Stagflation was not far from anyone's mind, as inflation was joined by an increasingly sharp recession. In September and October, unemployment reached 7.5 percent. Not to be forgotten, too, were the hostages. As much as Carter was hurt by the media obsession with the hostage crisis, it had been Carter himself who had stoked that obsession in late 1979 and who had benefited from it in the early primaries.

Every election is a mixture of prospective appraisals (What would the candidates do if elected?) and retrospective appraisals (What have the incumbent and his party done?). Carter was in the distinctly uncomfortable position of being an incumbent who hoped to tilt the balance of the election away from the retrospective. He hoped to accomplish this by stoking latent fears about Reagan and by focusing on the alternative "two futures" Carter had introduced in his nomination acceptance speech. Although they could hardly admit it publicly, Carter's strategists knew well that the future was better ground on which to wage a fight than was the present or past. According to internal White House polling, Americans gave the president a positive rating in only two of sixteen job areas; by more than a 2-to-1 margin, they wanted a new president. Campaign insiders joked grimly that "Why not the best?"—the Carter slogan of 1976—had been supplanted by "At least he's not the worst."[2]

The Carter campaign produced television advertisements on topics ranging from the equal rights amendment to Israel to Jimmy Carter's faith. However, the lion's share of the advertisements argued that Reagan was too big a risk and that Carter was a man of peace, a hardworking leader "for all the people." A series of ads asked, "What kind of person should occupy the Oval Office?" The answer on nuclear weapons, military deployments, energy, economic policy, and a number of other issues was: Not Reagan, who is too extreme. In the best example of such an ad, a narrator asked, "When it comes right down to it, what kind of a person should occupy the Oval Office? Should it be a person who, like Ronald Reagan, favors an immediate military arms buildup, opposes an arms limitation treaty, and calls the spread of nuclear arms around the world none of our business? Or should a man sit here, who, like every president since Truman, has worked tirelessly for the arms control that alone is our last best hope of survival? Figure it out for yourself." Man-in-the-street ads featured citizens calling Reagan "scary," "risky," "very apt to use military force," and possessed of a "shoot them dead type attitude . . . that could really get us into a lot of trouble."

Carter's strategists considered reprising their Rose Garden strategy of the primaries, but they concluded that the president would have to take a more active role in the fall campaign. The Rose Garden strategy had been overused, and, what was more important, Carter was faced with the difficult task of restoring his Democratic base. The divisions left by the Kennedy challenge had not fully healed. More broadly, as Carter complained, "I spent a major portion of my time trying to recruit back the Democratic constituency that should have been naturally supportive—Jews, Hispanics, blacks, the poor, labor, and so forth."³ The campaign assumed, too freely, that the "natural" coalition still existed and was simply in need of activation. Nevertheless, Carter was blessed with a strong and cohesive staff—Pat Caddell, Hamilton Jordan, Jody Powell, Gerald Rafshoon, and Tim Kraft—who had been battle tested in the general election of 1976, the Kennedy challenge of 1980, and three and a half difficult years of governing in between.

Ronald Reagan came out of the summer with a modest lead in most polls and a unified party. Over the summer he headlined a number of "unity dinners" to help his GOP rivals pay off their campaign debts. In early September he dined with Gerald Ford, who announced he was going on the road to campaign for Reagan for fifty-three of the next sixty days. Reagan possessed a strong message and an ability to deliver it that his foes could not match. However, he also faced a new level of scrutiny over his California record, his age, and his overall capacity to be president. For Reagan to win, the retrospective appraisals had to be predominant in the voters' minds. At the same time, though, he had to pass a minimum threshold in the prospective realm: Was he steady enough? Were the images of Reagan as a trigger-happy cowboy, popular in the salons of the East, false? Did he have a plausible prescription for the woes of the nation?

The resulting strategy emphasized attacks on Carter's economic performance and projection of Reagan as a "can-do" leader and a man of peace, albeit peace through strength. Conforming to Napoleon's dictum "Never interfere with the enemy when he is in the process of destroying himself," the Reagan camp also decided to maintain silence on the hostages, a posture Reagan maintained until near the end. One of Reagan's favorite lines throughout the fall was, "A recession is when a neighbor loses his job. A depression is when you lose yours. And a recovery is when Jimmy Carter loses his."

To raise the level of public familiarity with Reagan (a problem the president did not face), initial advertising focused on Reagan as a person and on Reagan's two terms as governor of California. Drawing implicit parallels between California in 1966 and the United States in 1980, a narrator intoned, "Ronald Reagan inherited the state in crisis. . . . Governor Reagan got things back on track. Governor Reagan dealt with California's problems. He will do as much for America." Once this foundation was laid well—and both campaigns' polling confirmed that

it had been—most ads addressed the economic crisis, particularly inflation. Playing to the candidate's strength, several featured Reagan himself speaking directly to Americans. Edward Kennedy, in the form of
news clips from the primary season, appeared in more Reagan ads than
Carter ads, once attacking Carter's foreign policy for its "surprises" and
once attacking Carter's inflation.

Set speeches also played a part in Reagan's message delivery, with two
standing out as particularly important. Reagan gave the first, announcing a comprehensive economic plan, on September 8 in Chicago. The
plan called for a five-point program consisting of restricting the rate of
growth of federal spending, cutting taxes for individuals and businesses,
deregulation, a stable monetary policy, and greater policy stability (in
contrast to Carter's economically damaging zigzags). It was put together by domestic adviser Martin Anderson as well as by such respected
Republican economic figures as former Federal Reserve chair Arthur
Burns, former head of the Council of Economic Advisers (and future
Federal Reserve chair) Alan Greenspan, and former Treasury secretaries
George Shultz and William Simon. The plan included detailed budget
figures purporting to show that the plan could be achieved while still bal-
ancing the budget by 1983. Questions remained about the numbers, but
the campaign achieved a new level of economic plausibility. The second
major speech came on October 19, when Reagan bought a thirty-minute
block of time on prime-time national television to deliver a well-received
address on peace and national defense.

Richard Wirthlin, Reagan's chief strategist and pollster, was one of
the best in the business and had spent two and a half years perfecting a
massive computer system designed to aid decisionmaking by simulat-
ing a variety of strategic moves by the campaign. Unlike Carter, however,
Reagan was surrounded by a staff that was disjointed and often quar-
relsome. Some were old-guard Californians who had been with Reagan
since his gubernatorial days; others had joined in the primaries of 1976
or 1980; two (James Baker and William Timmons) had been grafted on
from George Bush's campaign. After the Republican convention, it took
the group several weeks to coalesce and divide responsibility effectively.

However, if Carter had a bit of an advantage on top, Reagan had one
on the bottom, where his state and local organizations were widely conceded to be stronger and more enthusiastic than the president's. Reagan
was reaping the fruits of twenty years of grassroots organization by the

conservative movement. In addition, Republican National Committee chairman Bill Brock had overseen a GOP grassroots revival, and at least 16,000 local activists had been given campaign training since 1976.

Both major party candidates benefited from their running mates. Walter Mondale helped reassure Democratic liberals, as George Bush reassured Republican moderates, that the ticket was sound. Both men were more than able surrogates. However, personality conflicts and political distrust interfered, and one observer contended that the presidential candidates "never fully utilized their number two men."[4]

In addition to the Reagan campaign's own spending, a number of conservative groups spent $10.6 million in independent expenditures on his behalf. (In comparison, independent expenditures for Carter totaled $27,773.) The National Conservative Political Action Committee (NCPAC) and Americans for an Effective Presidency were two such groups. The independent expenditure groups helped Reagan and hurt Carter in several states, but they were loose cannons outside the control of the campaign or the party. Reagan's campaign manager William Casey did not like them, fearing they would divert resources away from party coffers and "make Reagan look harsher and more rightwing."[5] The Republican National Committee's Bill Brock asked them to exercise caution in order to avoid creating a public backlash. Their efforts were hindered by lawsuits filed by the Carter campaign and the liberal government-reform group Common Cause, which charged that the pro-Reagan groups were not fully independent.

John Anderson, as an independent challenger, had been the choice of 20–25 percent of voters in most polls during the spring and summer. Undergirding his own personal standing was the fact that about one-fifth of the electorate also expressed an abstract desire for a choice other than Carter or Reagan. Anderson had to make the case that Carter had failed, that Reagan was too old and too extreme, and that he was the right man at the right moment. As a liberal, he threatened to cut into Carter's base.

In late July, he met publicly with Ted Kennedy, told reporters that he might not run if Democrats nominated Kennedy, and in turn received the Democratic challenger's accolades. (Anderson later confided that the meeting was a mistake that alienated some of his erstwhile supporters.)[6] As a Republican maverick who had struck out against his own party, he might hope to cut into Reagan's appeal as an outsider, as well as to pick up the votes of the dwindling Rockefeller wing of the GOP. Carter was particularly worried about Anderson, complaining in his memoirs that he was a "chameleon" whose political support "was one of Governor Reagan's greatest assets, and one of my biggest liabilities."[7]

When the general election campaign got under way in earnest, Anderson named Patrick Lucey, a liberal Democrat, Kennedy supporter, and former governor of Wisconsin, as his running mate. The ticket wrote a platform calling for urban renewal, more mass transit, a fifty-cent-per-gallon tax on gasoline, a balanced budget, and such socially liberal policies as restricted guns and unrestricted abortion, including federal funding of abortions for poor women. It also proposed a smaller defense increase than either major party and—unlike both Reagan and Carter—no individual income tax cuts at all.

Framing his campaign around "sacrifice" and a "new public philosophy," Anderson succeeded in getting on the ballot in all fifty states, at a cost of $2 million. (Democrats spent $200,000 trying to keep him off the ballot.) He also received the coveted endorsement of the New York Liberal Party and was declared eligible for federal funds if he were to receive at least 5 percent of the vote in November. He employed noted media expert David Garth to draw up a media campaign, and he backed off his original vow to drop out of the race if it seemed that his presence might help elect Reagan. Anderson's challenge was to expand his committed support beyond the relatively narrow demographic base that he had held in the Republican primaries—young, white, upper-middle-class voters with college degrees and an attachment to gun control and abortion on demand. His regional support was concentrated in a handful of states in New England, the Great Lakes region, and the Pacific Northwest, though Garth thought he might be competitive in New York as well. His biggest—his only—hope of winning was that Carter and Reagan would somehow destroy each other, leaving him to pick up the pieces.

The parameters within which the general election campaign took place were both geographic and demographic in character. Because victory requires a majority of electoral votes and because electoral votes are determined on a state-by-state basis, every presidential election is, in a sense, fifty-one separate elections (in all the states and the District of Columbia). The task of every campaign is to assemble victories in states so that its candidate wins a total of at least 270 electoral votes. This means that geography is at the core of any presidential general election strategy.

By 1980 strategists knew that many of the old geographic assumptions of presidential politics were no longer valid. Republicans in 1964,

1968, and 1972 had reoriented the map by focusing on the "Sunbelt strategy." In 1976 Carter had disrupted the GOP's Sunbelt strategy by winning the South (except for Virginia, which now seemed solidly Republican). The states west of the Missouri River seemed to be the most solidly Republican area, and (thanks to California) the region had a large block of electoral votes. Johnson's 1964 landslide had demonstrated that Democrats could compete everywhere, and the Nixon landslide of 1972 had shown that no region was beyond the reach of the Republicans under the right circumstances, either. Many of Carter's 1976 wins had been very close (Texas, Florida, and Ohio, to name three), and in states that would clearly be up for grabs in 1980. Carter knew he had little margin to lose in 1980 states that he had won in 1976, though his campaign workers identified a few Ford states—such as Michigan and Washington—that they hoped could be swung.

Altogether, the Republicans started from an advantageous position. In the previous three elections, only Massachusetts and the District of Columbia, with seventeen electoral votes together, had voted Democratic all three times. Excluding the landslide year of 1972, another eight (mostly northeastern) states, with 124 electoral votes, had gone Democratic twice. On the other hand, twenty-three states, totaling 199 electoral votes, had voted Republican all three times since 1968. Eleven more, mostly in the industrial Midwest and the border and peripheral South regions, had given the GOP their 137 electoral votes twice. The Deep South was the greatest mystery. It had voted for Goldwater in 1964, Wallace in 1968, Nixon in 1972, and Carter in 1976.

History is not destiny. Majorities are made and unmade by circumstances and by the skills of the candidates, the party leaders, and the strategists. Nevertheless, history had posed but a handful of questions that would determine the presidency in 1980. Who would prevail in the big industrial states of the Midwest and Northeast, states that had wavered between the parties not just in the last three elections but since the 1940s? Before being fired, Reagan campaign manager John Sears had directed the campaign to look East, a strategic decision telegraphed in the choice of venue for Reagan's announcement speech: New York City. Could the Republicans regain their recently gained and even more recently disrupted hold on the peripheral South? For whom would the Deep South vote this time? And were there any subterranean trends that might produce a surprise in states that history suggested were solid? It is striking that although Reagan's strategists considered the peripheral

South and three Deep South states as "battlegrounds," they initially put only Texas, Florida, Virginia, Oklahoma, and South Carolina on their list of first-priority targets. Louisiana was added to the list in June. Not until October were Tennessee, Kentucky, Mississippi, North Carolina, South Carolina, Alabama, and Arkansas added on the basis of favorable polling data.

These questions led inexorably from geography to demography. States might cast electoral votes, but people tell them how to do it. If the big industrial states and the South were to be the pivot points of the electoral map, that meant that three types of people would be special targets.

The first consisted of the blue-collar white ethnic voters—most of them patriotic, economically besieged, and culturally conservative—who would decide states like Ohio, Michigan, Illinois, and Pennsylvania. Although he had won their votes in 1976, Carter was never really their type of man—perhaps too much of a cool engineer, perhaps too southern. The stagflation and the national humiliation of the Carter years provided an opportunity for a challenger. These voters were already loosened from the New Deal coalition—Wallace and Nixon had won a fair share of their votes in 1968 and 1972—and were not yet firmly attached to a new constellation of forces. This was especially true of unorganized blue-collar laborers, who were free to form their views without the direction of the union steward, but unionized workers were also targets.

Carter appealed to union workers by referring to the litany of popular Democratic presidents of the past; Reagan by reminding them of his six terms as a union president. Most unions endorsed Carter, but Reagan received the endorsements of the Teamsters, the National Maritime Union, and the Professional Air Traffic Controllers Organization (PATCO). (The Teamsters cited the economy and Carter's sponsorship of trucking deregulation; PATCO was enmeshed in a labor dispute with the administration; and the Maritime Union membership reversed its pro-Carter leaders by voting overwhelmingly on the floor of their convention to support Reagan instead.) Carter and the union leaders focused on frightening workers away from Reagan. Reagan focused on themes of economic renewal, while backtracking from earlier antiunion positions such as support for a national right-to-work law. Both Reagan and Carter spent a disproportionate amount of time at Slovenian festivals and Lithuanian bakeries in big states.

Heavily overlapping with the first constituency were Catholics, also concentrated in the Northeast and Midwest. Long a staple of the New

Deal majority, Catholics had shifted to Nixon in 1972. They had shifted back to Carter in 1976 but were not terribly comfortable with his
preachy style or with the outcome of his presidency. Catholics, on the
whole, were patriotic, culturally conservative, concerned by the fate of
their coreligionists besieged by communism in the old countries, and
inspired by the new Polish pope and the blossoming resistance of the
Solidarity movement in Poland, which was much in the news in the
fall of 1980. Both candidates tried to appropriate Lech Walesa's father,
symbolically important for the Polish vote. Carter tried to scare Catholics
away from Reagan by tying him to the Moral Majority. Reagan's pro-life
stand on abortion helped him among observant Catholics, though he
more often emphasized his support for tuition tax credits for parents of
students in private schools, a big issue for Catholics and one with little
downside among other voters.

Last, white evangelicals would decide the South and would help decide some northern states with large rural populations, such as Ohio. Patriotic, morally besieged, and culturally conservative, they had thought
in 1976 that Carter was their kind of man. By 1980 they were not so
sure. Relatively liberal Carter administration positions on abortion, homosexuality, drugs, and the tax status of Christian schools had led to
great disillusionment. They were only recently organized in the Moral
Majority and other groups, only recently finding a national voice through
the so-called televangelists, such as Jerry Falwell, Pat Robertson, and Jim
Bakker. Some evangelicals had taken the unprecedented step of joining
forces with Catholics on social issues like abortion, a nascent alliance
that may have blunted some of Carter's strategy of appealing to Catholics
by raising the specter of the Moral Majority. Though much more socially
conservative than most other voters, evangelicals were divided on non-
moral issues, including foreign policy and economic policy, as well as by
religious tenets—some were fundamentalist, others charismatic; some
were tied to established denominations, others independent; some were
recipients of a conversion experience, others not.

The leaders and the activists of the new religious Right had already
cast their lots with the Republicans, but would evangelical voters follow?
A September Gallup poll showed Carter leading Reagan among self-
described "born-again" voters (a category that did not necessarily include
all evangelicals and did include blacks) by a margin of 52 percent to 31
percent. Carter wooed evangelical leaders at a White House breakfast
in January 1980, reminding them that he was born-again. In the fall he

depended on his southernness and on his faith, which was highlighted in a campaign ad proclaiming, "Jimmy Carter is a deeply and clearly religious man. He takes the time to pray privately and with Rosalynn each day. . . . this man knows that one thing remains constant—his faith."

Reagan depended in wooing white evangelicals on his socially conservative positions on abortion and school prayer and on the organizing capacities of the new movement. Throughout the campaign, Reagan sent numerous friendly signals to this voting bloc, including a highly publicized meeting with Falwell in October. For Carter, the hard-hitting ads the Moral Majority ran against him in the South were a particular source of bitterness.

Although blue-collar ethnics, Catholics, and white evangelicals were foremost on the list of pivotal demographic groups in 1980, few groups were entirely ceded. The state of the nation encouraged Republicans to assume that all groups' previous ties to the Democratic Party were loosened. The GOP assiduously wooed Jews, whom the Carter administration had alienated with its serial blunders, culminating in the March 1980 U.N. vote that had undone Carter in the New York primary. Republicans also claimed that they hoped to attract inner-city blacks, and their selection of Detroit as a convention site was a means of furthering that goal. Reagan welcomed the endorsements of black civil rights leaders Ralph Abernathy and Hosea Williams.

For their part, Democrats hoped to pry away the voters at the left and middle of the Republican Party. Ford and Nixon might have been able to win New Jersey's moderate suburbanites, but could Reagan? Carter's strategists hoped these suburban moderates could make up for the losses they expected to suffer in rural, small-town America. Could women, who were widely perceived as having voted in a risk-averse way historically, be drawn away from Republicans with the war-and-peace issue coupled with the issue of the equal rights amendment? (Reagan tried to counter by promising that one of his first Supreme Court nominations would be a woman.)

Anderson also complicated the calculations for both major candidates. Would he take more votes from Carter than from Reagan? (Carter's campaign assumed so, but Reagan's was less certain.) If Carter managed to pry Republican moderates away from Reagan, would they vote for him or would Anderson be the beneficiary? Or would Anderson motivate a whole new cohort of voters who would otherwise have stayed at home on Election Day?

Not least, strategists had to grapple with the fact that a large and increasing number of Americans had decided to refrain from identifying themselves with a party. It was this phenomenon that gave Anderson what little hope he had, and it left both major candidates trying to find the key that would unlock the unaffiliated. To the extent that Americans identified with a party, Democrats held better than a 2-to-1 lead, roughly 45 percent to 20 percent. By 1980 this appearance of strength was only a chimera. Though it still had electoral consequences at lower levels, it was meaningless at the presidential level. The nation was in flux.

Reagan had a long-standing reputation for saying odd things. In the primaries, he had famously contended that most air pollution was caused by trees. Many of his gaffes were relatively harmless and were dismissed by voters, if not by the media. However, collectively they had called into question Reagan's steadiness and intelligence. In the atmosphere of international crisis that pervaded 1980—in which a president's utterances might make the difference between peace and war—this question had heightened importance.

In late August and early September, at the very moment the nation's attention was beginning to focus firmly on the choice, Reagan seemed determined to immolate himself. In the space of a few weeks, he was caught extolling states' rights to a southern audience and civil rights to the Urban League in the same day; repeated his "trees cause pollution" line; repeated an earlier assertion that the New Deal had had roots in fascism; called for "official government relations with Taiwan" just as he was sending George Bush to mainland China to reassure Beijing; called the Vietnam War "a noble cause" in a speech to the Veterans of Foreign Wars; and told a gathering of evangelicals that he favored teaching creation on an equal basis with evolution. Over the Labor Day weekend, Reagan, angered by Democratic attempts to link him to the Ku Klux Klan, wrongly accused Carter of opening his campaign in "the city [Tuscumbia, Alabama] that gave birth to and is the parent body of the Ku Klux Klan."

These gaffes must be separated into categories. Some, like the remarks about tree pollution and the Ku Klux Klan, were simply mistaken and careless, and Reagan's apology for the latter only focused more media attention on it. (The Ku Klux Klan remark may also have cost Reagan the endorsement of Alabama's Democratic governor, Fob James.)[8] Others, like the remarks about Taiwan, muddied his message. Reagan's

Carter opening his fall campaign in Tuscumbia, Alabama.

Ronald and Nancy Reagan campaigning in South Carolina.

analysis of the New Deal was not entirely off the mark: It had been rooted in the collectivist spirit of the time, and the National Recovery Administration actually did resemble a moderate form of Benito Mussolini's corporatism. The comparison, though, was exaggerated and impolitic, as Reagan had already drafted Franklin Roosevelt into service in his acceptance speech.

Some were not gaffes at all but were reported as such because of the predispositions of the media. There were a million Vietnamese boat people and two million dead victims of Pol Pot in Cambodia who vouched for the moral worthiness of the U.S. cause in Indochina. The evolution comment expressed views shared by a majority of Americans in polls and helped cement Reagan's ties to a critical voting bloc. And Reagan, who by all indications was a Jeffersonian but not a bigot, undoubtedly saw no contradiction at all between states' rights and civil rights. Only through a particular political lens could such remarks be viewed as gaffes.

Nevertheless, all the comments were thrown into the same heap of irresponsibility or stupidity by commentators and by Carter campaign spokesmen. The cumulative effect was that Carter had pulled even with Reagan by mid-September and had even established a small lead in one poll. From then on, Reagan stuck closer to his speech texts. Stuart Spencer, a longtime political pro who had helped Reagan in 1966 and 1968 (though he had aided Ford in 1976), began accompanying the candidate, in the view of many journalists, to keep him on track. In the recollection of press secretary Lyn Nofziger, Spencer was brought on board because Reagan needed someone on the campaign plane "who could take an overview of the campaign."[9]

The race, however, changed quickly again. Reagan first counterattacked on September 4 when he upbraided Carter for releasing information on the U.S. development of stealth aircraft. He charged the administration had improperly revealed the secret to shore up Carter's weak image on defense.

The "stealth issue" was soon supplanted by the "debate issue." The League of Women Voters had scheduled a presidential debate for September 21 and had invited Anderson to participate because he had reached the threshold of 15 percent or more in the polls that had been set by the league. Carter, however, wanted no part of a debate involving Anderson, believing that he stood to lose more votes to Anderson than Reagan did. When the White House had announced in May that Carter would not debate Anderson, Reagan had taken the opportunity to gently swipe at both Carter and Anderson: "Of course, he's reluctant to debate within his own party. . . . Maybe [Carter] thinks they might be appealing to the same voters."[10] In the end, Carter stayed away and looked petty. Reagan accepted and debated Anderson. The League of Women Voters threatened to set up an empty chair to represent (and shame) Carter but did not go through with it. In Reagan's debate rehearsals, Michigan congressman David Stockman played the parts of Anderson and Carter so well that it helped him land the job of Reagan's director of the Office of Management and Budget.

The debate itself was carried on CBS and NBC and was watched by an estimated 40 million to 60 million Americans. It ranged over topics such as inflation, energy conservation, the draft, the MX missile, urban issues, the deficit, and abortion. Anderson claimed that oil reserves would be completely depleted by the end of the 1980s, an assertion that Reagan refuted. Reagan claimed he could cut taxes, increase defense spending, and balance the budget, statements that Anderson attacked.

Although Anderson was crisp, Reagan was the big winner strategically, for three reasons. First, the content of the debate made it appear that Anderson was not the centrist candidate in the race but the candidate on the left. Anderson himself helped Reagan in this regard by pointing out that "Governor Reagan and I have agreed on exactly one thing [both opposed the peacetime draft]. . . . We have disagreed, I believe, on virtually every other issue."[11] Anderson hence reduced the threat that he might take Republican voters away from Reagan. Second, Reagan's style during the debate reassured many voters that Reagan was not really a dangerous bumbler with no control over his mouth. He appeared steady, reasonable, and well-spoken, undoing much of the damage of the previous month. Finally, the fact that Reagan had allowed the debate to go forward at all made Reagan appear more gracious than Carter. Both Reagan and Anderson had much fun at the president's expense. Reagan talked of the unfairness that would have resulted if Anderson had been denied the right to participate and thanked the League of Women Voters for holding to a course "with which I believe the great majority of Americans are in agreement." Anderson was forced to indicate his respect for Reagan "for showing tonight—for appearing here." Afterward, it was Reagan whose poll standings improved. Anderson's best chance to make a mark had passed.

Carter reduced his own standing by overplaying his hand. In highlighting Reagan's "gaffes," the president descended to the level of rough-

and-tumble campaigning, sounding eerie echoes of Pat Brown in 1966. In front of a black audience at the Ebenezer Baptist Church in Atlanta, Carter said, "You've seen in this campaign the stirrings of hate and the rebirth of code words like 'states' rights.' . . . Hatred has no place in this country. Racism has no place in this country." On the day after the Reagan-Anderson debate, the president declared that the election would determine "whether we have peace or war." Two weeks later, the president claimed in a speech in Chicago that Reagan would divide "black from white, Jew from Christian, North from South, rural from urban."

Having tarred Reagan as not just a nincompoop but a racist, a bigot, and a warmonger, Carter was soon criticized in the media, even by allies, as mean-spirited. Anderson weighed in on Reagan's side on the war-and-peace issue, calling Carter's comments "self-serving demagoguery." Reagan himself said that Carter was "reaching the point of hysteria and owes the country an apology." The president retreated, allowing that he had been "carried away on a couple of occasions" and promising in a televised interview with Barbara Walters that he would do his best to stop name-calling.

From a tactical standpoint, one could not blame Carter too much for his approach. He was merely following in the footsteps of Johnson's successful 1964 campaign against Goldwater. But Reagan was not Goldwater, and 1980 was not 1964. National conditions allowed the incumbent no cushion for being perceived as unfair. Furthermore, Carter chose to wield the bludgeon himself, unlike Johnson, who had mostly relied on surrogates and advertisements. Carter later said that he had decided on making his case against Reagan directly because his surrogates "were ignored by the press and the public."[12] Not least, Americans had had sixteen years of history to teach them skepticism about the sort of claims Carter was making. A well-worn joke of the late 1960s had gone, "Lyndon Johnson told me that if I voted for Barry Goldwater, we would be at war within six months. He was right: I did, and we were." Many Americans had not forgotten.

The impression of "meanness" left by Carter in this three-week window seriously undermined one of his few remaining strengths: that he was perceived as a "nice" man, a man of integrity. "Meanness" and "gaffes" had canceled each other out, though the campaigns had to continue dealing with the lingering effects of each. By the first week of October, Reagan had regained a lead of 5 percentage points or more, depending upon the poll.

The world, of course, continued to intrude into the race. The Ayatollah Khomeini issued terms for release of the hostages, but nothing happened. Then, on September 22, Saddam Hussein's Iraq invaded Iran. Carter ordered four Airborne Warning and Control System (AWACS) planes and three hundred support personnel to Saudi Arabia. In early October the president caught a rare break when economic data showed the recession was easing. But the campaigns slogged along with little change in the dynamic.

Carter tightened the race by pounding more adroitly at the theme of Reagan the dangerous, but the only major movement came in Anderson's numbers. After the September 21 debate, his support dropped steadily in the vicious cycle familiar to third candidates: a perception of unelectability was followed by declining support, which caused an even more pronounced appearance of failure, and so on. Anderson's fall was abetted by Carter, who released his surrogates (Mondale excluded) to begin attacking the independent candidate openly. "A vote for Anderson is a vote for Reagan," became the Carter mantra. The Carter campaign also produced radio ads attacking Anderson, and the administration quietly discouraged banks from loaning him money against his prospect of federal funds.[13] Anderson was unable to begin running television ads until October 17. By then, he had fallen below 10 percent in national polls.

Finally, after weeks of prodding, the Reagan camp agreed to a one-on-one debate with Carter. Describing the meeting in their memoirs, the two principals hardly seem to be talking about the same event, as if the spin-doctoring of the campaign had never ended. Carter recalled that he had challenged Reagan to debate but that "Reagan quickly rejected the challenge." In late October, "at last we had gotten agreement from the Republicans."[14] Reagan, for his part, held that "I was anxious to get Carter into a nationally televised debate, but his people wouldn't go for it. . . . Carter finally agreed to a debate."[15]

The full story is more complicated, and in a sense, both were right. The Carter camp had desired a series of debates, believing that Carter would show Reagan to be ignorant and dangerous. The traditional intellectual snobbery of Reagan's foes was surfacing again. The Carter camp's key requirements were that there had to be more than one debate (they believed that Carter's knowledge would be more telling over time), Anderson had to be excluded, and there had to be sufficient time before election day for Carter to recover from any mistakes. Reagan's team, for its part, preferred a single debate, including Anderson, as close to the election as possible.

As election day drew nearer, Carter's forces became more vociferous in their demand for a mano-a-mano debate. When Anderson dropped below 15 percent in national polls—the threshold for participation established by the League of Women Voters—their pressure for a debate increased. The Reagan camp was divided, with many fearing that Reagan would be endangering his small lead. If he was ahead, why take the risk? Others, concerned that the campaign seemed to have hit a plateau, hoped a debate could build a cushion against unforeseen last-minute developments. At a strategy session on October 16, Reagan said he preferred to debate. When he and Carter both appeared at the Alfred E. Smith Memorial Dinner in New York that same evening, Reagan spoke gracefully, in keeping with the light-hearted tenor of the event. Carter was tendentious, railing against the Moral Majority. This contrast may have influenced Reagan. In the end, though, contended Wirthlin—who opposed the debate—Reagan's sense of personal obligation was decisive. "If I want to fill [Carter's] shoes," Wirthlin reported Reagan saying, "I ought to be willing to stand up next to him and debate."[16]

On Carter's side, there had also been division. Pollster Pat Caddell had long opposed a debate on the grounds that Carter had little to gain and much to lose from it. He had almost convinced the campaign to pull the plug on the debate challenge when Reagan accepted. Some Carter aides were pleased that they had finally gotten the debate with Reagan that they had been calling for publicly, but Caddell was upset, asking Hamilton Jordan, "Is there any way we can avoid debating him?"[17] The answer, of course, was no: The president was for it, and it would look bad to back out now. The president was boxed in. His earlier refusal to debate Kennedy or Anderson meant that he had little latitude to refuse again.

The problem, as Caddell recognized, was this: Without help from external events, Carter's entire campaign now rested solely on proving Reagan to be ignorant and dangerous. But there was no guarantee that Reagan would cooperate when on the stage with Carter. To the contrary, he might succeed in passing the plausibility threshold just by remaining calm and making no major mistakes. Furthermore, Carter had not participated in a single candidate debate since October 1976. Reagan, meanwhile, had not only debated Anderson in September, to good effect, but had faced the Republican field several times in the spring. Two of his key primary victories—New Hampshire and Illinois—were at least partially traceable to his debate performances. And though Anderson would be absent, two of Reagan's three conditions had been met: There would be a single debate, very late in the season.

Why Carter or anyone on his staff ever saw a debate with Reagan as the key to victory is a bit mysterious. Caddell gave the president one chance in four of winning the debate, then supplied him with a strategy of methodically appealing to the multitude of "constituencies" that he took to represent Carter's Democratic base, including women, the poor, blacks, Hispanics, working families, and the young.

The debate was set for Tuesday, October 28, in Cleveland, Ohio, exactly one week before election day. Polls showed that the race was frozen, with Reagan slightly ahead, as Americans waited for the Big Event. The debate was a high-stakes event in every sense: an audience estimated to be between 100 million and 120 million, and little time for either candidate to recover from any missteps. It was a high-wire act without the net. As the ninety-minute format went on, Carter failed to land any serious blows. Reagan was given the opportunity to meet the war issue head-on, in the first question.[18] Asked to describe the differences between his and Carter's views on the uses of U.S. military power, he responded:

> I don't know what the differences might be, because I don't know what Mr. Carter's policies are. I do know what he has said about mine. And I'm only here to tell you that I believe with all of my heart that our first priority must be world peace, and that use of force is always and only a last resort, when everything else has failed, and then only with regard to our national security. . . . America has never gotten in a war because we were too strong. We can get into a war by letting events get out of hand, as they have in the last three and a half years.

Reagan disputed Carter's contentions about his "steady, carefully planned, methodical" defense increases. Carter pointed out that Reagan had "habitually . . . advocated the injection of military forces in troubled areas," but Reagan's opening seemed to preempt the criticism. Carter labored to put inflation "in perspective," while Reagan countered that the president had

> blamed the people for inflation, OPEC, he has blamed the Federal Reserve System, he has blamed the lack of productivity of the American people, he has then accused the people of living too well and that we

must share in scarcity, we must sacrifice and get used to doing with less. We don't have inflation because the people are living too well. We have inflation because the government is living too well.

Carter attacked the Kemp-Roth tax cut as "extremely inflationary." Reagan countered, "Why is it inflationary to let the people keep more of their money and spend it the way they like, and it isn't inflationary to let [Carter] take that money and spend it the way he wants?" When Reagan offered that when he was young, "this country didn't even know it had a racial problem," Carter noted that "those who suffered discrimination from race or sex certainly knew we had a racial problem." However, the voters stirred by such a recollection were mostly in his corner already. The discussion then coursed through terrorism.

Carter consistently came back to the theme of nuclear arms control and nonproliferation, attacking Reagan's opposition to SALT II as "dangerous and disturbing . . . extremely dangerous and belligerent." His thirteen-year-old daughter Amy, Carter confided, had told him nuclear proliferation was the number-one issue facing mankind. Reagan pleaded that "sometimes I have a hard time in connecting what he's saying with what I have said or what my positions are." Later, confronted with similarly stark accusations by Carter about environmental, Social Security, and Medicare policies, Reagan finally cocked his head and replied: "There you go again," to laughter in the house. Asked why the people should not vote for Carter and Mondale, Reagan responded with Carter's penchant for big-government solutions and with the "misery index," the combination of inflation and unemployment rates. When Carter had devised the index in 1976 to use against Ford, it stood at 12.5 percent. It was now in excess of 20 percent. Carter cited Reagan's "radical departure from the principles or ideals of historical perspective of his own party," as evidenced by his opposition to the equal rights amendment.

In conclusion, Carter referred to "the sharp differences between myself and Governor Reagan. . . . I consider myself in the mainstream of my party. I consider myself in the mainstream even of the bipartisan list of Presidents who served before me. . . . The final decision about the future of the nation—war, peace, involvement, reticence, thoughtfulness, care, consideration, concern—has to be made by the man in the Oval Office." Reagan had been given the last word by the Carter camp in exchange for agreeing to take the first question of the debate, Carterites hoping he would be particularly nervous as he opened the event. In his

*The October 28 presidential debate in Cleveland,
Ohio, may have been the critical turning point
in the 1980 campaign.*

closing statement, Reagan returned to the exclusion of Anderson, then framed the election as he had framed it in his July acceptance speech:

It might be well if you would ask yourself, are you better off than you were four years ago? Is it easier for you to go and buy things in the stores than it was four years ago? Is there more or less unemployment in the country than there was four years ago? Is America as respected throughout the world as it was? Do you feel that our security is as safe, that we're as strong as we were four years ago? And if you answer all of those questions yes, why then I think your choice is very obvious as to whom you will vote for. If you don't agree, if you don't think that this course that we've been on for the last four years is what you would like to see us follow for the next four, then I could suggest another choice that you have. . . . I would like to have a crusade today . . . to take Government off the backs of the great people of this country, and turn you loose again to do those things that I know you can do so well.

And that was it. Both Carter and Reagan had gotten some facts mixed up, and Carter drew considerable ridicule for consulting Amy on nonproliferation, but both had stuck to their themes. As the president reflected in his October 28 diary entry, "Both sides felt good after the debate . . . he accomplished his purpose; we accomplished ours."[19] For Carter, though, this was not enough. Reagan had deflected most of Carter's jabs, showed steadiness and good humor, and belied the picture Carter had been trying to paint for months. Whatever else he was, he did not look dangerous, disturbing, or belligerent. His conclusion was also crucial. Carter's struggle was always to try to have it both ways, gaining credit for the experience of incumbency without bearing responsibility for the intolerable state of the nation. Ultimately, he had to do what no other incumbent of the twentieth century had been able to do successfully: turn his reelection campaign into a primarily prospective rather than primarily retrospective evaluation. With Reagan's closing statement in the Cleveland debate, that effort ended in failure.

An ABC News instant poll, in which people could vote for the debate winner by calling in and paying fifty cents, showed Reagan beating Carter by a 2-to-1 margin. Although this poll may have been unscientific and impersonal, Hamilton Jordan conducted his own unscientific and very personal poll: He asked his brother, who said, "Reagan looked good. He did better than Carter."[20] More-scientific surveys, such as a

focus group convened for the *Wall Street Journal* by Democratic consultant Peter Hart, showed Reagan to have scored heavily against Carter.
Other scientific polls had Reagan winning the debate by anywhere from
8 to 18 percentage points.

The national polls showed Reagan opening up a bigger lead, though
there was a short lag; as in debates before and since, the subsequent
interpretation and rehashing of the debate may have influenced voters
as much as the debate itself. Richard Wirthlin, Reagan's pollster, found
a dip in the number who considered Reagan "dangerous," as did the
public polls. On the question of which candidate was the stronger figure, Wirthlin's post-debate polls showed Reagan beating Carter by 2 to 1.
In total, by Wirthlin's calculation, Reagan's lead had grown from 5 percent to 7 percent on the Thursday after the debate. Caddell's figures also
showed Reagan's lead growing from a hair's breadth to 4 or 5 points.

Three years later, a miniscandal erupted when former Reagan campaign officials admitted that in the days before the debate they had received a copy of Carter's debate briefing book from a "mole." The use of
the briefing book was undoubtedly unethical, but there is little reason
to believe that it made much difference. Reagan's two most noted lines
were "There you go again," a response to a series of attacks Carter had
been making publicly since August, and "Are you better off?" a restate-
ment of one of the key themes from his July acceptance speech.

What happened over the next five days is unclear, even a quarter of a
century later. By Wirthlin's calculation, Reagan's lead continued growing
through the weekend before the election as debate impressions hard-
ened and bad economic data again came to the fore. (After a brief lull,
inflation was raging at a 12.7 percent annual rate, and the prime interest
rate reached 14.5 percent after a brief drop in the summer.) Caddell, on
the other hand, found Democrats "coming home" to Carter, so that the
president drew even over the weekend, until the bottom fell out on Monday. Most public polls like Gallup, NBC, and Harris showed Reagan with
a modest lead, though the *Washington Post* showed Carter ahead. Most
stopped polling on Saturday.

After little movement for months, it appeared on the weekend before
the election that Iran might be preparing to release the hostages. The
Iranian parliament, the Majlis, began debating terms for such a release.
For a time, a militant minority boycotted the proceedings, preventing

the Majlis from attaining a quorum. Reagan, who had only recently departed from his long reluctance to criticize Carter about the hostages, went silent again. Once the quorum was reached, it passed a resolution stating four conditions. Carter himself suspended campaigning in Illinois, making a dramatic return to Washington on Air Force One. Hope was built up; the nation waited.

Cynical Republicans had suspected since Carter's Wisconsin primary morning press conference that they might face an "October Surprise," a release of the hostages engineered just in time to tip the election to Carter. They had been strenuously preparing the public for such a possibility since July. However, it turned out upon translation that the conditions set forth by the Majlis were the same as those Khomeini had issued two months before—nothing new, and nothing that could be executed immediately. On Sunday afternoon, Carter told the nation that the developments were "positive" but that "I wish I could predict when the hostages will return. I cannot." This announcement came just in time for an onslaught of media commemorations of the first anniversary of the embassy invasion.

The effect of this turn of events is hard to assess. By Caddell's reckoning at the time, only after the hostage release fell through did the numbers turn sharply against the president, as if all of people's pent-up frustration had suddenly burst forth. Caddell saw a substantial increase in those not expecting the hostages to be released anytime soon, ominously concentrated among Catholics and union workers. On the other hand, by Wirthlin's reckoning (and, to a lesser extent, that of most other polls), Reagan had already pulled beyond easy reach. The failure to achieve a last-minute breakthrough was bitterly disappointing for many Americans, but in Wirthlin's data there is little evidence to suggest that Carter would have won even without the disappointment.

A tougher question is whether Carter would have won had the Majlis actually released the hostages. If the race was as close as Caddell thought on Saturday, it may well have been tipped; the potential effect of an event of that magnitude cannot be dismissed. Yet all else continued to work against the president, and the timing would have raised questions. How was it that Carter could not secure the release of the hostages for a year and then suddenly could—two days before the election? What did he give up to get them back at such a convenient time? A foretaste of what such questioning would have been like came on Sunday, when Gerald

Ford, Henry Kissinger, and George Bush took to the airwaves to express concern about the "manipulation" of the U.S. election by the Iranians (or, implicitly, by Carter).

Polls found that one-third of Americans believed Iran was indeed manipulating the election, and another one-third thought Carter was— twice as many as had accused the president of the same thing only six weeks before. Just in case, setting aside $200,000 for the contingency, the Reagan camp cut four last-minute television ads as well as radio ads tailored to address a variety of hostage-release scenarios but focusing on the themes that a hostage return was "simply a political expedient" and "why weren't they returned earlier?"[21] They were never used.

A decade later, former Carter National Security Council staff member Gary Sick claimed in a book entitled *October Surprise* that key members of Reagan's staff, including William Casey, had entered into secret negotiations with the Iranians with the aim of preventing the release of the hostages until after election day. The book caused a major stir when it was released in 1991, though the lurid tale had been circulating in less-respected conspiracy circles since 1987. However, conflicting evidence soon discredited it. Sick's sources were highly questionable, as he himself admitted, and records showed the alleged participants could not have been where Sick said they were.

Ultimately, both House and Senate investigations—at a time when Congress was still under Democratic control—concluded in 1993 that there was "no credible evidence" to support Sick's assertions. The House investigation cost $1.35 million, interviewed 230 people, uncovered reams of previously hidden documentation, and produced a 968-page report. The 1993 House report still stands as the definitive exposition on the matter, and no one has come close to refuting it since.

Except to dyed-in-the-wool cynics, the premise has always been far-fetched. Even if one is willing to accept the possibility that Reagan's team was capable of such a thing—which would have amounted to treason— it is hard to believe that they would have taken the risk. At a minimum, discovery would have been political suicide. And if a deal was struck, what was the point of holding the hostages a full two and a half months after election day? And what exactly was the Majlis doing over the weekend, shaking fists at each other and engaging in bitter boycotts? Why would the Iranians give up a deal in the hand for the uncertain prospect of a Republican win? And why would they make the Americans a last-minute offer, as the Majlis did, when Carter might actually accept it and

After learning from Pat Caddell that his reelection bid was doomed, Carter closed his campaign with a nostalgic speech in Plains, Georgia.

upset the whole apple cart? The release of the hostages a few minutes after Reagan's inauguration on January 20, 1981—taken by conspiracy theorists as circumstantial evidence for the existence of a plot—was always more easily explainable by Khomeini's deep hatred of Carter and by the fact that the fortieth president, unlike the thirty-ninth, appeared ready to impose a firm deadline on Iran backed up by military force.

Americans went to the polls on the one-year anniversary of the seizure of the hostages. In the dark, early-morning hours of election day, Tuesday, November 4, Jimmy Carter had been informed by Pat Caddell that the race could not be won. Carter then returned to Plains to end his campaign. Reagan had been told by Richard Wirthlin that the race was won. Around noon eastern time, the networks' exit polling was already indicating a swell for Reagan. As voting places closed across the United States, the results confirmed what the exit polls had been saying. NBC News called Indiana, Virginia, Mississippi, Alabama, and Florida for Reagan (as well as Georgia for Carter) at 7:01 P.M. eastern time. At 7:30, Ohio joined them, as did Kentucky two minutes later. When, at 8:01, anchor John Chancellor declared Connecticut, New Jersey, Pennsylvania, Michigan, Illinois, North Dakota, South Dakota, Kansas, Missouri, Tennessee, Oklahoma, and Texas for Reagan, it was clear that an electoral vote landslide was in the making. At 8:15 Chancellor called the race for Reagan. Altogether, twenty-five states were called first by NBC, which was the first network ever to use exit polls to project a winner.

Thus, at the absurdly early hour of 8:30 P.M., Carter placed what must have been the most difficult phone call of his life: to Reagan, who was in the midst of taking a shower. Years later Reagan would recall that "standing in my bathroom with a wrapped towel around me, my hair dripping with water, I had just learned I was going to be the fortieth president of the United States."[22] At 9:52 P.M., Carter appeared at the Sheraton Washington Hotel to give his concession speech. It was the earliest concession since Alton B. Parker was swamped by Theodore Roosevelt in 1904. Carter had had all day to prepare. His supporters had not. Since the polls had not yet closed on the West Coast, some Democrats, including Speaker of the House Tip O'Neill, urged Carter to wait to concede so as not to depress Democratic turnout where there were still live races. However, the president did not want to "appear to be a bad loser, waiting until late at night to confirm what everybody already knew."[23] "I can't stand here today and say it doesn't hurt," Carter acknowledged. "I've not achieved all I set out to do. But we have faced the tough issues. . . . The great principles that have guided this nation since its very founding will continue to guide America through the challenges of the future."

Anderson then appeared to concede a race he and his advisers had long known was lost. Carter may have had a day to polish his statement, but Anderson had had a month or more. Still looking forward to the possibility of leading a future movement of the affluent center-left, Anderson conceded that "I was not destined to be the next President of the United States—that is a decision deferred."

Finally, at 11:45 P.M. eastern time, 8:45 on the West Coast, Reagan stepped out before an enthusiastic crowd at the Century Plaza Hotel in Los Angeles to claim victory. "There's never been a more humbling moment in my life. . . . I am not frightened by what lies ahead, and I don't believe the American people are frightened by what lies ahead. We're going to put America back to work again."

Reagan received 51 percent of the nationally aggregated popular vote, winning forty-four states and 489 electoral votes. Carter finished with 41 percent, prevailing in six states with 49 electoral votes. Anderson won nowhere, but gained nearly 7 percent of the vote, enough to qualify for federal funds. He broke the 10 percent mark in only nine states, doing best in Massachusetts with 15.2 percent. The Libertarian candidate, Ed Clark, won 921,000 votes (about 1.1 percent of the national total, including 11 percent in Alaska), that party's best showing ever. A total of 86,515,221 Americans voted, or 52.6 percent of the voting-age population. This proportion represented a slight decline from 1976.

In the chief battleground of the election, Reagan scored solid wins in the industrial Midwest and Northeast. The marriage of the Republican Sunbelt "L"—West plus South—was consummated. Reagan won all the contiguous states west of the Missouri River and lost only Mondale's Minnesota in the upper Midwest. In the South Reagan may have surprised even himself by the breadth of his victory. In a region where Reagan's campaign had identified no more than five states as first-priority targets until early October, Carter won only his native Georgia.

Because Reagan was instrumental in attaching the South to the GOP after 1980, it is easy to forget how hard-fought the battle there was in that year. Reagan barely prevailed in Alabama, South Carolina, Mississippi, Tennessee, Arkansas, and North Carolina. In none of these states did Reagan break the 50 percent mark; in none was his margin greater than 2.1 percent, and five of the six gave him a margin of 1.3 percent or smaller. Texas and Florida, two key battleground states, went to Reagan by more comfortable margins, as did Louisiana and Virginia. In Texas 43,000 GOP volunteers got out the vote, and did it so successfully that some voters in Republican suburbs had to wait in line for three hours before casting their ballots.

Aside from the home states of Carter and Mondale, the Democratic ticket won only West Virginia, Maryland, Rhode Island, Hawaii, and the District of Columbia. In twenty-five states Reagan obtained an absolute majority of the vote; in another nineteen, a plurality. He won in some unexpected places, finishing ahead of Carter in New York (where he had spent zero dollars on advertising) and in Massachusetts, which only eight years before had been the only state in the union to vote for George McGovern. In every state the total Democratic presidential vote share was less in 1980 than in 1976. Removing Anderson and other non–major party candidates from the picture, Carter's two-party share was also less in 1980 than in 1976 everywhere but Rhode Island, Vermont, and the District of Columbia. Reagan polled a plurality in every region of the nation—East, West, Midwest, South.

By any standard, the election was an electoral vote landslide. Prior to 1980, only two winners had ever received more than 489 electoral votes: Roosevelt in 1936 and Nixon in 1972. Johnson had not in 1964; FDR had not when he unseated Hoover in 1932; Eisenhower had not, despite his wide appeal in 1952 and 1956. The 1980 results seemed even more like a landslide given press predictions of a tight finish and given the GOP's takeover of the Senate on election day. By all indications, voters who had made up their minds in the last week went overwhelmingly for Reagan.

On the other hand, the Californian won with only 51 percent of the total popular vote. Had just 2 percent of the voters shifted from Reagan to the president across the board, eleven more states, with 124 electoral votes, would have been Carter's. Anderson did not do well nationally, but he may well have siphoned enough votes from Carter to give Massachusetts, New York, and perhaps Connecticut to Reagan. In other elections that are widely considered "landslides," such as 1964 and 1936, the winners had not gained so much by such thin margins. However, Reagan's 51 percent majority was more impressive in that it was achieved in a three-way-race, a feat that had not been matched by Nixon in 1968, Truman in 1948, or Wilson in 1912. When calculated in two-party terms, Reagan received 55 percent to Carter's 45 percent, right at the 10 point spread that is often used to delineate a "landslide." What mattered in the end was that Reagan won, and with quite a bit of room to spare.

He did it by making serious inroads into the groups that were understood by both campaigns to be pivotal. Indeed, the New Deal coalition, or what was left of it, was exploded on November 4, 1980. This can be seen by examining each of the major groups targeted by the parties:[24]

- *Blue-collar workers:* Carter, who won this group against Ford in 1976 by a 3-to-2 margin, only broke even in 1980 (losing by 1 point in one exit poll, winning by 2 points in another). Even labor-union families supported him by only a margin of 5 to 7 points, compared with margins of up to 27 points in 1976. White union voters actually gave Reagan a plurality. Blue-collar voters who believed that their economic condition would be worse in a year backed Reagan by a 2-to-1 ratio. Another way of getting at this question is by looking at educational attainment. Those with a college education (53 percent Republican in 1976) and those with only a grade school education (58 percent Democrat in 1976) hardly changed their vote pattern at all in 1980. Only those with a high school education flipped, from 54–46 Carter to 51–43 Reagan.
- *Ethnics:* All three big ethnic blocks—Irish, Slavs, and Italians—shifted to the Republicans. Reagan won the Irish vote in every major state, including New York (by a margin of 53 percent to 35 percent). Carter held a plurality of the Polish and Slavic voters in only Pennsylvania, Maryland, and Ohio. In New Jersey, Polish and Slavic voters gave Reagan a 31 percent margin, in Illinois a 10 point margin, in Michigan a 5 point lead, and wins of one sort or another in all other major states. The Italians supported Reagan over Carter by 60 percent to 33 percent in New Jersey, 57 percent to 37 percent in New York, and 64 percent to 26 percent in California.
- *Catholics:* In 1976 Carter had won by a margin of 15 points among this group. In 1980 he lost it to Reagan by anywhere from 2 to 7 points. Reagan beat Carter by 11 points among all white Catholics and by a 2-to-1 margin among white, middle-class Catholics.
- *Evangelical Protestants:* White fundamentalist or evangelical Christians gave Reagan a 2-to-1 edge over Carter (though Southern Baptists, the president's denomination, gave him a

bigger proportion of their votes than did other white Protestants). This was almost exactly the same edge Reagan gained among all white Protestants, and some analysts held that they "had no measurable effect on the outcome."[25] However, Carter's vote share in this group fell by about one-fourth from 1976 to 1980. The strongest fundamentalists voted more heavily for Reagan than did other voters, and evangelicals were more likely to participate in the election than were others. Richard Wirthlin contended that gains among evangelicals gave Reagan his wins in North Carolina, Kentucky, Tennessee, Alabama, and Mississippi. Some also argued that the religious Right helped Reagan indirectly by politicizing a set of social issues that benefited Reagan with a majority of Americans. The Moral Majority's positions, it was noted, were much more popular than the Moral Majority was as an organization. By 1984, 78 percent of white born-again Christians voted for Reagan.

- *Jews:* Against Ford, Carter had compiled a lead of 30 points among Jewish voters. In 1980 he still won, though only by 6 points. Jews in critical Pennsylvania actually gave Reagan their plurality. Brooklyn Park, New York, the largest concentration of Orthodox Jews in the United States, gave Reagan 63 percent.
- *Blacks and Hispanics:* Black voters remained loyal to the Democrats, giving Carter a margin of 85 to 11. However, Reagan polled more than a third of the Hispanic vote.
- *Men and women:* The 1980 election also gave birth to the modern "gender gap." Carter flipped his position of 1976, when he had won among men but lost among women. In 1980 he still lost among women, but he lost by a much bigger margin among men. Campaign ads hitting Reagan for abandoning the equal rights amendment were judged by Carter's strategists to have been effective, but the war-and-peace issue helped him much more. For the rest of the 1980s, this form of the gender gap would persist, with Republicans winning big among men and winning by a smaller margin among women. Journalists and feminist leaders focused on the women, but the striking turnaround was among men, who had traditionally voted Democratic. Not until the 1990s did pluralities of men and women actually support opposing candidates.

Otherwise, Reagan held on to all his party's bases while making substantial forays into what used to be solidly Democratic terrain. And no analysis of demographic groups should obscure the point that Reagan's victory and Carter's loss were exceptionally broad, with Reagan winning all but the poorest, all but the very youngest, and all but the least-well-educated voters. Reagan won the independent voters by nearly 2 to 1, and he even gained an edge among self-described "moderates." In no region or demographic group did Carter do better in 1980 than in 1976. In the end, Reagan lost only one in twelve Republican voters to Carter, but Carter lost one in four Democrats to Reagan.

For his part, Anderson was hurt by the "wasted vote syndrome," though, interestingly, an ABC News exit poll showed him doing better among voters who had decided in the last week than among other voters. By the end of the campaign, voters identified Anderson as a liberal, placing him to the left of Carter on the ideological scale. And his votes reflected those perceptions. He did significantly better than his national vote average among the young, the college-educated, independents, and self-described liberals. He did particularly well among Jewish voters (winning around 15–20 percent), and did abysmally among blacks, high school dropouts, southerners, evangelicals, conservatives, and farmers. Anderson got roughly the same percentage from Democrats as from Republicans, and did about twice as well among professionals as among blue-collar workers. Exit polls showed that his voters would have split roughly evenly between Carter and Reagan if he had not been in the race—49 percent for Carter to 37 percent for Reagan—and that about one-third would not have bothered voting at all.

However futile Anderson's quest may have been, he also broke important ground in terms of ballot access and finance. His campaign spent $14.4 million, and he was the first non–major party candidate to qualify for federal funds. In sum, according to campaign finance expert Herbert Alexander, independent and third-party expenditures in 1980 represented a "historic breakthrough."[26]

The top two reasons given by Reagan voters for their vote were "It's time for a change" (38 percent) and "He's a strong leader" (21 percent). The top reason given by Carter voters was a fear that Reagan would lead the United States into war. Voters gave Reagan significantly higher marks than Carter on strengthening national defense, reducing inflation, improving the economy, spending tax money wisely, increasing respect for the United States overseas, and reducing unemployment. Carter had the advantage on improving things for minorities, keeping the United States out of war, helping the poor, fostering women's rights, dealing with racial problems, and advancing peace in the Middle East.

Surveys clearly demonstrated two important features of the 1980 issue environment. First, the economy (especially inflation, then unemployment and a balanced budget) was the top issue on people's minds, followed by foreign policy. Second, foreign policy was much more important in 1980 than it had been in 1976. Data collected by the Survey Research Center at the University of Michigan showed that in 1980 economic issues outweighed foreign policy in voters' minds by a margin of 56 percent to 32 percent. Four years earlier, the margin in favor of economic issues had been 76 percent to 4 percent.

Why did Reagan win and Carter lose? Campaign analysts are always torn between contingency and determinism. Campaign insiders and journalists dissect every move on the chessboard, looking for the keys to victory in specific strategic decisions and in flukes of happenstance. On the other hand, many political scientists are inclined to dismiss the importance of campaigns and to look instead at the underlying national conditions and structural factors within which the candidates operate. At the extreme, some have argued that campaigns are not important at all, that everything rides on the bigger picture and is hence easily predictable.

In the category of contingency, there are a number of possible explanations that could be offered for the results of the 1980 election:

- Reagan's field organization is generally judged to have been superior to Carter's. In a number of states this may have been decisive.
- Local factors were important to Reagan's success in specific key states. These included the influx of Cuban refugees in Florida and Arkansas, the decline of the auto industry in Michigan, the grain embargo in the farm belt, and the possession of the Texas governorship by Republican Bill Clements, who some observers argued was in a position to pull away some of the south Texas Hispanic vote.
- The Republicans were better with money. Their local organizational superiority was abetted by the fact that state and local party organizations, which were allowed to raise money

outside the regular national party and candidate limits, raised three times as much on the Republican side as on the Democratic side. The Reagan field operation was largely funded through this mechanism. At the same time, on the national level, the Reagan-Bush team conserved its resources and was able to pour 40 percent of its advertising budget into the last two weeks of the campaign.

- Carter strategists severely misjudged their opponent. They could never really envision Reagan as the winner. Despite being warned not to underestimate Reagan by Jesse Unruh, Reagan's 1970 gubernatorial opponent, and Bob Morretti, the California Assembly leader in Reagan's second term, Carter confessed that he had been "pleased that Governor Reagan was the nominee. . . . all my political team believed that he was the weakest candidate the Republicans could have chosen."[27] Even in early October, Carter's press secretary, Jody Powell, was privately arguing that Howard Baker would have been "a much more formidable candidate" than Reagan.[28]

- Kennedy hurt Carter. Many of his attacks were recycled by Republicans in the fall. More generally, the Kennedy challenge forced Carter to the left in the primaries (which was Kennedy's goal), possibly damaging Carter's centrist image in the fall. Carter was unable to focus his undivided attention on the fall campaign until August, and the Democratic National Committee could spend no money for him as long as the nomination was uncertain. Kennedy was said to have pushed the Senate Judiciary Committee to investigate Billy Carter, and he drew blood from Carter at the convention. In the fall, Kennedy demanded that the Carter campaign pay off his campaign debts as a price for campaigning for the president. Theodore White recounts an instance (which he heard secondhand) during the fall campaign in which Kennedy pulled out some private polls of Pennsylvania, asked, "Do you want to see some good news?" and proceeded to display polls showing Carter behind.[29] Jody Powell contended that a Kennedy man, Paul Corbin, was somehow involved in the case of the purloined debate briefing book.[30]

- The Anderson factor hurt Carter. The president found himself fighting a two-front war. Anderson hoped to seize the middle, but he failed. He was identified on the left and had his greatest support among self-described liberals. This meant that Carter had to protect his left flank, which was already crumbling, without giving up ground to Reagan in the center. Anderson also complicated the debate picture in ways that hurt Carter, and he may have cost Carter a few states in November. Political scientist Gerald Pomper observed that "concern about Anderson dominated and warped many of Carter's strategic decisions."[31]

• Events worked against Carter. Of the five key factors in the campaign—Reagan's "gaffes," Carter's "meanness," the two debates, and the last-minute hostage flurry—four turned against Carter. At least two of the four were self-inflicted wounds. First, Carter went on the attack so directly and so vehemently that he looked "unpresidential" and "mean," undercutting two of his key strengths (incumbency and a reputation for personal rectitude). Second, he agreed to the debate with Reagan. Pat Caddell argued that "the biggest mistake we made in this campaign was not to cut off the possibility of a debate."[32] The hostages, on the other hand, caused Carter supporters to curse their bad luck. If only Iraq had not invaded Iran, causing Iran to put hostage negotiations on the back burner. If only the apparent breakthrough on the last weekend had not fallen through.

• The media were unhelpful through their day-by-day hostage coverage and, in exaggerated form, through their coverage in the days prior to the one-year anniversary of the hostage crisis. The media also damaged Carter when it came time to assess his "meanness" and his debate performance. In Carter's view, the unwillingness of the media to "expose" Reagan—that is, to serve as a willing handmaiden of the Carter campaign strategy—was what drove him to his more aggressive stance. Reagan was endorsed by newspapers with twice the overall circulation of the papers endorsing Carter, and one study showed that Carter received more negative coverage than Reagan on CBS news and in UPI wire reports.[33] Commentator Jonathan Alter complained that journalists covering the challenger had been "rooting for Reagan" in hopes of landing a spot on his White House beat.[34]

Each of these arguments has some merit, but they also have serious limits as explanations for the 1980 outcome. For example, though the Kennedy and Anderson factors demonstrably made life harder for the president, they cannot be considered decisive. Despite the Kennedy challenge, Carter gained a significant bounce from his convention. Even if every Anderson voter had voted for Carter, he still would have lost the election by a substantial margin in the Electoral College. Nor did the Kennedy challenge lead to Carter's November defeat; Carter's preexisting troubles led to both the challenge and the defeat. Democrats (and Americans in general) were noticeably angry at national conditions and at the administration even in early 1979. Many influential Democrats were casting about for an alternative. Eyes fixed on Kennedy as the heir apparent, but Kennedy could have been Jerry Brown or Hugh Carey or Edmund Muskie or any number of other figures. Kennedy had the political stature to mount a serious campaign—which is precisely why liberals fixed on him—but his candidacy was more a symptom than a cause of Carter's difficulties. Can one imagine Kennedy running if Carter's approval rating in mid-1979 had stood at 59 percent instead of 29 percent? In the same way, Anderson was drawn to the race not just by his dislike of Reagan and Reaganism but by his calculation that Carter was vulnerable. Historically, both strong intraparty challenges and strong third-candidate efforts are associated with incumbents who are already perceived as weak, and 1980 was no exception.

Media may have been at the center of the campaign, but two of the biggest media-driven stories—Reagan's gaffes and Carter's meanness—essentially canceled each other out. However much hoopla surrounded it, the hostage crisis was a real event. The same study that showed Reagan with better press than Carter on average also showed that Reagan's advantage was slight. Indeed, Reagan actually had the worst coverage of any of the three major candidates in two of the three months of the general election period, and researchers were most struck by the degree to which both Carter and Reagan were consistently pummeled by the media, especially on television. Political scientist Michael J. Robinson argued that media, both free and paid, probably had less influence in 1980 than it had had in 1976.[35]

One can pinpoint at least three specific failures that flowed from the Carter campaign's underestimation of Reagan. One was a failure to anticipate how adept Reagan was at sidestepping and redirecting attack. This was a crucial error in a campaign that was based on little more than attack. Second, the campaign underestimated Reagan's southern appeal, mistakenly assuming that its southern base, with a few possible exceptions, would not desert it. The third was the confidence—not shared by

Caddell—that debates would redound to the president's favor. However, the debate issue is clearly more complicated than that. Carter had been hurt in September for not debating, and ducking again in October might have hurt him more. That, at any rate, was the campaign's calculation, and it is hard to say that they were wrong. Furthermore, by most indications, the debate only lengthened Reagan's already-existing lead.

Then there was the last minute flurry about the hostages. It is impossible to know for certain which version of how this affected the race—Wirthlin's or Caddell's—was closer to the truth. Neither was flatly impossible, and each pollster had a vested interest in his own account. However, it seems much more likely that Wirthlin was right. A closer examination of Caddell's data showed that the Carter "trend" actually consisted of a one-day blip—occurring on Saturday—bracketed by a consistent Reagan lead on either side.[36] Other public and private pollsters uniformly failed to find the phenomenon described by Caddell in either national or state surveys, and most who were interviewed about it found the notion implausible.[37] Caddell himself seemed to downplay the significance of the Carter blip when he later acknowledged, "None of this analysis suggests that Carter would have been reelected, absent the events of the final weekend. There is only a slim possibility that he could have won."[38] In Caddell's view, the debate, rather than the final weekend, was ultimately decisive, though the weekend events converted Reagan's win into a landslide by refocusing attention on Carter and inviting a referendum on his presidency.

Strategically, both camps knew what they had to accomplish. Reagan stressed prosperity, where Carter was weak, and called for a referendum on four years of crisis; Carter stressed war and peace, where Reagan was weak, and looked to the future rather than the more troubling present. If anything, it was in the area of execution that Reagan had the advantage. He did a better job of framing the election than Carter did. He carried off his good plan; Carter did not.

In all, this litany of chessboard moves and untoward events does not add up to the whole. Indeed, even some of the contingencies that seem to have genuinely contributed at least something to the fact and the size of the Reagan victory—Kennedy and Anderson, superior Republican organization at the local level, and Reagan's greater success in executing his strategy—were actually connected intimately with the bigger picture, the "fundamentals" that political scientists emphasize.

The biggest part of the big picture was that the nation was in terrible shape. The election result on November 4, 1980, was exactly what one would have predicted on July 15, 1979—Kennedy or no Kennedy, Anderson or no Anderson, hostages or no hostages. Indeed, since the day of the "malaise" speech, inflation and interest rates had worsened, personal income had fallen dramatically, unemployment had increased (to depression levels in some industrial cities), a decade of U.S. retreat had been laid bare in Iran, and the Soviets had invaded Afghanistan. Levels of public confidence in the future were extremely low, and the president's approval ratings were hardly better. No president should expect to win reelection who spends most of the sixteen months before the election—except for a brief crisis-induced rally—with approval ratings in the 20s and 30s. It was these national conditions that drove Carter into attack mode, an awkward position for an incumbent. That the attack mode did not work for Carter, despite his relentless drive, was testament to the difficulty for incumbent presidents of preventing their reelection races from becoming a referendum on themselves, especially under bad conditions.

Furthermore, the structure of the issues did not favor Carter. Reagan, who emphasized his promise of prosperity, struck at the issue considered most important by a substantial majority of Americans. Worse for Carter, he was long past the point of being able to affect the public perception of his economic performance. On the other hand, "peace" was outranked by prosperity as a concern in polls by a 2-to-1 or even a 3-to-1 margin. It was also an issue on which Reagan had compensating advantages. If people worried about his trigger finger, they also respected and approved his strength, considering him much better able than Carter to restore U.S. prestige, rebuild U.S. defenses, and stand up to the Soviets. His defense stand particularly helped Reagan in the South. Thus, Carter's advantage on "peace" largely disappeared when considering foreign policy as a whole. Carter had no such compensating advantage on the economy. And Reagan could—and did—affect how voters understood the peace issue, reducing its potency over time. His October 19 foreign policy speech went some distance in that direction, as did his late-October endorsement by former Democratic senator and 1968 antiwar presidential candidate Eugene McCarthy. The two debates were critical for helping to reassure voters. In any event, by nearly a 2-to-1 margin, Americans said they wanted the United States to be more forceful in its dealings with the Soviets "even if it increased the risk of war."

In a similar vein, the structure of the electorate gave an advantage to Reagan. Recall that the three most pivotal groups—blue-collar ethnics, Catholics, and evangelicals—were all culturally conservative. Even if the specific issues of the campaign did not often revolve around the social issues, they were a powerful undercurrent, in the same way that Prohibition in 1932 and campus unrest in 1968 had been. All three groups were also unashamedly patriotic, and the weakness of the Carter foreign policy was another undercurrent. Seeking the votes of the key groups of the election, Carter was swimming upstream. When Reagan attacked the Democratic coalition, he was appealing to the old Democrats—the Democrats who still adhered to the old values. These were the "Reagan Democrats."

On top of this, Reagan had three other built-in advantages. First, looking at the campaign state by state, it was clear from the outset that Reagan had more room for maneuver, more margin for error. The electoral map favored him. By mid-September, despite the zigzags of the polls, most analysts agreed that Reagan had seized a sizable lead in electoral votes, and he never relinquished it for the remainder of the race. The geographic base of the Republicans had always been an advantage for Reagan. To win, Carter had to "run the table."

Second, it was also clear from numerous indicators that Reagan's support was more enthusiastic than Carter's. Union and black leaders warned throughout the fall that their troops were not excited about the Democratic ticket. When the votes were counted, only about three in five of Carter's 1976 voters who voted again in 1980 voted for him; about 30 percent defected to Reagan and 10 percent to Anderson. On the other hand, only about 10 percent of Ford's 1976 voters switched to Carter in 1980, and only about 5 percent switched to Anderson. Carter's 1976 supporters were four times as likely as Ford voters to report that they did not vote at all in 1980.[39]

Third, Reagan stood to benefit from both the nation's move to the right and its embrace of the outsider. Unlike Carter, he had a ready-made reserve of enthusiasm and organization in the form of the conservative movement. His views on issues like government regulation, federalism, and defense spending were markedly more popular than they had been before the onset of the decade of disaster. His disdain for the Washington bureaucracy and his vow to clean up the mess in the federal government echoed Carter's own campaign of 1976. Indeed, though there were many disputes between Reagan and Carter on specific issues—

Carter kept talking about the "stark differences" between them—Carter had already been pulled along a considerable distance in Reagan's direction. He was, it turned out, a transitional figure caught between the Great Society and Reaganism. The weakness of this position is clear: If Carter was moving in a more conservative direction, establishing lower expectations for government, cutting food stamps, advancing deregulation of certain industries, and rallying the nation against the Soviets, why not vote for a real conservative? And if the voters need an outsider, why choose the incumbent president? It was this strategic conundrum that largely explained Carter's apparent "vacillation" and "inconsistency" throughout his tenure in office.

Thus, the big picture showed a race in which the incumbent's base was far from secure. Carter was playing a defensive game throughout the general election, on ground not of his choosing. Nothing symbolized the incipient bankruptcy of American liberalism better than the self-conscious way Carter sought to weave back together the scattered strands of the Democratic coalition—something for the feminists, something for the blacks, something for the Chicanos, something for the teachers' union. He was sent scurrying to New York, Massachusetts, and the South, fighting for votes there long after they needed to be secure for him to win. Indeed, the election ultimately showed that virtually nothing had been secure. Afterward, one Carter aide concluded that "there was an illusion created—it just occurred—at the time of the Democratic Convention, and continuing through the period of Reagan's mistakes early in the fall, that we were building on the base of the Democrats. It was an illusion because the base wasn't there."[40] The big question of 1980—had Carter's 1976 win restored the New Deal coalition, or was it really just a last gasp?—was answered resoundingly.

In sum, Carter was plagued by certain objective conditions. No campaign, no matter how well run, could change the inflation rate, undo the embassy seizure, or wish out of existence the decay of the Democratic coalition. No campaign could write the conservative movement out of being, abolish the Electoral College, or change the basic contours of public opinion. Campaigns, for the most part, must work with what they have. In 1980, Jimmy Carter did not have much to work with.

Looked at in this way, Reagan's victory seems almost inevitable. Bill Casey later said, "It would have been hard to lose that election."[41] Carter's campaign chairman Robert Strauss concurred, lamenting, "I think I could have stayed in bed the last ninety days and he [Carter] would have got exactly the same number of votes he had."[42] In a volume published in 2000, eminent political scientists wrote seven articles putting forward alternative formulas for predicting presidential election results based on economic performance and some other external circumstances. All seven, applying their formulas to the relevant 1980 data, came up with a Carter defeat.[43] Yet just as it would be a mistake to focus solely on the minutiae of the campaigns, it would be a mistake to completely disregard the importance of contingency. After all, political scientists with their forecasting models uniformly predicted that Al Gore would win the 2000 election, many saying he would do so by a wide margin. Gore's temperament, the debates, and the complications posed by the sitting incumbent undid Gore, despite the models.

So neither approach—focusing on contingencies or focusing on deeper fundamentals—is fully satisfactory. Theodore White argued that "in no other campaign had events so intruded."[44] On the other hand, one has to go back to 1932 to find a race that was more structurally tilted toward one side. Carter faced heavy odds, heavier than he or his campaign ever seemed to grasp. Yet one cannot rule out the possibility that he might have won, had every (or nearly every) contingency gone his way instead of against him.

In the end, both approaches miss an important fact. Elections come down to a choice between candidates. Whatever the structure, whatever the circumstances, candidates matter. This is perhaps the biggest contingency of all. One cannot rule out the possibility that Carter might have won if he had faced a different opponent. Jody Powell thought that Howard Baker would have been a stronger candidate than Reagan, an assessment that was seconded by James L. Sundquist and Richard M. Scammon, who argued in 1981 that "in retrospect, it seems clear that if the GOP had settled on a more typical politician as their candidate—George Bush or Howard Baker—there would never have been a contest."[45]

There is no way of knowing with certainty whether this view was right, but it seems highly unlikely. Indeed, it is probable that Carter and his team had things exactly wrong. Baker had elicited no enthusiasm in the Republican primaries, seemed to have little to say, was not impressive in debates, and may have been deserted by the conservatives had he somehow attained the nomination. Almost certainly, neither he nor Bush would have driven Anderson into an independent general election campaign, thus freeing Carter from the two-front war that vexed him so much. Neither Baker nor Bush would have been able to capitalize on the national sentiment favoring an outsider. No one in the Republican primary lineup could match Reagan's appeal to blue-collar voters, evangelicals, or southerners; Reagan had demolished Bush on exactly those lines in primary after primary. Only Reagan had spent years developing and advancing a public argument that served as the basis for his campaign; only he had behind him the concerted efforts of a swelling popular movement.

Above all, Reagan was a superb campaigner, in terms both of technique and of substance: He clearly won all three of the key primary debates in which he participated. No Republican was better than Reagan at offering a compelling vision of a free, dynamic, prosperous, and strong United States. In the "era of limits," Reagan spoke the language of hope; in an age of the cynic, he spoke the language of idealism; in a time of tyrants, he spoke the language of defiance and of liberty. And no candidate in the Republican field was as good at slipping away from the punch as Reagan was, though most of them were on record as supporting more or less the same positions and doubtless would also have come under severe attack from Carter. It was, after all, Carter's weakness, not anything Reagan did, that was the fundamental reason for the president's onslaught.

A little-noted but critical battleground in the race was a struggle between Reagan and Carter over the question of whether the presidency was a capable institution. Reagan said yes. Carter, following the tack of Herbert Hoover in 1932, pleaded that there was not much that he or any president could do to solve the nation's difficult problems. Throughout the campaign, Carter did best among voters who agreed. To defeat Carter, one had to first persuade Americans that the presidency could matter again. With his confident words and presence, Reagan succeeded. It is far from clear that a Howard Baker would have. Overall, Carter, though tenacious, was clearly outmatched by Reagan, who touched a chord among Americans that inspired and persuaded at the same time. Carter and Powell should have been wishing for a different opponent.

Top Reagan operatives have no doubt that it was their candidate who made the difference. In Lyn Nofziger's view, "Carter was a weak president, but he had tremendous resources at his disposal. . . . It always takes a good candidate to beat an incumbent. I don't think just anybody could have beaten Carter."[46] To Richard Wirthlin, "Reagan was clearly the strongest candidate against Carter. . . . Ronald Reagan had the most articulate and believable positive vision of any of the candidates," a key asset against Carter, whose pessimism ran contrary to Americans' ingrained values.[47]

For his part, Carter, although severely damaged by a wide range of circumstances, was also not Reagan's equal as a candidate. He was often humorless, preachy, or shrill. The novelty of his 1976 candidacy had long worn off. He seemed to offer no vision and no way out of the morass into which the country had fallen. The president faced the same problem George H. W. Bush would face in 1992, except to an even greater degree: He was politically and intellectually exhausted. His campaign offered little rationale for his reelection except that he was not his opponent. Consequently, in order for him to win, millions of Americans in the privacy of the voting booth had to be willing to inflict on themselves what must have seemed like the certainty of another four years of futility. In the final event, 59 percent of voters chose not to do so.

Out of that plain fact came a pair of opposing interpretations of the presidential election of 1980: Either it was a mandate for conservatism or it was a simple repudiation of Carter. The first interpretation was most frequently offered by journalists, Republicans, and conservative activists, though some shell-shocked Democrats voiced it as well. The second interpretation represented the view of many Democrats as well as the near consensus of academic specialists.

As the academics pointed out in article after article, the "conservative mandate" explanation had many shortcomings. The proportion of Americans who called themselves conservative had not grown during the campaign, and only 12 percent of Reagan's voters said explicitly that they had voted for him because of his conservative stands. In polls, Americans favored maintaining or increasing government spending for most social welfare programs. The most thorough examination of public opinion trends in this era concluded that, on balance, there had not been a consistent and drastic shift to the right on specific issues. And, as more than one left-leaning observer asked, how could 1980 represent an ideological mandate when both candidates were relatively conservative? One poll, taken in January 1981 for *Time* magazine, showed that 63 percent of Americans—including 54 percent of Republicans and 57 percent of self-described conservatives—viewed the election as "mostly a rejection of President Carter and his Administration" rather than as "a mandate for more conservative policies."[48]

Wirthlin, Reagan's pollster, agreed.[49] Nor had Reagan explicitly sought an ideological mandate. His campaign was deliberately framed to elicit a negative retrospective judgment on Carter. Voting choice was highly correlated with approval of Carter's economic and foreign policies and with voters' assessments of their own personal financial prospects. Clearly, 1980 must be seen, first and foremost, as a repudiation of Carter, in the same way that 1932 was, first and foremost, a repudiation of Hoover.

However, to say that 1980 was a repudiation of Carter is not the same as saying that it was only a repudiation of Carter. For one thing, 1980 was clearly a Republican victory as much as a Reagan victory. By mid-1980 Republicans were leading Democrats in polls as the party best able to cut inflation, maintain U.S. military strength, control government spending, hold down taxes, increase energy supplies, and even reduce unemployment. Republicans were perceived, for the first time since the 1920s, as the party of prosperity. With a bit of hyperbole, Gerald Pomper pointed out of Reagan that "for the first time in fifty years, a President has been elected who admits that he is a Republican."[50] It was entirely plausible to see 1980 as part of a growing Republican trend starting in 1968 and only temporarily interrupted by Watergate.

When it came to issues and ideology, polls actually did indicate a slight shift toward conservatism during the course of the campaign. More important, the proportion of conservatives in the electorate had outnumbered liberals by a 3-to-2 margin for a decade and a half. Perhaps election results were starting to catch up with this no-longer-new reality. Furthermore, as already mentioned, there had been numerous indications for some time that the "philosophical conservatism" of the electorate—that is, its general approval of principles like limited government and decentralization—had been growing substantially in the half decade before 1980. There had also been rightward movement in the years before 1980 on a number of specific issues, including crime and the death penalty, defense spending and relations with the Soviet Union, the degree to which government was to blame for inflation, and the degree to which the economy and energy production should take precedence over the environment.

On other issues like support for school prayer and a balanced budget amendment and opposition to forced busing and racial quotas, the conservative position had long enjoyed a substantial majority. More broadly, William G. Mayer, author of the aforementioned study, concluded that "the major problem with contemporary American liberalism is not that public opinion has grown more conservative, but that liberalism itself has moved too far to the left," especially on social issues.[51] Wirthlin, who disclaimed a specific ideological mandate for Reagan in 1980, nevertheless argued that Reagan's "moral traditionalism" had been a key to winning over the pivotal groups.

Nor can one discount the fact that politicians in the executive and legislative branches, whose jobs depended on sensitivity to shifts in public opinion, had decided they needed to shift rightward. Although only inferential, this is no small evidence that the political climate in the United States had changed in Reagan's direction. Just as astronomers had deduced the existence of Pluto long before it was seen by observing its gravitational effects on nearby objects, observers could have predicted the Reagan surge long before it manifested itself on election day 1980 by the way it changed the behavior of other elected officials in the late 1970s. Wirthlin reinforced this point, noting that the issues and solutions offered by both major candidates were relatively conservative. In this broad sense, the election ratified a move to the right more than it mandated one.

Polls also showed that in the course of the campaign, voters increasingly came to see Carter as a liberal. A Center for Political Studies survey showed that on a seven-point ideological scale, public perceptions of Carter went from seeing him as slightly right-of-center at the beginning of 1980 to seeing him as slightly left-of-center in September and October. Two spring 1980 polls (one by CBS and the *New York Times* and one by Gallup) showed Carter rated moderate by a plurality and rated conservative more than liberal. By election day the image had flipped. A plurality still labeled him moderate, but Carter was now considered more liberal than conservative.

In all cases, voters clearly identified Reagan as conservative. Big majorities also agreed that Reagan had "clear positions." And Pat Caddell's surveys showed that, by a 2-to-1 margin, voters did not think Reagan was too conservative to be president. As analyst William Schneider pointed out, although the biggest reason Reagan supporters gave for their vote was that it was "time for a change," voters had a good general idea what they were changing from and what they were changing to. At the very least, the election was an indication of a public willingness to give Reagan's conservatism a chance to work.[52]

A highly respected team of voting behavior analysts reached the following conclusions, on the basis of the extensive 1980 National Election

Survey conducted by the University of Michigan's Survey Research Center: On seven of nine key issues, voters wanted a government policy that was more conservative than the status quo. The median voter was slightly closer to Reagan's perceived position on those issues than to Carter's. At least two-thirds of voters cast their ballots for the candidate closest to them on issues, though Carter's median voter was actually closer to Reagan's positions than to Carter's. Retrospective (or referendum) evaluations "appear[ed] somewhat more important" than prospective evaluations in 1980, the analysts found, but "on balance, prospective comparisons had a much more independent impact on voting choices in 1980 than in 1976."[53] This analysis is hardly a ringing endorsement of the pure version of the referendum interpretation. Carter lost, but Reagan also won.

And to the degree that the election was a repudiation, there was more to the repudiation than a simple rejection of Carter. Everett Carll Ladd and Daniel Yankelovich, two respected public opinion pollsters, concluded that the electorate did not intend a full-scale embrace of conservatism but that it did more broadly reject the liberal economic regime of the previous half century. Support for specific liberal programs remained high, but confidence in the federal government as a national economic planner—and the high taxes, big spending, and aggressive regulation that such a role required—collapsed. As Ladd argued, "When Keynesianism ran afoul intellectually, the Democrats got into trouble politically."[54] In the same way, 1932 had represented not just a personal rejection of Hoover but a repudiation of a general economic and political approach.

In an overlapping vein, the Washington that liberals had created over the previous five decades was repudiated. Carter, the outsider of 1980, became, "however reluctantly, a Washington man."[55] But Carter, if anything, had merely left Americans with a greater hunger for change than he had tapped in 1976. The *Washington Post*'s Bill Prochnau argued that Americans "were rebelling against the symbol of the federal city, too, the symbol of a city and a government out of control, of decades of federal programs that became so complex and, to many, so ridiculous that the time finally had arrived to call a halt."[56]

Reagan's anecdotes of government run amok, which were ridiculed by the sophisticated, touched a nerve among average voters because they spoke to a fundamental reality of American life in 1980. For the previous fifty years, tax had been piled upon tax, regulation upon regulation, program upon program. Almost every piece of the edifice had been popular in its own right (if not always wise), but sometime around 1964 the advocates of the new order had stopped adding up what the pieces meant in the aggregate. If the world in 1980 seemed out of control to most Americans, so did their government. The election was an opportunity for Americans to regain control of the "court," as the English Whigs had styled it. The country party was in.

Finally, there was a distinct sense in which Americans were repudiating not just the failures of Carter's stewardship but the failures of his imagination. Reagan was the only candidate among the three who did not accept the widespread assumption that the United States must simply accept its fate as a power and a society in decline. (Kennedy had also attacked Carter on this point, and a race between him and Reagan would have offered two competing visions of dynamic growth.) To Carter and Anderson, the unbearable complexities of modern challenges prescribed limits to growth at home and limits to power abroad. Reagan was unwilling to concede that the nation's problems were too complicated to be solved, and he was equally unwilling to place the blame on "malaise." Remember that you are Americans, he told his countrymen. Remember what you have done. Be confident about what you can do. Take control of your destiny. On election eve, Reagan contended in a nationally televised address that "the question before us tonight [is] does history still have a place for America, for her people, for her great ideals?" Answering his own question, he quoted John Wayne as telling him, "Just give the American people a good cause, and there's nothing they can't lick." It was here that Reagan's appropriation of Roosevelt rang most true.

Altogether, 1980 could be considered a repudiation of Carter, of the excesses and failures of liberalism, of government run amok, and of the very un-American failure to insist upon a future better than the past. It was, at the same time, an endorsement of Reagan's leadership potential and of movement in a generally conservative policy direction. For further evidence that 1980 was something bigger than a mere personal defeat for Carter or personal victory for Reagan, one has only to look to the other election taking place at the same time. Just after casting their votes for president, Americans looked down the ballot and checked names that would decide who controlled the Congress of the United States.

5

CONGRESSIONAL AND STATE ELECTIONS A REPUBLICAN TIDE

By their nature, presidential elections, featuring a handful of highly visible protagonists, lend themselves to dramatic narrative. Congressional elections, which can be just as important, do not. In 1980 there were 435 U.S. House elections, and 34 U.S. Senate seats were up for election. The story at the state level was even more convoluted, with 13 governorships and around 5,000 legislative seats in dispute. Although each contest was unique and each individual winner had a story to tell, it was the sum total of the elections that determined control of Congress and statehouses. Below the level of the U.S. Senate, rarely did individual races appear on the national radar screen, either before or after the votes were counted. Thus, any account of those elections must focus on broad trends and aggregate results. If 1980 was a defining year in U.S. electoral history, the nonpresidential contests went far to making it so.

At the moment in summer 1979 that Carter was preparing to deliver his "crisis of confidence" speech, congressional Democrats could look at the world with both satisfaction and trepidation. The satisfaction was due to their seemingly permanent majority status in both chambers. Democrats had controlled both the House and the Senate continuously since the elections of 1954 and had been in the minority in both for only four years since the Democratic landslide of 1932. At no time since 1958 had those partisan majorities been seriously threatened. After the 1978 elections, Democrats had outnumbered Republicans in the Senate by 58 to 41 (there was 1 Democratic-leaning independent) and in the House by 276 to 157.

The cushion afforded by those majorities allowed both House and Senate Democrats to retain substantial independence from both their party and the White House, despite efforts in the mid-1970s to strengthen the Speaker and the party caucus in the House. The Subcommittee Bill of Rights adopted by House Democrats in 1973 decentralized the structure of the House and gave greater opportunities for semiautonomous "policy entrepreneurs" to advance their own agendas. At the same time, the power of incumbency had grown. In 1976, during the previous presidential election, House incumbents had been reelected at a rate of 96 percent, Senate incumbents at a rate of 64 percent. In July 1979 *Congressional Quarterly* reported that Senate incumbents had "collected record amounts of campaign money at an early stage in the 1980 election season."[1] Incumbency thus supplied what strong parties used to provide: resources and a solid base of support. It was no coincidence that these individualistic tendencies coexisted with a weak (and financially broke) Democratic national party structure, which was focused on Carter's reelection and still paying off 1968 campaign debts. All in all, Democrats were in a defensive posture.

Congressional Democrats did as much as they could to insulate themselves from national political trends, but they could not help noticing the potential drag on their reelection efforts emanating from a failing White House. This threat was the source of their trepidation. The response of Democrats on Capitol Hill to the developing Carter-Kennedy race was based less on ideology than on their calculation of how the presidential ticket might affect their reelection campaigns. Fearing the undertow from Carter, a parade of northern Democratic senators lined up in the summer of 1979 to encourage Edward Kennedy to run. Of the thirty-four Senate seats up for election in 1980, twenty-four were held by Democrats. Many House Democrats made similar calculations. As one representative said, "A lot of us could lose, and Carter isn't worth it."[2] Many congressional Democrats were also upset with Carter's outsider approach and lack of competence in his dealings with Congress. Furthermore, the decentralizing reforms of Congress, which might have made sense as a response to the adversarial climate of the Nixon-Ford years, made governing all the more difficult in a situation of unified Democratic control of the legislative and executive branches. Finally, many Democrats in Congress were spooked by the elections of

1978, when they believed they had mitigated their losses only by shifting sharply to the right. It would be a serious understatement to say that there were tensions between the Democrats at opposite ends of Pennsylvania Avenue. One could no more count on a unified Democratic Party campaign effort than on a unified Democratic strategy for governing.

Congressional Republicans, on the other hand, were the mirror image of Democrats: frustrated but optimistic. Their frustration grew out of the impotence and indignities of their extended time in the minority. From this frustration grew, in the House, a new aggressive strategy. Using parliamentary procedure to full advantage, a hungry group of junior Republican congressmen took every opportunity to embarrass the majority party and draw sharp contrasts with it on issue positions. Led by Representative Robert Bauman of Maryland, the group specialized in forcing Democrats to take recorded votes on politically charged amendments and giving tough speeches using C-SPAN, the new cable network that was broadcasting House proceedings on television. Although not a member of the Republican leadership team, Bauman came to have "more of an impact on the day-to-day conduct of the House of Representatives than all but a handful of Congress' most senior members."[3] Bauman's strategy was the forerunner of Newt Gingrich's guerrilla warfare of the 1980s and early 1990s. Between the dysfunctional decentralization of the Democratic majority and the renewed aggressiveness of the Republican minority, observers noted that throughout 1979 "the House continually teetered on the brink of chaos, and occasionally fell over."[4]

Bauman's efforts raised Republicans' spirits (and gave Republican challengers useful campaign ammunition), but Republicans also had other, more substantial reasons for optimism. The same presidential travails that worried Democrats gave hope to the GOP. Furthermore, they could expect more help from their party than could their opponents. Whereas Democrats would be running as individuals, Republicans would be running as members of a team. In contrast with the dilapidated Democratic National Committee, the Republican National Committee under chairman Bill Brock had constructed a viable plan for a national party campaign.

Such a campaign was possible because Republicans had adapted much more successfully than Democrats to the 1974 campaign finance laws, which required parties to cultivate small donors. In 1979–1980, the Republican National Committee raised ten times as much through direct mail and phone solicitation as did the Democratic National Committee (about $40 million to $4 million). The Republicans funneled this money into training for activists, candidates, and campaign managers, the development of a major grassroots organization, recruitment of strong candidates for both Congress and local offices, research resources, a surrogate speaker program, polling and data analysis, direct financial assistance to congressional candidates, help with political action committee (PAC) fund-raising, and broadcast studios for radio and TV ad production, which were made available to the party's candidates at one-sixth the commercial cost.

Republicans also planned a national advertising campaign to put a new face on the party. Republican pollsters had discovered to their amazement that many Americans who blamed Congress for the nation's woes did not know Congress was controlled by the Democrats. The ad campaign would seek to educate them. A key figure in implementing the plan in House elections was the aggressive Representative Guy Vander Jagt (R-Mich.), who chaired the National Republican Congressional Committee (NRCC). Vander Jagt had at his disposal a staff of forty and, ultimately, $26.1 million to spend. His counterpart, James C. Corman of California, chairman of the Democratic Congressional Campaign Committee (DCCC), had a bare-bones staff and a budget of $2 million. The disparity of party resources was nearly as great on the Senate side, where the National Republican Senatorial Committee would spend $21.2 million to the Democratic Senatorial Campaign Committee's $1.6 million.

Outside the Republican Party's own campaign, Republicans hoped to benefit from major efforts by groups like NCPAC and Paul Weyrich's Committee for the Survival of a Free Congress. In 1978 Free Congress had given substantial support to twenty-six nonincumbents, of whom sixteen won. In 1980 NCPAC and Free Congress vowed to up the ante. In June 1979 NCPAC began running television advertisements against targeted liberal Democratic senators. Altogether, the campaign finance reforms of 1974 had spawned a quadrupling of PACs, whose spending grew by 67 percent from 1978 to 1980. In 1980 ideological PACs would account for about one-third of all PAC spending, and three-fourths of that was by conservative groups. Altogether, PACs in the 1980 election cycle gave a smaller percentage of their money to Democrats (52 percent) than at any previous time; in races involving incumbents, they gave the largest percentage ever to challengers (47 percent).

The broad contours of the race for Congress followed those of the contest for the White House. As Carter's national poll numbers rose in late 1979, the Kennedy fervor among congressional Democrats quieted. The senators who had lined up at Kennedy's door to urge him to run made themselves scarce. As Carter collapsed in the polls in the summer of 1980, a large number of congressional Democrats joined the open convention bandwagon. Many did not come to the Democratic national convention at all, hoping to avoid the taint of an unpopular president.

Throughout 1980 media attention was focused on the battle in the Senate, where Democrats appeared to be especially vulnerable and where journalists could follow the more manageable number of races. In early 1980 whispers were heard of a potential Republican takeover of the Senate. Over the summer Senate majority leader Robert Byrd privately warned the White House that trends pointed to potentially high losses. By September—perhaps not coincidentally, when Carter had pulled even with Reagan—Democrats sighed with relief that they seemed to have turned the corner and were no longer facing disaster. According to local polls, many of the party's vulnerable senators had come from behind to pull even or gain a small lead. A month before election day, *Washington Post* correspondent David Broder held that "there is no evidence of a dramatic upsurge in Republican strength or a massive turnover in Congress."[5]

Key races included the reelection bids of Birch Bayh (D-Ind.), Frank Church (D-Idaho), Alan Cranston (D-Calif.), John Culver (D-Iowa), John Durkin (D-N.H.), Thomas Eagleton (D-Mo.), Gary Hart (D-Colo.), Warren Magnuson (D-Wash.), George McGovern (D-S.D.), Robert Morgan (D-N.C.), Gaylord Nelson (D-Wisc.), and Herman Talmadge (D-Ga.). There were also several competitive open seats caused by Republican retirements in Pennsylvania, Oklahoma, and North Dakota; Democratic retirements in Connecticut and Illinois; and the defeat of Democratic incumbents in primary elections in Alaska, Alabama, and Florida. In New York, incumbent liberal Republican senator Jacob Javits was defeated in the Republican primary by conservative Alfonse D'Amato but was given a place on the Liberal Party ticket, creating a three-way race in November. Republican Barry Goldwater, the dean of conservatism, was facing a tough reelection in Arizona. A number of the endangered Senate Democrats were high-profile liberals. Only Culver campaigned as a proud liberal. The rest, even McGovern, hedged in their campaigns. A full year before, Church had used the controversy over the Soviet combat brigade in Cuba as the vehicle for moving to the right.

On the House side, few observers expected dramatic change and no one expected Republicans to gain the fifty-nine seats they needed to win control. There were only twenty-seven open Democratic seats (and sixteen Republican open seats); thirty-seven House Democrats had no Republican opponent at all. However, a number of observers agreed that Republicans had recruited a stronger field of House candidates in 1980 than in recent years. This success was partially due to the deliberate efforts of the party and partially due to the more hospitable political environment in 1979 and 1980. Republicans contemplating a House run found the national circumstances encouraging.

Guy Vander Jagt and the NRCC made a decision in 1980 to target Democrats in positions of party or committee leadership, in the hopes that some would be defeated and "the survivors will be frightened enough so that they will become more conservative once they return."[6] Vander Jagt also hoped that the targeted leaders would soak up financial resources that might otherwise be directed toward lower-profile races and that they would be prevented from campaigning hard for their colleagues around the country. Altogether, the Republicans kept an evolving list of up to eighty districts that warranted special national attention. For their part, House Democrats put defense of incumbents as first priority and holding on to Democratic open seats as second. Far lower in importance were races against the nineteen incumbent Republicans deemed vulnerable. However, the national Democratic Party had little to give to any of these efforts.

Throughout the race, the Republican campaign took a toll on the Democrats. The $9.5 million Republican television ad campaign featured a truck driver, an unemployed factory worker, and a Tip O'Neill look-alike. Early on, Bill Brock had decided to focus on the economy, and the ads addressed economic issues, "getting government off people's backs," and rebuilding defense. The slogan "Vote Republican—for a Change" held it all together, inviting a retrospective appraisal of Democratic governance. In Brock's view, where it was used, the ad campaign "just about eliminated the net negative to being Republican" and was essential to "establish the parameters of the debate."[7] Vander Jagt agreed that "for the first time since the 1930s, the Republican label is not baggage."[8] (Of course, Republicans had also won in 1946 and 1952, but they had had to overcome strong negative party images left over from the Great Depression.) Republicans also credited the ad campaign with making it more difficult for individual Democratic incumbents to distance themselves from Congress as a whole. As NRCC executive director Steve Stockmeyer argued, "The Democrats' secret weapon for years was that no one made the connection between their local Democrat and the Democratic majority in Congress."[9] In early 1980 a CBS–*New York Times* poll showed confidence in Congress as a whole had fallen to 18 percent.

Underscoring the degree to which the Republican presidential and congressional candidates were running a unified campaign, Reagan and Republican congressional leaders formulated a joint strategy pushing an immediate 10 percent tax cut in mid-June of the election year, a push that divided and embarrassed Washington Democrats. Reagan then appeared on the steps of the Capitol on September 15 with several hundred Republican members of Congress and congressional candidates. Reagan proclaimed that "we are proposing a solemn covenant with the American people. . . . Each of us here pledges that if elected we will begin working the day after election as a solid, unified team, and we pledge that within a year from today we will achieve five major goals for America."[10] The pledges, called the "Capitol Compact," were to reduce waste, fraud, and abuse in federal spending, to cut expenditures on Congress itself, to cut federal income taxes across the board, to encourage private investment and inner-city jobs, and to strengthen U.S. defenses. Republicans aimed to demonstrate party unity, promote their common program, and show that they—unlike Carter and the Democratic Congress—could cooperate to get things done. (Fourteen years later, reporters, who apparently did not remember the Capitol Compact, would treat the Contract with America as an unprecedented tactic.)

Outside political groups, mostly conservative, also campaigned hard until election day. NCPAC initially targeted McGovern, Bayh, Cranston, Church, and Culver, then added Eagleton. It spent a total of $1 million on advertising, running ads that focused on defense and on social issues, such as abortion. Likewise, the Moral Majority particularly targeted McGovern, Bayh, Cranston, Church, Culver, and Nelson. However, these efforts became quite controversial in several states. Democratic incumbents often turned NCPAC itself into an issue, imploring voters not be driven by outsiders intervening in a local election. In Iowa Culver called on Iowans to turn against "the hate factories of the East."[11] In South Dakota the ad campaign became so counterproductive that NCPAC temporarily shifted resources away from the race against McGovern and opened a new front against Eagleton in Missouri.

And, of course, whatever national issues might overlay them, every race was a local race as well. In Georgia and Washington, Democratic incumbents suffered from perceptions that they were too old or too stale in their careers. Talmadge was sixty-seven, seeking a fifth term. Magnuson

*Reagan and Republican congressional
candidates announce the Capitol Compact
on September 15, 1980.*

turned seventy-five on election day. He had been serving in Congress since 1937 and had not aged well. He was seeking his seventh Senate term. His opponent, Slade Gorton, staged a fifty-mile relay run to file his ballot petitions with the Washington Secretary of State's office. In Colorado Republican chances were hurt by internecine quarreling. In New York the liberal vote was split between Javits and Democrat Elizabeth Holtzman. Republican congressman Robert Bauman's reelection was considered a sure thing until he was charged on October 3 with soliciting sex from a sixteen-year-old boy. Other scandals played a role in several races, especially the "Abscam" sting in which seven House members (six of them Democrats) accepted bribes from undercover FBI agents posing as Arab sheikhs.

A late Republican surge was detected by some analysts, but on the eve of the election *Congressional Quarterly* estimated that Republicans would pick up only ten to fifteen House seats and two or three Senate seats. Though *Congressional Quarterly* conceded that many races were still toss-ups, not even the most daring prognosticators predicted that the GOP would pick up more than seven seats in the Senate and thirty in the House. When all was said and done, the Republican tidal wave had come farther inland than anyone had imagined it would. The GOP gained a net of twelve Senate seats, enough to win a majority there (split fifty-three to forty-six) for the first time since 1954. In doing so, Republicans ended the longest period of one-party dominance in the history of the Senate. Not since 1958 had either party gained so many Senate seats in one election. Of the eighteen Senate freshmen, sixteen were Republicans. Republicans also gained thirty-three seats in the House, their biggest gain since 1966. No presidential coattails had been as long since at least 1964, when Democrats had gained thirty-seven seats in the House (though only one in the Senate). Through 2004, no coattails have been that long again.

As the networks reported results, the endangered Senate liberals were mowed down from east to west: Bayh was defeated by future vice president Dan Quayle; he was followed by Nelson, Culver, McGovern, Church, and Magnuson. Four of the six liberals had been targeted by NCPAC, five by the Moral Majority. Talmadge went down in Georgia, ending a twenty-four-year Senate career, victim of a denunciation by the Senate for personal misconduct. Other Democratic incumbents lost: Durkin of New Hampshire and Morgan of North Carolina were both defeated. Altogether, Republicans unseated nine Democratic incumbents with a total of 155 years of Senate service, including four powerful committee chairs. Republicans also picked up all three of the open seats created by the defeat of Democratic incumbents in the primaries. The GOP held on to all its own open seats as well as New York, where D'Amato defeated Javits and Holtzman. No other Republican incumbent lost, though Goldwater nearly did.

Republican gains were won in many cases by the barest of margins. A shift of but 50,000 votes in Senate elections nationwide, if properly distributed, would have saved seven seats for the Democrats, and with them control of the Senate. (On the other hand, a 23,000-vote shift would have given Colorado and Vermont to the Republicans, and Democrats retained Missouri with only 52 percent of the vote.) Nationally, because of huge Democratic margins in the California, Ohio, and Illinois Senate races, Republicans won only 47.5 percent of all votes cast for the Senate. These indications of a close call were small comfort for Democrats. When it mattered, where it mattered, Republicans got the votes they needed. An aide to Senator Warren Magnuson said, "There was nothing personal" about his boss's defeat: "It was like dying in a plane crash. Everybody was killed."[12]

In the House, Speaker Tip O'Neill called the results "a disaster for the Democrats."[13] Republican gains were broadly won, as the GOP picked up eleven seats in the East, nine in the South, seven in the West, and six in the Midwest. They gained a majority of House seats in the Midwest and drew nearly even in the West. Broken into smaller areas, Republican gains were biggest in the Middle Atlantic (plus seven), outer South (plus seven), and Pacific Coast (plus five) regions. They also gained in the border states (plus four) and the Great Lakes region (plus three), with a smattering in other areas. After having survived the elections of 1976 and 1978 relatively unscathed, the Democrats' liberal class of 1974 lost nine members. Although many of the Democratic losers were unknown outside their own districts, many were not.

Republicans beat twenty-seven Democratic incumbents. Of that number, two-thirds had been part of the majority leadership. House majority whip John Brademas (D-Ind.) fell to twenty-seven-year-old businessman John Hiler in the same statewide tide that beat Birch Bayh. In Oregon, House Ways and Means Committee chairman Al Ullman, seeking a thirteenth term, was shown the door by his constituents. Another three committee and fourteen subcommittee chairs were undone. These included the chairmen of the Public Works and Transportation

Committee, the Appropriations Subcommittee on Military Construction, and the Ways and Means Subcommittee on Public Assistance and Unemployment Compensation—panels that were supposed to confer great electoral advantage. A total of eight Democrats who had served in the House eighteen years or longer were toppled. In contrast, only three Republican incumbents lost, including Bauman; only one was senior. A handful of Democratic leaders in tough fights survived. These included House majority leader Jim Wright of Texas (later to be Speaker) and Interior Committee chairman (and 1976 presidential candidate) Morris K. Udall of Arizona.

Scandal struck hard, as five of the losing Democratic incumbents had been touched by Abscam or had been hurt by other allegations of financial wrongdoing. One of the losers was Representative John Jenrette of South Carolina, who had been caught on videotape saying, "I've got larceny in my blood." As reporters summarized it, Jenrette's lawyer argued that the congressman was "a drunk with financial problems whom the government lured into committing a crime."[14] This line may have been the best legal argument the attorney could muster, but it was hardly calculated to inspire confidence among Jenrette's constituents.

The GOP also won about two of every five open Democratic seats. Examinations of demographic data showed that the House Democrats' electoral coalition was much the same as Carter's coalition, but stronger by about 10 percentage points. However, the gender gap at the presidential level was reversed in House elections, with men more likely than women to vote Democratic. (For those concerned with demographic representation: The number of black congressmen increased from fifteen to seventeen, the number of women from fifteen to nineteen. In the Senate races, four of five women lost; even so, the addition of Florida's Republican Paula Hawkins doubled the number of women serving in that chamber.) Overall, Democrats gained a bare majority (50.4 percent) of the national House vote, but if uncontested races were excluded, Republicans actually had the edge.[15] Not since 1950–1952 had Republicans had two good congressional elections in a row.

At the state level, Republicans also gained for the second consecutive election. As in the congressional races, the national Republican Party took a close interest in the outcome. In 1980 the Republican National Committee spent about $3 million on state legislative races, the Democratic National Committee zero. Worse for Democrats, their state and local parties were outspent by Republican state and local parties by a margin of $26 million to $9 million. Because state legislative contests take place even further under the national radar than U.S. House campaigns, virtually none was familiar to Americans as a whole. Even within the same state, only the politically active knew much about campaigns occurring in other districts. Some 5,000 legislative races were on the ballots in 43 states.

Yet out of these highly fragmented pieces came a mosaic that illuminated the story of 1980. Nationwide, Republicans gained over 200 legislative seats. By contrast, they had gained only 51 in Nixon's 1972 landslide. More to the point, with redistricting battles on the near horizon, they took unified control of four new legislatures. In the wake of the 1980 vote, Republicans held 49.5 percent of state legislative seats and a majority of legislative chambers outside the South.

At the same time, the GOP made a net gain of four governorships, adding to its column Missouri, North Dakota, Washington, and Arkansas, where a young Bill Clinton fell after one term. In Washington, Democratic governor Dixie Lee Ray, one of only two female governors in the United States, lost her primary, and Republican John Spellman beat her replacement. None of the three Republican governorships at stake in 1980 were lost. Democrat Jay Rockefeller won the West Virginia governor's race by spending a record $9.5 million, or $25 per vote that he received. Over the previous quarter century, most states had shifted to four-year gubernatorial terms, with elections held in midterm years. As a result, only thirteen states had gubernatorial elections in 1980. Had it not been for this relatively recent separation of gubernatorial and presidential elections, it is not hard to imagine that 1980 might have brought a much more dramatic Republican gain in governorships.

As it was, the combined effects of 1978 and 1980 nearly doubled the number of Republican governors from their post-Watergate low and added approximately 500 Republican state legislators. The party had achieved "redistricting insurance"—that is, control of at least one point in the redistricting process where they could stop action—in thirty-two states. Those gains were partly a consequence of success at the top of the ticket and of the nationalization of the election in 1980 itself. They were also a continuation of the trends of 1978 and a confirmation of Brock's wisdom in focusing more attention on state elections throughout his chairmanship.

Reasons could be found for each individual Democratic loss, but the nationalization of the election had to be considered a crucial explanation for the overall congressional and state results. In nearly every detail, the congressional elections confirmed the rather complicated picture that emerged from the presidential race. Voters conferred no blanket mandate for a specific conservative program. Even in the Senate, not all liberal Democrats lost; not all Democrats who lost were liberal; not all Republicans who won were conservative, and at least one Republican (Arlen Specter in Pennsylvania) was not as conservative as the Democrat he defeated. At the same time, the congressional wipeout itself argued against viewing the election as nothing but a rejection of Carter. If all voters had wanted to do was punish Carter, why did they throw out Birch Bayh and Al Ullman?

Clearly, an anti-Carter tide did play a part, both by affecting voter choice and by affecting turnout. The congressional elections in 1980 were connected with the presidential campaign to a degree unmatched between 1964 and 2004. The lack of enthusiasm for Carter among Democratic voters hurt Democratic candidates down the ballot by keeping many of those voters at home. The degree to which local Democratic organizers saw Carter as a drag could be observed in white ethnic South Philadelphia, where Democratic ward leaders threw away Carter-Mondale literature so their other candidates would not be hurt by association.[16]

How much help Reagan provided to Republicans down the ballot is not completely clear. In some states, enthusiasm for Reagan carried the day. Idaho's Frank Church blamed his 4,262 vote loss in a state that voted 76 percent for Reagan on that enthusiasm, and some analysts claimed that GOP Senate wins in New York, Arizona, and North Carolina were also due to Reagan's coattails.[17] Looking at the raw number of votes cast, Reagan outpolled the Republican winner in eleven of the sixteen key Senate races (the nine defeated Democratic incumbents, six open seats, and New York). In only five races did the Republican Senate candidate outpoll Reagan, even though Reagan was locked in a three-way race and they were not (except for D'Amato). Looking at vote percentages, however, Reagan outperformed only eight of the sixteen. Some academic analysts contended that "Reagan was a significant asset to Republican congressional candidates";[18] others argued that in the House, the Reagan landslide "probably made the difference in some of the Democratic losses" but that "the congressional candidates and their campaigns were dominant."[19] Reagan ran ahead of about one-third of the winning GOP House candidates.

After the dust had settled, presidential pollster Pat Caddell maintained that Democratic congressional losses were mostly traceable to the national repudiation of Carter, and Tip O'Neill's pollster told him that the Reagan landslide had cost the Democrats thirteen of the thirty-three seats the party lost in the House. However, since repudiation of Carter was only one factor explaining the Reagan win, Reagan's coattails are not purely synonymous with an anti-Carter referendum. Indeed, the same analysts who declared Reagan "a significant asset" also found little independent relationship between voters' approval of Carter and their congressional vote choice.[20]

Developments in the presidential race may have helped Republicans in another way as well. In the summer of 1980, some Republican insiders were concerned that a strong run by independent John Anderson might hurt GOP candidates down the ballot. In this view, Anderson might bring out liberal voters who would have otherwise stayed at home, and these voters were not likely to vote for Republican congressional hopefuls. In Connecticut some local Republican candidates tried to protect themselves against this danger by running on both the Republican and Anderson lines. Some analysts disagreed with this Republican conclusion, thinking Anderson's affluent and educated supporters were likely to vote in any case, but Anderson's collapse in the fall made it a moot point.

However, the state and congressional elections also showed that Republicans had generated a party tide with the help of Reagan and their coordinated national campaign. One academic analyst suggested that "perhaps the most significant quality of the 1980 elections at the national level will be the judgment of party victory."[21] A key group of voters did not merely vote against Carter, they voted against Democrats and for Republicans, proving that retrospective judgments could be leveled at parties as well as at individual officeholders. The 1980 congressional elections were the first since 1952 to be so deliberately and successfully nationalized by a party. Republicans tied individual Democrats to the Democratic Congress, and then tied Congress to Carter (though Carter and Congress had often been at odds). In Senate general election races Republican candidates slightly outspent Democratic candidates. In the House Democratic candidates had a slight advantage. The big difference came in spending by party committees, where Republicans had a huge edge ($50.7 million to $5.1 million). The fund-raising negligence of Democratic National Committee chair John White became "a matter of bitter resentment among the congressional Democrats."[22]

Even if there was not a mandate for a specific programmatic agenda in 1980, it would be obtuse to deny that there was a general conservative trend to the congressional results. Most of the Republican Senate challengers were conservative, and the Senate liberals lost disproportionately. Of the eighteen Senate freshmen of both parties elected in 1980, fourteen were more conservative than those they replaced. In some measure this was because many of the liberals had long eked out an existence in such conservative states as South Dakota, Idaho, and Indiana, where Bayh had not won any of his three terms with more than 51.7 percent of the vote. In 1980 the clock ran out for them. Nevertheless, the reassertion of a native conservatism in these states was itself significant. Two incoming Republican Senators, Don Nickles of Oklahoma and former admiral Jeremiah Denton of Alabama, were particularly identified with the Moral Majority. Denton was Roman Catholic, indicating the degree to which the new socially conservative coalition crossed traditional boundaries. Another, John East, a political science professor who defeated Morgan in North Carolina, was aided tremendously by Jesse Helms's Congressional Club. Above all, the 1980 congressional campaigns were fought out on conservative ground. Congressional scholars Thomas Mann and Norman Ornstein concluded that

> There can be no question that in 1980 the electorate opted for a much more conservative Senate (as it had in 1978). With the exception of John Culver, most liberal Democratic incumbent senators were on the defensive throughout the 1980 campaign, tempering their viewpoints and downplaying their voting records. Conservative challengers were clearly on the offensive, proclaiming proudly their ideological points of view. The nature of the campaign, combined with the highly visible defeats of Church, McGovern, Bayh, Culver, Magnuson, Nelson, and Durkin and the victories of a dozen staunchly conservative freshmen, leads to the inescapable conclusion that 1980 was partly a referendum on liberalism and conservatism—and liberalism lost.[23]

The ideological character of the House elections was less obvious. Some saw little clear pattern (except that the generally more conservative party gained). Generally speaking, House elections tend to be more parochial and less ideologically charged than Senate elections: NCPAC endorsed 103 House candidates, of whom 57 lost. However, most Democratic House losses were suffered by northern liberals and southern moderates—that is, the leftmost edge of the party in both regions. The southern House Democrats who were removed were more liberal than those who were retained; in the Senate, the ideological placement of the average northern Democrat, southern Democrat, and Republican all shifted to the right.[24] Analysts showed that conservative evangelical voters probably played a larger role in Democratic congressional losses than at the presidential level.[25]

Not least, the outsider appeal finally reached congressional elections after having percolated at the presidential level since 1964. Mann and Ornstein noted that seniority was highly correlated with defeat among Democrats. In the Senate, those liberals who were most clearly tied to the Washington power structure fared worst. Junior liberals escaped relatively unscathed. Magnuson of Washington was president pro tem of the Senate and chairman of the Senate Appropriations Committee. The last time either an Appropriations Committee chair or a president pro tem had lost a general election was in 1932. Likewise, Republicans in the House elections made their biggest gains against incumbents, not in open seats, and struck hardest against the insiders who ran Congress. Although the overall incumbent reelection rate remained at 91 percent in the House (falling from 96 percent in 1976), it was only 55 percent in the Senate, the chamber more visibly tied to national government and issues. Even Goldwater, "Mr. Conservative," came within a few thousand votes of losing his quest for a fifth term. Many Arizonans thought he had been in Washington too long. All of this suggests that the appeal of outsiders did not end with the presidential race but deeply affected the congressional contests as well.

In sum, the congressional elections underscored the themes of the presidential election: Reagan's coattails, rejection of Carter, a Republican victory, a repudiation of philosophical liberalism and of Washington insiders, held together by a reaction against the events, at home and abroad, that seemed to indicate the bankruptcy of the ruling order. Although it was possible to distinguish among these factors in theory, to voters they may often have seemed interlocking. The problem faced by senior and visible Democrats was that they were part of the president's party, were mostly liberals, and were vested insiders, all at once.

Two examples showed how difficult it was to untangle these effects in individual contests. In the Senate, George McGovern was the liberal of liberals, running in a conservative state. In 1972 he had taken the Democratic Party by storm, riding to its presidential nomination on the strength of the left-wing new politics movement. In November 1972 he could not even win South Dakota's electoral votes, though he was reelected to the Senate in the 1974 Democratic wave with only 53 percent of the vote.

In 1980 he was hammered by NCPAC, the Moral Majority, and opponent James Abdnor for his liberal positions on defense, abortion, and the Panama Canal Treaty. At the same time, McGovern was seeking a fourth term and was vulnerable to the charge that he had been in Washington long enough. As ammunition, Abdnor was able to use the fact that McGovern was denied a South Dakota resident hunting license because he no longer possessed a South Dakota driver's license. The challenger also attacked the incumbent for not having owned land in South Dakota until shortly before the election and for ignoring his constituents while he traveled the country on an extensive speaking tour. Reagan polled 8,000 more votes than the Republican senatorial candidate, but this was far from enough to account for Abdnor's win. James Abdnor beat George McGovern with 58 percent of the vote.

California's Twenty-first House District was represented by James C. Corman, an insider of insiders, a subcommittee power broker and the head of the national House Democratic campaign effort. Having served since 1960, he was seeking his eleventh term. Corman, too, was a liberal—the strongest supporter of national health insurance in the House—whose opponent, Bobbi Fiedler, had made her name fighting forced busing. The congressman was also one of the rare Carter loyalists in Congress, casting the deciding vote for the president's energy package in conference committee. Fiedler took to calling him "a puppet of Carter." Reagan's coattails touched him directly when Carter's early concession speech kept Democrats away from polling places on the West Coast; a Corman aide estimated that 2,000 Democratic votes were lost in the Twenty-first District alone. When the ballots were counted, Corman was defeated by 752 votes.

Democrats later complained that Carter's concession speech had cost them not only Corman's seat but perhaps Al Ullman's and several other congressional and legislative seats in the western United States. Outside of Corman and a few legislative candidates who lost by very narrow margins, these objections were probably overblown—after all, the presidential race was hardly in doubt any longer, and NBC News had called it for Reagan a full one hour and thirty-seven minutes earlier. Carter was simply acknowledging what most people already knew. As they were to be again in 2000, the network projections were a more plausible villain. The moaning is perhaps better seen as one last testimony of the bitterness felt toward Carter by many of the Democratic party regulars. However much (or little) Carter's concession speech actually changed the course of events, it joined the "malaise" speech as oratorical bookends of Democratic disaster. Carter's words may not have brought down the Democrats, but his presidency surely did.

6

THE RETURN OF CONFIDENCE AND THE TRANSFORMATION OF AMERICAN POLITICS

Like the National Football League playoffs, the 1980 presidential selection process had one ultimate winner and a slew of losers. The losers went on to a variety of endeavors. John Connally dropped out of politics, losing so much money in real estate in the 1980s that he was forced to auction his belongings. Phil Crane continued serving in the House, finally losing his bid for a nineteenth term in 2004 one day before his seventy-fourth birthday. Howard Baker remained in the Senate, served as Senate majority leader until 1985, then became Reagan's chief of staff in the last months of his presidency. Bob Dole remained in the Senate, became Senate majority leader in 1985, failed in his 1988 bid for the GOP nomination, won the nomination in 1996, left the Senate, and lost to Bill Clinton. John Anderson, eligible for federal matching funds in 1984, formed the National Unity Party, dropped out when no groundswell developed, and won 1,486 votes. Jerry Brown finished his second term as governor of California in 1982 after the Mediterranean fruit-fly crisis made hash of his popularity. As unpredictable as ever, he ran once more for the Democratic presidential nomination in 1992, was beaten by Bill Clinton, and retired from public life until becoming mayor of Oakland in 1998. Ted Kennedy considered a presidential run in 1984, declined, and never ran again; 1980 turned out to be his one shot. He remained in the Senate as a champion for liberalism, and is still there in 2005. When Kennedy's presidential ambitions waned in 1984, Walter Mondale's nomination by the Democrats led to the second worst electoral vote defeat in

U.S. history. In 2002 Mondale came out of retirement to run for the U.S. Senate in the week following the death of Minnesota senator Paul Wellstone, and he promptly lost to Norm Coleman. George H. W. Bush served as vice president from 1981 to 1989, won the Republican nomination for president in 1988, and beat Michael Dukakis to become the forty-first president. Four years later, he was beaten for reelection by Bill Clinton. Eight years after that, his eldest son, George W. Bush, redeemed the family name by defeating Clinton's vice president, Al Gore.

Indeed, Clinton played a bit part in the drama of 1980, too, when he lost his bid for reelection as governor of Arkansas after one term. Two years later he reclaimed his post, winning the moniker "The Comeback Kid." In many ways Clinton's presidency reprised Carter's, as he tried to remake the Democratic Party in a more moderate mold that embraced balanced budgets, welfare reform, the death penalty, and limits to government activism. And though Clinton refined it to an art, it was Carter who pioneered the use of empathy as a political tactic, the first to promise a president "who feels your pain" in both his 1976 nomination acceptance speech and his 1979 "crisis of confidence" speech. Clinton, blessed with superior political skills and a less troublesome world, had considerably greater success than Carter.

Carter himself retired to Plains, Georgia, to write his memoirs, then took up an active life of charity and peacemaking. He could be counted, by his friends or his foes, as either the best or the worst of former U.S. presidents. More than any other former president, he devoted his remaining time to acts of goodness, exemplified by his deep involvement in Habitat for Humanity, a group that builds houses for the poor at home and abroad. Yet more than any other, Carter also violated the long-respected custom of former presidents to refrain from criticizing subsequent presidents when they are making difficult decisions: Carter accepted a Nobel Peace Prize in 2002 even though the prize committee had made it clear that they conceived of their decision as a means of undermining the policies of the sitting president. And Carter continued showing the same tendencies in foreign policy that had so vexed his critics during his presidency. The 1994 deal "stopping" North Korea's nuclear program—a deal Pyongyang began flouting the moment it was signed—was largely Carter's handiwork.

And Ronald Reagan was left—king of the hill, president of the United States.

The electoral earthquake of 1980 was felt immediately, though its full significance could not be known or appreciated for some time. For one thing, the 1980 elections offered a glimpse into the future of presidential selection. Although the nominating system had been reformed after the 1968 election, many of its features were not fully apparent until 1980. The strategy of running hard early and everywhere—pioneered by Carter in 1976—became conventional wisdom for the first time in 1980. The phenomenon of early withdrawals from the race likewise exploded that year, fueled by the fund-raising restrictions imposed by the campaign finance reform regulations of 1974, which punished candidates who did not win an early primary. And 1980 was the last year that any drama surrounded the national conventions, the last time a convention began with any doubt at all as to its outcome.

The inflexibility of the new system was demonstrated in both parties, as Gerald Ford found when he concluded that March was too late to enter the race and as perceptive Democrats who hoped to escape the Carter undertow found in their unsuccessful drive for an open convention. All of this meant that 1980 was a key step on the long road to today's highly front-loaded primary calendar.

In the primaries, the first cracks appeared in the system of public financing when Connally gave up matching funds so he would not be bound by the attendant spending limits. It would be another twenty years before the experiment was repeated, more successfully, by George W. Bush in 2000. In 2004 both men who were ultimately nominated by their parties used the Connally strategy, which seems destined to become the rule rather than the exception. In the general election, the practice of projecting the winner on the basis of exit polls was begun in 1980 by NBC News, a practice that has become increasingly controversial. Faulty projections were a central factor in the 2000 election imbroglio.

More substantively, the congressional elections of 1980 were momentous. Republican control of the Senate gave Reagan a stronghold in the legislative branch that served as a launching pad for his initiatives for the next six years. As congressional scholars Roger H. Davidson and Walter J. Oleszek observed, the Senate "provided the motor power for the administration's legislative victories."[1] Control of committee chairmanships shifted along with the majority. In the most dramatic examples, Edward Kennedy was replaced by Strom Thurmond as chairman of the Senate Judiciary Committee and Barry Goldwater took the place of Birch Bayh as chairman of the Select Committee on Intelligence. Of the fifty-three Republican senators after the 1980 election, twenty-seven had gained their seats in either 1978 or 1980, meaning that Reagan had an unusual opportunity to shape his party. It is no exaggeration to say that without control of the Senate, there would have been no "Reagan Revolution."

In the House, Republicans did not have a majority, but the so-called conservative coalition of Republicans and southern Democrats was back. In 1981–1982 Republicans had needed the aid of only twenty-six conservative Democrats to form a majority; they typically had the support of thirty-five to fifty. (There was even short-lived talk that the coalition might form an alliance to depose Tip O'Neill as Speaker.) In 1981, when the conservative coalition appeared in floor votes—on about one vote in five—it prevailed 88 percent of the time in the House and 95 percent of the time in the Senate. Thus, Reagan enjoyed de facto unified conservative government for the first two years of his presidency, a critical moment that saw the passage of his economic plan and defense buildup.

When losses in the midterm elections of 1982 put liberal Democrats firmly back in control of the House, Congress settled into a stalemate with the president. This highlighted another feature of the 1980 elections: Before 1980, only a handful of times in U.S. history had different parties controlled the Senate and the House, and never for more than one two-year congressional session at a time. The parties had most recently split Congress in 1931–1932. For the six years after 1980, divided government featured a split in Congress, and the potential for one has remained high ever since (it occurred again in 2001–2002).

The elections of 1980 also proved that under the right conditions and with the right preparation, a party could turn a congressional election into a national referendum. Republicans used this strategy again in 1982, with the national slogan "Stay the Course," and it probably helped them mitigate their House losses in a year of deep recession. They returned to the strategy in 1994, when they sought to use the Contract with America as they had the Capitol Compact in 1980. More important than the two contracts, whose fine print escaped most voters in both elections, was the overall approach: aggressive tactical maneuvering within Congress, the drawing of sharp distinctions between the parties, and the transmission of those distinctions to the voters in such a way that individual incumbents could not easily escape connection to their party's national record. In this sense, 1980 was very much a model for 1994. At the same time, though, the House Republicans' drive for a majority suffered a setback in 1980 when they lost Representative Robert Bauman at the peak of his effectiveness. Democrats did not stand still. They were driven by the 1980 results to emulate the GOP's aggressive small-donor fund-raising and its tactical sophistication.

Although the overall reelection rate remained quite high in the House and was over 50 percent in the Senate, the 1980 elections showed that incumbents were not invincible in either chamber. Members redoubled efforts to find electoral security. If a large number of incumbents had failed in their task of running against Congress while serving in it, many who remained responded by working even harder at running against Congress. The security of incumbents was threatened by the unprecedented prominence of PACs and by the PACs' new willingness to underwrite challengers. House Democrats responded in the 1980s by co-opting the business PACs, directing their substantial resources toward those with power: incumbents of the majority party in Congress. In the early 1980s, Representative Tony Coelho (California) and Senator Lloyd Bentsen (Texas) led Democrats in Congress to apply the lessons of 1980.

With a quarter century of hindsight, it is also clear that the 1980 election was an important moment in the increase of congressional partisanship. Partisan polarization—instances in which a majority of one party voted against the majority of the other party—characterized an average of 37 percent of House votes and 42 percent of Senate votes from 1970 to 1980; from 1981 to 1991, this increased to 51 percent of House votes and 45 percent of Senate votes. In the 1990s, partisan polarization continued growing in both chambers. The transformation of the 1980 election into a partisan referendum contributed to this heightened partisanship. Furthermore, besieged House Democrats turned to a stronger party leadership and to increased use of controlled procedures (for example, the increased use of the Rules Committee to strictly limit floor amendments) to protect them from excessive individualism and political embarrassment in the future.

At the same time, rejuvenated Republicans, perceiving that the confrontational experiment of 1979–1980 had paid off, were even less inclined to demur to Democratic control. The victory of five new southern Republican senators foreshadowed the partisan realignment that rolled through the South, in fits and starts, beginning in the 1980s and reaching a crescendo in 2004. As conservative southern Democrats were gradually replaced with Republicans, the congressional parties became more homogeneous.

Reagan's attempt to impose a significant change in policy direction, as well as his rhetorical emphasis on philosophical first principles, meant that Congress faced more issues on which compromise was difficult. The rise of groups like NCPAC and the Moral Majority, important in its own right, contributed to the polarized atmosphere. Above all, the liberal consensus on public philosophy had shattered. Democrats could no longer afford to be gracious to Republicans, secure in the knowledge that their majorities and the New Deal/Great Society policy regime were untouchable; Republicans, confident that they represented the future and angry at the obstructionism of their opponents, no longer felt compelled to be gracious to Democrats. On November 4, 1980, Congress turned from an English manor, in which civility was maintained by virtue of the gross inequality of the parties, into a fight club.

A number of other political milestones were marked in 1980. The following facts revealed a great deal about the state and future of U.S. politics:

- The Sunbelt reigned supreme in national politics. In both parties, the candidates whose greatest appeal lay in the Northeast—Kennedy, Bush, and Anderson—were trounced. In the general election, the candidate who assembled a Sunbelt coalition was the big winner.

- After the dominance of the 1960s and 1970s by both liberal secularism and counterculture irreverence, religion in the public square was making a comeback. In 1976 Carter had raised eyebrows by declaring himself "born again"; in 1980 all three general election candidates were publicly devout in their own ways. At the same time, conservative evangelicals flexed their political muscles at the grassroots for the first time, and the Republican platform became an unambiguous instrument of social conservatism.

- The old gender gap—with women more likely than men to vote Republican in presidential elections—was replaced with a new and reversed gender gap, one that has endured for a generation.

- The day of the independent candidate—as opposed to the third-party candidate—had fully arrived. Anderson's 1980 run, devoid of even the pretense of a party, paved the way for Ross Perot's 1992 effort. Perot, who was more charismatic than Anderson and had a more genuine claim to the political center, tripled Anderson's percentage.

- The United States was also on the edge of a new era of political dynasties. The election of 1980 was filled with dynastic intrigue. No fewer than four of the candidates for party nomination— Edward Kennedy, Edmund Brown, Howard Baker, and George Bush—had inherited national political ambitions from their fathers (and in Baker's case, from his father-in-law as well). Although the political family was hardly new in the United States, a republican concern for meritocracy had limited such instances in presidential politics. Those limitations were quietly swept away in 1980, though none of the legatees actually acquired a nomination. In 2000 both major party nominees came from prominent political families.

Most important, the nation's repudiation not only of Carter but of Democrats, philosophical liberalism, insiders, and "malaise" and its embrace of conservatism's chief public spokesman in the United States set the nation on a course for the foreseeable future. Conservatism was a respectable option now, and voters were ready to try it.

As in other change-oriented years, the election itself provided an opportunity, but no guarantees, to the winners. Even conservative activists like Paul Weyrich conceded that the long-term consequences of the 1980 elections would depend largely on the performance of the Republican victors. This was no more—and no less—than the opportunity FDR had been given in 1932.

The winners sought to install a new public philosophy to fill the void, to give a point to the "equilibrium without purpose," described by political scientist Samuel Beer in 1978. As Hugh Heclo observed, Reagan was among a small handful of presidents "who have conducted their careers primarily as a struggle about ideas" and was probably the only one in the twentieth century "so thoroughly devoted to contesting for the public philosophy."[2] The New Deal era, in which every problem was presumed to have a federal solution, was over. Reagan's drive for a new conservative public philosophy contained three intertwined elements—policy, institutions, and politics—all undergirded by the consistent use of the bully pulpit to advance his argument. In his inaugural address, Reagan proclaimed:

> In this present crisis, government is not the solution to our problem, government is the problem. . . . So, as we begin, let us take inventory.

We are a nation that has a government—not the other way around. And this makes us special among the nations of the Earth. Our Government has no power except that granted it by the people. It is time to check and reverse the growth of government which shows signs of having grown beyond the consent of the governed.

It is my intention to curb the size and influence of the Federal establishment and to demand recognition of the distinction between the powers granted to the Federal Government and those reserved to the States or to the people. All of us need to be reminded that the Federal Government did not create the States; the States created the Federal Government. . . .

Now, so there will be no misunderstanding, it is not my intention to do away with government. It is, rather, to make it work—work with us, not over us; to stand by our side, not ride on our back. Government can and must provide opportunity, not smother it; foster productivity, not stifle it.

It is no coincidence that our present troubles parallel and are proportionate to the intervention and intrusion in our lives that result from unnecessary and excessive growth of government. It is time for us to realize that we are too great a nation to limit ourselves to small dreams. . . . So, with all the creative energy at our command, let us begin an era of national renewal.

Almost immediately, Reagan, with the help of the Republican Senate and the conservative House, shifted the national agenda in a conservative direction. Reagan won his biggest economic policy victories in 1981, when Congress passed his package of spending cuts totaling $130 billion over three years and tax cuts estimated to be worth $1.8 trillion through 1990. Ultimately, discretionary domestic spending by the federal government fell from 4.7 percent of gross domestic product in 1980 to 3.1 percent in 1989. The 1981 tax bill speeded the depreciation of business investments and cut personal income taxes by 25 percent across the board over three years, at which time the tax brackets were indexed to inflation to prevent "bracket creep." The top rate was cut from 70 percent to 50 percent. Reagan also backed the tight money policy of the Federal Reserve Board under Chairman Paul Volcker, reappointing Volcker in 1983 and then appointing inflation-fighter Alan Greenspan in 1987. Deregulation was extended to other industries, and pages in the *Federal Register*—a rough measure of federal regulatory activism—fell

Ronald Reagan, fortieth president of the United States, being sworn in.

from 87,012 in 1980 to 53,376 in 1988. Overall, the Reagan administration issued 6,000 fewer rules in its first four years than had been issued during the Carter administration. Reagan's energy policy consisted of getting the federal government out of the energy business; he ended oil price controls only eight days after taking office.

In keeping with an early campaign promise to forge a "North American Accord," Reagan pursued free trade in the form of the Caribbean Basin Initiative and the U.S.-Canadian trade accord. In 1986 he signed the most significant overhaul of federal income taxes since their institution in 1913: Fourteen brackets were reduced to two, the top tax rate was cut to 28 percent, many loopholes were abolished, and four million working poor were removed from the tax rolls. Significantly, his administration laid the groundwork for the rise of the "small investor," for the 1981 tax bill gave tax deductions for individual retirement accounts (IRAs), and a key IRS decision paved the way for the establishment of 401(k) plans.

Reagan restored the respectability of federal inaction as a legitimate economic policy option. Indeed, what he did not do was as important as what he did. He pursued no major new federal domestic programs, and he resisted calls for such government interventions as mandating equal pay for comparable worth, setting industrial policy, and taking a hard turn toward trade protectionism. Altogether, the Reagan economic policies aimed to restore prosperity by restoring economic freedom, rejecting federal planning, and revitalizing the capitalist system.

Reagan's foreign policy likewise aimed to defend freedom, in this case by prosecuting the Cold War to the fullest extent. Although Reagan was generally cautious about the use of force, he put into effect the principles of "peace through strength" that he had long extolled. He began by shoring up the defensive posture of the West. Reagan restored the policy of containment by aiding El Salvador against Communist guerrillas and strengthened the policy of deterrence by engaging in a big buildup of conventional and nuclear arms. From 1980 to 1985 real defense spending grew by 35 percent. Reagan also bolstered U.S. alliances by refusing to cancel the Euromissile deployment despite severe public pressure by the antinuclear movement (recall that Carter had canceled the neutron bomb). To this extent, Reagan reinvigorated an old policy.

However, he went much further. Believing that a posture limited to defensive containment could not endure indefinitely, Reagan sought to end the stalemate of Cold War by actively bringing down the Soviet colossus. The new strategy was encapsulated in National Security Decision

Directive (NSDD) 75, a secret 1983 document declaring that the rollback of Soviet influence, and ultimately a change in the Soviet system, was now a key U.S. objective. Reagan went on the propaganda offensive, calling the Soviet Union the "Evil Empire." He went on the economic offensive, systematically cutting off Soviet access to Western technology. He went on the military offensive, invading Grenada directly in 1983 and (in what became known as the Reagan Doctrine) giving aid to anticommunist forces in Afghanistan, Angola, Cambodia, and Nicaragua. He went on the diplomatic offensive, accusing the Soviets (correctly) of treaty violations and pressing proposals to reduce nuclear arms rather than merely limit them. And Reagan took the scientific offensive, threatening the massive Soviet investment in offensive ballistic missiles by launching the Strategic Defense Initiative, a research program seeking an effective defense against attack.

The shift in policy from containing the Soviet threat to defeating it was dramatic. Eisenhower promised rollback but could not deliver; Goldwater asked "Why not victory?" but lost the 1964 election. Reagan turned the idea into policy. At the same time, he hoped that U.S. pressure would result in a chance for real negotiations with a chastened Soviet leadership. He genuinely sought the ultimate abolition of nuclear weapons. When Mikhail Gorbachev rose to the top of the Politburo, Reagan took advantage of the opportunity.

In both the economic and foreign policy realms, several of Reagan's policies were extensions of Carter's. Carter had tried to restrain federal social spending, had appointed Volcker to the Federal Reserve, had deregulated some industries, had launched the military buildup, and had even given aid to the Afghan resistance. Reagan took these policies to their logical conclusion, added to them, and wrapped them in a coherent public philosophy. He happily surrendered Carter's ambiguity, enhancing Carter's conservative strands while letting the other half of the Carter formula fall away.[3]

Reagan's foreign and economic policies have received the lion's share of attention since 1980, but in some respects, the deterioration of social indices since 1960 presented a more difficult challenge than did foreign affairs or the economy. Ultimately Reagan's results were much more mixed here, and his achievements were often more symbolic than concrete. Nevertheless, his social policy represented a notable counterrevolution against the moral permissiveness of the 1960s and 1970s. Reagan appreciated Alexis de Tocqueville's complex understanding of a free society, and he quoted the Frenchman at least fifty-eight times in public statements. To Reagan, liberty depended on strong families, religion, and civil society. Atomistic individualism was not his aim. In this view, Americans could solve many of their own problems without federal interference, but only if they were connected to their communities through voluntary associations.

Likewise, they would have fewer problems to solve if they returned to the moral values of the nation's Judeo-Christian heritage. At his inauguration, Reagan had the Bible on which he placed his hand for the oath of office opened to 2 Chronicles 7:14: "If my people, which are called by my name, shall humble themselves, and pray, and seek my face, and turn from their wicked ways; then I will hear from heaven, and will forgive their sin, and will heal their land."

Reagan pursued tough policies on crime, supporting stricter sentencing and declaring a new "war on drugs." He endorsed a welfare reform measure in 1988 that served in some respects as the intellectual starting point of the 1996 welfare overhaul. He regularly extolled religion and the traditional family in his rhetoric. He rejected the recently ascendant absolutist view of the First Amendment, an interpretation that insisted on the elimination of religion from public life. Reagan also issued Executive Order 12606, requiring that all new policy proposals include a family impact statement. He sought to overturn abortion on demand and launched a variety of initiatives to promote voluntarism. Broadly speaking, Reagan held that a strong civil society cannot take root if centralized government insists on co-opting its functions. Limited government was thus necessary to leave open the space that a free society requires for growth.

Institutionally, Reagan saw the crisis of 1980 as nothing less than a constitutional crisis in which the chickens were coming home to roost after decades of ignoring crucial constitutional principles. Using rhetoric, legislation, administrative action, and judicial appointments, he tried to restore the vitality of a number of principles that had been downgraded since the New Deal. For instance, he argued that legitimate federal authority was limited to the powers enumerated in Article I, Section 8 of the Constitution. Reagan resuscitated at least the metaphor of enumeration of powers by forcing a reappraisal and prioritization of spending.

In a number of court cases, including one challenging the independent counsel law, his administration also argued for a more traditional version of separation of powers and for individual (as opposed to group) rights. He defended private property rights and opposed racial preference schemes as a violation of the constitutional mandate of equal protection under the law. In the area of federalism, Reagan failed to win a comprehensive sorting out of federal and state responsibilities, but block grants shifted power to the states in a more ad hoc manner, also anticipating the welfare reform of the 1990s. Two executive orders (12372 in 1983 and 12612 in 1987) required agencies to engage in consultation with the states and to consider the effects of new programs on the balance between the federal and state governments.

What held these principles together was Reagan's conviction—the bedrock foundation of his policies—that the federal government could not simply do whatever it wanted, that the Constitution limited as well as empowered Washington. In this, too, Reagan broke sharply with the New Deal legacy.

In one sense, though, Reagan's task was the same as FDR's had been: to restore Americans' confidence in their institutions, in democracy, and in the future of their country. Reagan undertook this mission at a time when many Americans questioned whether the presidency was a viable institution. No president had served two full terms since Eisenhower in the 1950s. Kennedy had accomplished little before being assassinated; Johnson had been forced to forgo his reelection bid in 1968; Nixon had been driven from office by the threat of impeachment; Ford had been defeated; Carter had been defeated after basing his reelection campaign on the argument that no president could really deal with the nation's problems. Reagan's words aimed to restore confidence, though his optimism was not Pollyannish. As he said in his first inaugural address, "We are not, as some would have us believe, doomed to an inevitable decline. I do not believe in a fate that will fall on us no matter what we do. I do believe in a fate that will fall on us if we do nothing." As powerful as his words often were, the restoration of U.S. confidence hinged most of all on successful deeds.

Two standards are especially appropriate measures by which to judge the Reagan presidency. One was the standard set by most Americans: Did Reagan deal successfully with the crises that had contributed so much to his election? The other was the standard he set for himself: Did he advance the cause of liberty as he understood it? To Reagan, his first objective, overcoming the crises of 1980, was intertwined with his second objective, to advance the cause of freedom, because the first required the second.

It is difficult to review the history of the 1980s without concluding that Reagan did, indeed, pass these tests. In broad terms, by 1989 the economic crisis of stagflation was a thing of the past. The energy crisis was gone in short order as the government regulatory schemes that caused market distortions were ended. Inflation, judged by the public to be the greatest economic threat in 1980, fell from 13 percent to 3.5 percent. Unemployment fell from 7.5 percent to 5.3 percent; interest rates were halved. The economic recovery that began in January 1983 lasted ninety-two months, then a new record, and produced over 19 million new jobs. In late 1982 the Dow Jones Industrial Average began a rally that ultimately tripled its value by the end of the decade. Furthermore, Reagan succeeded in revitalizing the free-market economy by using policies of greater economic freedom. Roosevelt's supporters have long contended that FDR saved capitalism by taming it. Reagan could claim to have saved it by unleashing it. By the end of the 1980s no one but doctrinaire Marxists were asking whether the free-market system was doomed, and there were fewer and fewer of those.

The foreign policy crisis was a memory as well. In 1987 the Soviets agreed to Reagan's "zero option" eliminating intermediate-range ballistic missiles in Europe. In 1988 they withdrew from Afghanistan. In 1989, months after Reagan had left office, the Berlin Wall crumbled, along with communism in eastern Europe. Only two years later, the Soviet Union itself reached the "ash heap of history" that Reagan had predicted in a 1982 speech to the British parliament. The Cold War ended, not with Soviet world domination or nuclear war (both of which were real possibilities in 1980) or with the "convergence" touted by some intellectuals who had predicted the Soviet and Western systems would gradually merge, but with the total victory of the United States. The decline of U.S. power in the world, far from proving inevitable, was reversed. Success in the Cold War—a global conflict that may rightly be considered the third world war—was a victory against totalitarianism and for freedom that rivaled World War II in importance. The goose-stepping boots arrayed against the West were worn by different opponents, but the fundamental character of the enemy was the same in 1981 as it had been in 1941.

During the Reagan years, many aspects of the social crisis set in motion in the 1960s also quietly abated. What Reagan perceived as the foundation of free society was stabilized and at least marginally strengthened. One key indicator, the illegitimacy rate, continued worsening, but the stage was set for its stabilization and modest improvement in the 1990s. Across a range of other indicators, U.S. society was healthier in 1990 than it had been in 1980. The overall crime rate, the murder rate, and drug usage fell. Divorce rates declined for the first time since 1960. The abortion rate stabilized, then fell a bit for the first time since *Roe v. Wade*. SAT scores rose, and high school dropout rates fell. There was something of a religious and moral revival, and voluntarism and charitable giving among citizens rose dramatically, having declined in the 1970s.

At best, this progress was partial, and social indicators remained much worse than they had been in 1960, but for the first time Americans who were watching closely could imagine that an important corner had been turned. Of course, Reagan could claim only partial credit for such social improvements, but it was possible to argue that a combination of policy and presidential rhetoric had served as a rallying point and had contributed to nudging things in the right direction.

Institutionally, one of Reagan's signal accomplishments was proving Carter (and a raft of pundits and presidential scholars) wrong about the presidency. Commentator Richard Reeves argued in 1984 that Reagan "made a mockery of the conventional wisdom that the country was ungovernable."[4] Princeton political scientist Richard Nathan agreed, saying, "The executive office needed resuscitation, and Ronald Reagan, in a way that surprised many observers, has accomplished precisely that."[5] Noted presidential scholar Richard Neustadt concluded that Reagan had "restored the public image of the office to a fair (if rickety) approximation of its Rooseveltian mold."[6] Reagan's August 1981 confrontation with PATCO, the Professional Air Traffic Controllers Organization, was a crucial step on that road. When he fired the striking controllers for violating their federal contracts, the public (and, it turned out, the Soviets) sensed that this was a president to be reckoned with.

Reagan also incrementally advanced several key principles of the Constitution, which he called the blueprint of national liberty. His judicial appointments bore some fruit over time when court decisions demanded stricter separation of the branches, defended federalism, trimmed affirmative action, and even interpreted the Constitution's commerce clause narrowly for the first time in fifty years. By Reagan's conception of freedom—for the most part, the conception of limited government and individual rights advanced by the Founders—the United States was freer when he left office than it had been when he entered. He was quick to argue that this was precisely why the crises he had inherited were vanquished or controlled. Perhaps most important of all, Reagan restored to prominence a consideration of first principles, an insistence that the claims of liberty not be given short shrift. He did more than any U.S. political figure of the twentieth century to refute the notion that centralization and government planning was (and should be) the wave of the future. He reforged the link, central to American thinking until the New Deal, between freedom and progress.

Taken all together, the "crisis of confidence" that had served as the backdrop for the whole 1980 campaign—starting with Carter's speech of July 15, 1979—was overcome. The unprecedented pessimism of 1979 and 1980 gave way to renewed confidence about the future of the country. Almost all observers noted a profound resurgence of patriotism during the 1980s. Some public confidence was also restored in government. Voting turnout stabilized in 1980 and then actually increased in 1984, the first uptick in more than two decades. After two decades of decline, the number of Americans saying that government could be trusted all or most of the time grew, increasing from 26 percent in 1980 to 45 percent in 1984, those believing government was run for the benefit of all grew from 23 percent to 41 percent, and those thinking government wastes a lot of money fell from 80 percent to 66 percent.

By no means was the loss of confidence since 1960 entirely made up—and a bit of the gain was lost again because of the Iran-Contra affair at the end of the decade—but the downward spiral of cynicism was halted. The nation no longer seemed to be unraveling. When Americans reflected on the Reagan years, it was often this recovery of confidence that was most fondly remembered. In his January 1989 farewell address, Reagan declared that recovery to be one of the "great triumphs" of his presidency.

To achieve enduring change, Reagan had to construct a new politics for the United States. He contributed to a revival of the political parties, another crucial (though extraconstitutional) institution in U.S. politics. For years, state and local party organizations had atrophied, party loyalty in the electorate had fallen off, and there had been little party discipline in Congress. In 1972 political correspondent David Broder had declared "the party's over." One of the key contrasts between Carter and Reagan was the way they interacted with their parties. Carter remained aloof from the Democratic Party for four years, exercising a highly personal style of leadership. In return, the Democratic Party had little to offer his reelection effort. Reagan, on the other hand, benefited from and applauded a revival of Republican party politics. As candidate and as president, Reagan relished his role as party leader, consciously seeking to transform the GOP into a more powerful force. Larry J. Sabato argued in 1988 that "Ronald Reagan has been the most party-oriented president of recent times."[7]

Reagan aimed to build a Republican majority on the basis of the policy and institutional changes he wrought. He succeeded in forming a new and more powerful Republican coalition that could regularly compete for a majority. Although in 1984 Reagan did not press as hard as he could have for a broad party victory, he did solidify his 1980 coalition. That coalition has remained the core of Republican support. Reagan clearly fomented a Republican realignment in the South, where voters' self-identification did not shift to the Republicans until the 1980s. In the view of southern politics experts Earl and Merle Black, Reagan accomplished this by "realigning" conservative Democrats to the Republicans and "dealigning" white moderate Democrats, who became a swing group.[8] By 2004 headline writers could declare, "GOP Has Lock on South, and Democrats Can't Find Key."[9]

White evangelicals, first mobilized into a cohesive voting bloc and turned into Republicans by Reagan, have remained one of the GOP's most loyal groups. And Reagan's dealignment of Catholics and blue-collar voters from their traditional Democratic loyalties has not been undone, though those groups remained up for grabs. Catholics gave Clinton majorities in the 1990s but split evenly between Bush and Gore in 2000 and gave Bush a majority in 2004. Gore lost in part because George W. Bush carried white, working-class males by a 15 percentage point margin in 2000.

In sum, Reagan redefined the political self-identification of several key groups, teaching middle-class voters to think of themselves as taxpayers rather than as government beneficiaries, refocusing the attention of workers on cultural issues, convincing white southerners to vote as patriots and evangelicals, and melding big business with small.[10]

The Reagan era did not bring about a classic realignment, with Republicans immediately dominating at all levels as Democrats had dominated after 1932. The catalytic crisis was less severe in 1980, the electorate was less amenable to straight-ticket voting for any party, congressional incumbency and gerrymandered districts insulated more House members from national tides, and the enormous largesse distributed by government meant that there was probably a fairly high floor below which the party of big government could not fall. Even so, Reagan launched a fundamental transformation of U.S. politics. The augmented GOP coalition proved strong enough to win three presidential elections in a row—the only time either party accomplished that feat from 1952 through 2004—and five of seven presidential elections between 1980 and 2004. It was essentially the Reagan limited-government coalition, finally brought down to the congressional level, that led to Republican control of Congress starting in 1994. In 1994 Republicans also gained a majority of the nation's governorships, a majority they continued holding for the next decade, and achieved rough parity with Democrats in state legislatures.

The Republican gains inspired by Reagan first produced a twenty-year stalemate that ended the national dominance of the Democrats. From 1961 through 1980, Republicans had controlled the three elected institutions of the federal government—the presidency, the House, and the Senate—a combined total of eight out of sixty years and were entirely shut out of the federal government for twelve years. From 1981 through 2000, Republicans controlled the institutions a combined total of thirty out of sixty years and were shut out for only two years. The new coalition institutionalized the ambivalence toward government that Everett Carll Ladd held was at the core of the 1980 vote. These Republican gains in the electoral arena had policy consequences: Many conservative policies advanced, and the most dramatic liberal policy departures were turned aside. Then, Republican wins in 2002 and 2004, putting them in control of all three elected federal institutions, showed that Reagan's "rolling realignment" was still unfolding. It was no coincidence that George W. Bush's biggest bloc of voters in the 2004 election came from those thirty to forty-four years old, the "Reagan cohort" that came of political age in the 1980s.[11]

Furthermore, Reagan largely remade the Republican Party in his own conservative image. In doing so, he also remade the image of conservatism: He was more likely to quote Tom Paine ("We have it in our power to start the world anew") than Edmund Burke. In the modern Republican Party, nearly all presidential contenders vie to be seen as the authentic "Reagan Republican," though they often disagree about exactly what that means. Altogether, conservatives who had hoped for total control of the federal government under Reagan were not satisfied, but conservatism was much stronger after 1980 than before both inside and outside the GOP. Not only was the Republican coalition strengthened over the long run, but Reagan's political successes ultimately cemented a "philosophical realignment" in which Democrats had to imitate Republican coloration to prosper. Such imitation is a strong sign of the influence of Reagan's public philosophy.

It is conceivable that if Reagan had lost to Carter in 1980, Democrats would have moved rightward sooner rather than later, with Carter as the leader; perhaps Reagan's win had the effect of retarding for twelve years the Democrats' adjustment to post–New Deal realities. Balanced against this possibility, though, are several powerful rejoinders. First, one cannot ignore Carter's poor record of party leadership or Kennedy's "moral victory" in the Democratic primaries. Though Kennedy lost the nomination, he "carried the platform and essentially won the party."[12] Thus, even a Carter victory in November 1980 would not have guaranteed Democratic adjustment. To the contrary, if Reagan and congressional conservatives had lost in 1980, the rightward pressure building on Democrats since 1978 would have been relieved. Any gain that might have been won for conservatism within the Democratic Party would have been more than offset by the weakening of Republican conservatism that would probably have followed a Reagan defeat in 1980. And if Reagan had won in 1980 but then failed as president, the Democrats who stood to pick up the pieces were liberals like Kennedy and Mondale, not centrists.

For these reasons, Clinton's presidency has been rightly considered by many a political consequence of Reagan's success. Clinton can be seen as the Democratic equivalent of Eisenhower, a figure who accommodated himself to the new political realities and "put a tepid but confirmatory seal of approval on popular policies of the other party."[13]

Altogether, in the quarter century after the election of 1980, the political world has changed dramatically, in ways Reagan would have generally approved. Republicans have put together a (narrow) national majority to control the full federal government for the first time since 1952. An ideological and geographical sorting of the parties has taken place, with conservatives concentrated in the Republican Party rather than divided between the two parties. Conservative ideas have gained ascendancy, bolstered by an extensive infrastructure of think tanks and journals. And, in a way that was scarcely imaginable in 1980, a new media—based in the Internet, talk radio, and the "blogosphere" and much friendlier to Republicans and conservatives than the old mainstream media—has arisen to challenge the old. Even here, Reagan was not a passive observer: The rise of conservative talk radio would have been impossible without a 1987 Reagan administration decision to abolish the so-called Fairness Doctrine prohibiting political use of the airwaves without "equal time" for opposing views.

The effusive praise of Reagan that dominated the news after his death obscured the fact that his attempt to forge a new public philosophy was highly controversial at the time. His 1980 campaign was shadowed by protestors with signs reading "Reagan for Shah" and "Fascist Gun of the West." None of Reagan's policy innovations escaped severe criticism from opponents who warned that the tax cuts would fuel inflation, that aid to El Salvador would bring another Vietnam, and that the defense buildup would lead to Armageddon. Also obscured in the funerary pomp was the degree to which analysts today, including his critics, disagree about Reagan. On the one side are those who consider Reagan to have been generally benign but not as influential as his strongest supporters claim. On the other side are those who consider Reagan to be the decisive figure of recent U.S. history, but not at all benign.

Critics in the first category note the limits of Reagan's accomplishments. These limits are not difficult to discern: He stopped the growth of government, but he did not shrink it; he legitimized and advanced conservatism, but he did not bring its unalloyed triumph; the social problems facing the nation were mitigated during his tenure but far from solved. Many of his policy successes were partial, incremental, and (to the degree that they relied on executive orders or judicial decisions) highly vulnerable to reversal. In areas as diverse as natural resources, Social Security, and civil rights, his policy preferences were often overruled by a restive Congress. Although he made an effort, he failed to deliver much of what he had promised to the social conservatives—school prayer, restrictions on abortion, tuition tax credits—owing in part to an unfriendly House and in part to his own decision to make economic and national security issues a higher priority.

However, no president achieves all he sets out to do. Franklin Roosevelt failed to solve the Great Depression, even though solving it was the chief rationale of his first two terms. Measuring Reagan against what was actually possible is more reasonable. What was possible was conditioned by divided government and narrow majorities, by entrenched groups fighting hard to retain their spots at the public trough, by media and an intellectual elite that were mostly hostile, and by a national situation that was disastrous in January 1981. Measured against those limits, what Reagan accomplished looks substantial indeed.

A second question is whether Reagan's innovations were durable enough to be significant. Some clearly were. For example, his economic prescription—slowing the growth of federal spending, holding down regulation, cutting taxes, and elevating (at least in theory) the importance of trying to balance the budget, of maintaining a tight grip on inflation through monetary policy, and of free trade—endured for at least two decades. There were, to be sure, zigs and zags, including two major tax increases, in 1990 and 1993. However, what stands out in retrospect is the continuity of policy since 1980. Even Clinton raised the top income tax rate to only 39.6 percent; in 1980 it had been 70 percent.

Likewise, in foreign policy, the assertive United States of the Reagan years never reverted back to the docile United States of the early Carter years. Indeed, George H. W. Bush and Clinton both used military force abroad much more often than Reagan did. When the U.S. response to the attack of September 11, 2001, took shape, it bore an uncanny resemblance to the Reagan strategy of the 1980s: Take the offensive and go to the root by bringing down the regimes that serve as the incubator of the threat. Missile defense, requiring the 2002 abrogation of the Anti-Ballistic Missile Treaty, is another example of Reagan's ongoing influence, as is U.S. support for democratization abroad and George W. Bush's embrace of the natural rights theory of the Declaration of Independence as a foundation for foreign policy. Reagan's human rights strategy, aimed at the fundamental systemic reform of despotic governments, has proven more effective and more lasting than Carter's more acclaimed alternative, which aimed at the mitigation of repression in individual cases.

Welfare reform and the devolution movement in the 1990s meant that federalism continued gaining. Even in the social arena, many of the modest improvements of the 1980s—for example, in divorce rates, crime rates, and abortion rates—turned into more substantial gains in the 1990s. In the quarter century since the election of 1980, the United States has never reprised the malaise of that era, and the presidency has never sunk to the level of institutional ineffectiveness it suffered in the 1970s, even during the impeachment episode of 1998–1999.

In other areas, the verdict on Reagan's innovations is not so clear. The moral counterrevolution against the counterculture that Reagan represented has endured, even deepened, but has not appreciably broadened and certainly has not prevailed; it has suffered serious setbacks on such issues as abortion and homosexual rights. The southernization of the Republican Party, key to its political success, has also brought a backlash in which states like California, Illinois, and New York are now consistently Democratic at the presidential level. The Republican geographical coalition of 2004 was not the same as that of 1980, when Reagan struck hard to the East and won much of the South by a whisker.

Not least, one of the defining characteristics of the Reagan era—Reagan's commitment to a discourse of first principles and his consequent commitment to both a rhetoric and a policy of constitutionalism—has not been consistently followed since his presidency. Republicans drew heavily from that well during their next surge in the 1990s, but in their third surge, under George W. Bush, it has been largely absent. The narrative Reagan offered the nation as a substitute for the progressive narrative—that founding principles, far from having become obsolete, still provide a road map into the future—has been, for the most part, left to wither from neglect. It cannot be judged good for the long-term future of Reaganism that his constitutional principles have not had the staying power or widespread acceptance of his policies.

George W. Bush's presidency has been more ambivalent toward Reaganism than much media commentary would have one believe. On one side lies an explosion of domestic spending in Bush's first term, his near-total abandonment of a rhetoric of limited government, and his signing into law of the first major federal entitlement since the Great Society era: a Medicare prescription drug program. On the other hand, Bush has exhibited a Reaganesque commitment to tax cuts, social conservatism, strict constitutionalism in judicial appointments, and a foreign policy based on the natural rights doctrine of the Declaration of Independence. Bush's long-term strategy seems to be to produce a fundamental shift in public policy in the direction of greater self-reliance and stronger civil society. Should he succeed, as one journalist noted, "he will move us toward an America Ronald Reagan would have been happy to call his own."[14]

Another critique of Reagan's presidency holds that his successes should largely be ascribed to good fortune. This theme stresses that correlation is not the same as causation. In this view, many of the good things that happened in the 1980s were really the result not of Reagan's policies but, rather, of salutary coincidences. He was, in this view, "lucky" in his economic policy (OPEC stopped driving oil prices up) and in his foreign policy (Gorbachev happened along at just the right time).

Luck, though, hardly seems a sufficient explanation. For one thing, Reagan often made his own luck. OPEC stopped driving oil prices up in no small part because Reagan worked behind the scenes to forge a close strategic relationship with Saudi Arabia. As for Gorbachev, the new Soviet premier in 1985 had taken a more, not less, aggressive posture toward the West, initiating a new strategic arms buildup, increasing aid to Nicaragua and Libya, pouring more troops into Afghanistan, and launching a propaganda offensive (the "common European home") designed to split western Europe from the United States. Not until he took the measure of Reagan at the Reykjavík, Iceland, summit did Gorbachev noticeably soften. As John W. Sloan remarked in his book *The Reagan Effect,* "luck" is a "particularly weak argument" and "can hardly be relied on to explain why Reagan was elected governor of California and president of the United States."[15]

Of course, neither Reagan's supporters nor his critics can provide definitive evidence regarding how much his policies caused the U.S. recovery of the 1980s. However, logic can point to some conclusions. That such a dramatic turnaround in conditions would come accidentally in so many areas at exactly the time that the nation was implementing a dramatic turnaround in policy seems unlikely. Furthermore, broad agreement has emerged among analysts across the political spectrum that Reagan's tax cuts helped fuel the two-decade-long economic expansion and that his foreign policy did indeed contribute to the end of the Cold War. The argument now is largely about how, not whether, Reagan influenced events. Supply-siders attribute the economic boom to cuts in marginal tax rates; Keynesians attribute it to the demand effects of the tax cuts. Scholars like John Lewis Gaddis argue that Reagan's strength combined with his diplomacy helped push the Soviets into surrender; others like Beth Fischer claim that it was only Reagan's softening and willingness to negotiate that was decisive.

On the other side of the ledger, a number of critics concede the importance of Reagan's presidency but argue that his influence was highly pernicious. One scholar argued that Reagan had produced "a transformation in [U.S.] political institutions and its philosophy of governance of a magnitude not seen since the 1930s." The results were "untold damage to the structure of governance" and the onset of "early-stage plutocracy."[16]

One exhibit in this charge was the federal deficit, which ballooned in the first Reagan term. Ultimately, the national debt nearly tripled during the Reagan presidency. In the standard account, Reagan's tax cuts and defense spending increases were responsible for the deficit, which was an economic disaster. The deficits were indeed a highly problematic feature of the Reagan years, and he himself admitted that the deficit was "one of my bigger disappointments as President."[17] On the other hand, there is little evidence that the deficits inflicted long-term harm on the economy. Furthermore, due to congressional and executive action, by 1989 the federal deficit was almost exactly the same proportion of the economy as it had been in 1980, before Reagan took office.

Above all, there are good reasons to question the standard account of how the deficits occurred. Federal revenues under Reagan were a higher proportion of the economy than they had been in 1960—when there was a balanced budget—and defense spending was a lower proportion. The increased deficit from 1960 to the 1980s was therefore entirely the result of a growth in domestic social spending. Even in the 1980s defense spending accounted for only 30 percent of the increase in noninterest annual spending from 1980 to 1989. As for the tax cuts, federal revenue grew by 27 percent in real terms from 1980 to 1989, faster than in the 1970s. Thus, the deficits of the 1980s are more easily traced to New Deal and Great Society entitlements than to anything Reagan did. This interpretation would explain why administrations from Eisenhower through Reagan saw steadily higher real average annual deficits.

Observers like Elizabeth Drew hold that Reagan's call for limited government and his skepticism about federal authority contributed to public cynicism. However, as we have already seen, measures of public confidence in government actually rose during the 1980s.

The central critique made by Reagan's detractors, however, focuses on the question of equity. This critique holds that the Reagan boom was won at the cost of higher income inequality, worse poverty, a declining middle class, and declining incomes for most. Reaganism produced, in this oft-stated view, a "decade of greed." This argument is bolstered by the fact that Reagan did not emphasize equalization of economic conditions between rich and poor; his chief concern was with liberty. It is also true that he cannot escape some measure of responsibility for the deep recession of 1981–1982, which flowed from the Federal Reserve policies he endorsed.

However, no credible evidence has ever been offered to support the notion that there was more greed in the 1980s than in any other decade of human history. Indeed, a number of indicators contradict this critique:

- Poverty rates declined every year from 1983 through the remainder of Reagan's presidency.
- Income inequality had been growing since 1973, and Reagan policies contributed no more than one-fifth of the increase in the 1980s.
- Inequality in consumption expenditures did not grow at all.
- Economic mobility remained high.
- Real household incomes in all quintiles, including the lowest, grew from 1983 through the end of the Reagan presidency.
- The aggregate movement of people from the middle class was into higher, not lower, income groups.
- The number of the homeless, the cause célèbre of the 1980s in some quarters, was found in a number of scholarly studies to have been greatly exaggerated by their advocates.

In sum, the egalitarian argument against Reagan, though pursued doggedly by believers, has little to support it. Reagan's ideological rejection of redistributionism and his embrace of limited government and free markets seem to account, more than any actual fact, for the distaste of egalitarians for his program.

Other more genuine blemishes appear on the Reagan record. They include an imprudent peace-keeping mission in Beirut, Lebanon, which cost 241 American lives, and the Iran-Contra affair, in which arms were secretly sold to Iran and the proceeds funneled to the Nicaraguan resistance. Reagan's penchant for delegation and loose management contributed to the collapse of the savings and loan (S&L) industry, although the S&Ls were already $120 billion in arrears when Reagan took office. Some critics objected that Reagan violated his own standard of advancing liberty by supporting draconian tactics in the war on drugs or by aggrandizing executive authority.

Looking back, even many conservatives cannot abide Reagan's easy acceptance of massive immigration, and some question whether he did everything possible to forestall the rise of Islamic terrorism. On the one hand, he took more dramatic action than had Carter, tilting against Iran in its war with Iraq, intercepting an Egyptian plane carrying Palestinian terrorists who had hijacked the cruise ship *Achille Lauro* and murdered one American passenger, and bombing Libya in retaliation for a terrorist act in Berlin. On the other hand, he took little action against the perpetrators of the Beirut bombing, and when his behind-the-scenes dealings with Iran were revealed, much of his antiterrorist effort was undercut. The administration's tilt toward Iraq has been the target of critics since the first Gulf War, but that tilt has been much overstated—the Soviet Union always provided the vast majority of Saddam's arsenal, followed by France—and at the moment Khomeini was clearly the bigger threat. Above all, terrorism was a relatively low priority much of the time for Reagan, who had bigger fish to fry in the Kremlin.

Taking everything into account, the bottom line for most Americans was that Reagan had inherited a disaster and left a revival. The United States had weathered the multifaceted crisis of the late 1970s. Indeed, one is hard-pressed to find a more dramatic reversal of bad fortune in any comparably short period in U.S. history. Reagan accomplished the most important things he had promised—a return to economic stability, the restoration of national strength, and a check on the big government Leviathan—and then some. When Reagan left office in January 1989, he did so with the highest approval rating of any departing president since FDR. With the exception of a brief dip in the early 1990s, the next fifteen years saw little change in this assessment, despite significant efforts by Democrats to redefine the Reagan years to their own advantage. (This strategy was outlined in 1991 by pollster Stanley Greenberg, who later served both Clinton and Gore.) When Reagan died in June 2004, Americans lined the streets in gratitude and affection.

In a more reserved fashion, a host of noted presidential scholars have declared Reagan to have been one of the most consequential presidents of the last hundred years. Aaron Wildavsky called him "one of the two most influential of the modern era," along with FDR.[18] Marc Landy and Sidney Milkis argued that among presidents from the latter half of the 1900s, Reagan and Johnson were the only ones with a plausible claim to greatness.[19] Stephen Skowronek listed Reagan as one of only five fundamentally transformative presidents in all of U.S. history, in the company of Jefferson, Jackson, Lincoln, and Roosevelt.[20]

As a result, the election of 1980 is one of only a handful of twentieth-century elections that must be considered truly pivotal. Wilson's victory in the three-way race of 1912 had a more dramatic institutional effect than did Reagan's victory, as Wilson modeled the modern plebiscitary presidency and rewrote the theory of the presidential nominating system; in policy and public philosophy 1912 was comparable with 1980. The Kennedy election, which led to the New Frontier/Great Society era, was responsible for dramatic policy developments. Nixon's 1968 win was politically momentous, setting the stage for the dismantling of the New Deal coalition. Political scientist David R. Mayhew has made a strong case for adding 1920 and 1948 to the litany of key U.S. elections because of the way they reoriented the winning parties, the 1920 Republicans toward decentralized limited government and the 1948 Democrats toward black civil rights.[21]

But only the election of 1932 rates as clearly more important than 1980 in terms of its impact on policy, institutions, politics, and public philosophy, and the crises with which Roosevelt contended—the Great Depression and war with the Axis powers—were more severe than those Reagan faced. Altogether, only 1912, 1932, and 1980 offered a new public philosophy around the nexus of institutions and policy; only 1932 and 1980 saw the formation of fundamentally new and durable electoral coalitions; only 1932 and 1980 faced and ultimately resolved potentially existential crises. It is difficult to escape the conclusion that 1980 was the second or third most significant election of the twentieth century.

With journalistic hyperbole, the *Washington Post* declared 1980 to have been "the most astonishing landslide in election history." There were many Americans for whom it was not all that astonishing: campaign pollsters, political scientists who predict elections, people who had closely followed Reagan's career, conservatives who thought only that common sense had returned at last. Astonishing or not, it was an election that changed the United States.

APPENDIX A
1980 DEMOCRATIC PRIMARY RESULTS

		Carter Votes	%	Kennedy Votes	%	Brown Votes	%	Others Votes	%
Feb. 17	Puerto Rico	449,681	51.7	418,068	48.0	1,660	0.2	826	0.1
Feb. 26	New Hampshire	52,692	47.1	41,745	37.3	10,743	9.6	6,750	6.0
Mar. 4	Massachusetts	260,401	28.7	590,393	65.1	31,498	3.5	25,031	2.7
	Vermont	29,015	73.1	10,135	25.5	358	0.9	195	0.5
Mar. 8	Alabama	193,734	81.6	31,382	13.2	9,529	4.0	2,819	1.2
Mar. 11	Florida	666,321	60.7	254,727	23.2	53,474	4.9	123,481	11.2
	Georgia	338,772	88.0	32,315	8.4	7,255	1.9	6,438	1.7
	Illinois	780,787	65.0	359,875	30.0	39,168	3.3	21,237	1.8
Mar. 18	Connecticut	87,207	41.5	98,662	46.9	5,386	2.6	19,020	9.0
Mar. 25	New York	406,305	41.1	582,757	58.9				
Apr. 1	Kansas	109,807	56.6	61,318	31.6	9,434	4.9	13,359	6.9
	Wisconsin	353,662	56.2	189,520	30.1	74,496	11.8	11,941	1.9
	Louisiana	199,956	55.7	80,797	22.5	16,774	4.7	61,214	17.1
Apr. 5	Pennsylvania	732,332	45.4	736,854	45.7	37,669	2.3	106,368	6.6
Apr. 22	Texas	770,390	55.9	314,129	22.8	35,585	2.6	257,250	18.7
May 3	D.C.	23,697	36.9	39,561	61.7			892	1.4
May 6	Indiana	398,949	67.7	190,492	32.3				
	North Carolina	516,778	70.1	130,684	17.7	21,420	2.9	68,380	9.3
	Tennessee	221,658	75.2	53,258	18.1	5,612	1.9	14,152	4.8
	Maryland	226,528	47.5	181,091	38.0	14,313	3.0	55,158	11.6
May 13	Nebraska	72,120	46.9	57,826	37.6	5,478	3.6	18,457	12.0
May 20	Michigan					23,043	29.4	55,381	70.6
	Oregon	208,693	56.7	114,651	31.1	34,409	9.3	9,451	2.5
May 27	Arkansas	269,375	60.1	78,542	17.5			100,373	22.4
	Idaho	31,383	62.2	11,087	22.0	2,078	4.1	5,934	11.8
	Kentucky	160,819	66.9	55,167	23.0			24,345	10.1
	Nevada	25,159	37.6	19,296	28.8			22,493	33.6
June 3	California	1,266,276	37.6	1,507,142	44.8	135,962	4.0	454,589	13.5
	New Mexico	66,621	41.8	73,721	46.3			19,022	11.9
	New Jersey	212,387	37.9	315,109	56.2			33,412	6.0
	Montana	66,922	51.5	47,671	36.7			15,466	11.9
	Ohio	605,744	51.1	523,874	44.4			56,792	4.8
	Rhode Island	9,907	25.8	26,179	68.3	310	0.8	1,931	5.0
	South Dakota	31,251	45.4	33,418	48.6			4,094	6.0
	West Virginia	197,687	62.2	120,247	37.8				
	TOTALS	9,593,335	51.2	6,963,625	37.1	573,636	3.1	1,617,229	8.6
	Total Vote:	18,747,825							

Source: *Congressional Quarterly's Guide to U.S. Elections,* 2d ed. (Washington, D.C.: Congressional Quarterly, 1985), 429–435.

1980 REPUBLICAN PRIMARY RESULTS

		Reagan Votes	%	Bush Votes	%	Anderson Votes	%
Feb. 17	Puerto Rico			111,940	60.1		
Feb. 26	New Hampshire	72,983	49.6	33,443	22.7	14,458	9.8
Mar. 4	Massachusetts	115,334	28.8	124,365	31.0	122,987	30.7
	Vermont	19,720	30.1	14,226	21.7	19,030	29.0
Mar. 8	South Carolina	79,549	54.7	21,569	14.8		
Mar. 11	Alabama	147,352	69.7	54,730	25.9		
	Florida	345,699	56.2	185,996	30.2	56,636	9.2
	Georgia	146,500	73.2	25,293	12.6	16,853	8.4
Mar. 18	Illinois	547,355	48.4	124,057	11.0	415,193	36.7
Mar. 25	Connecticut	61,735	33.9	70,367	38.6	40,354	22.1
Apr. 1	Kansas	179,739	63.0	35,838	12.6	51,924	18.2
	Wisconsin	364,898	40.2	276,164	30.4	248,623	27.4
Apr. 5	Louisiana	31,212	74.9	7,818	18.8		
Apr. 22	Pennsylvania	527,916	42.5	626,759	50.5	26,890	2.1
May 3	Texas	268,798	51.0	249,819	47.4		
May 6	D.C.			4,973	66.1	2,025	26.9
	Indiana	419,016	73.7	92,955	16.4	56,342	9.9
	North Carolina	113,854	67.6	36,631	21.8	8,542	5.1
	Tennessee	144,625	74.1	35,274	18.1	8,722	4.5
May 13	Maryland	80,557	48.2	68,389	40.9	16,244	9.7
	Nebraska	155,995	76.0	31,380	15.3	11,879	5.8
May 20	Michigan	189,184	31.8	341,998	57.5	48,947	8.2
	Oregon	170,449	54.0	109,210	34.6	32,118	10.2
May 27	Idaho	111,868	82.9	5,416	4.0	13,130	9.7
	Kentucky	78,072	82.4	6,861	7.2	4,791	5.1
	Nevada	39,352	83.0	3,078	6.5		
June 3	California	2,057,923	80.3	125,113	4.9	349,315	13.6
	New Mexico	37,982	63.8	5,892	9.9	7,171	12.0
	New Jersey	225,959	81.3	47,447	17.1		
	Montana	68,744	86.6	7,665	9.7		
	Ohio	692,288	80.8	164,485	19.2		
	Rhode Island	3,839	72.0	993	18.6		
	South Dakota	72,861	82.2	3,691	4.2		
	West Virginia	115,407	83.6	19,509	14.1		
	Mississippi	23,028	89.4	2,105	8.2		
	TOTALS	7,709,793	60.8	2,958,093	23.3	1,572,174	12.4

Total Votes Cast: 12,690,451

Source: *Congressional Quarterly's Guide to U.S. Elections*, 2d ed. (Washington, D.C.: Congressional Quarterly, 1985) 429–435.

ker es	%	Crane Votes	%	Connally Votes	%	Dole Votes	%	Others Votes	%
934	37			1,964	1.1	483	0.3	3,050	1.6
943	12.1	2,618	1.8	2,239	1.5	597	0.4	1,876	1.3
366	4.8	4,669	1.2	4,714	1.2	577	0.1	8,814	2.2
55	12.3	1,238	1.9	884	1.3			2,458	3.7
	0.5			43,113	29.6	117	0.1	380	0.3
63	0.9	5,099	2.4	1,077	0.5	447	0.2	685	0.3
45	1.0	12,000	2.0	4,958	0.8	1,086	0.2	2,275	0.3
71	0.8	6,308	3.2	2,388	1.2	249	0.1	1,009	0.5
51	0.6	24,865	2.2	4,548	0.4	1,843	0.2	5,169	0.5
46	1.3	1,887	1.0	598	0.3	333	0.2	4,564	2.5
03	1.3	1,367	0.5	2,067	0.7			10,860	3.8
98	0.4	2,951	0.3	2,312	0.3			9,607	1.1
								2,653	6.4
846	2.5			10,656	0.9			18,344	1.5
								8,152	1.5
		270	3.6					261	3.5
43	1.5	547	0.3	1,107	0.7	629	0.4	4,538	2.7
	*	1,574	0.8	1	*			4,998	2.5
		2,113	1.3						
		1,062	0.5			1,420	0.7	3,467	1.7
								15,047	2.5
		2,324	0.7					1,265	0.4
		1,024	0.8					3,441	2.6
								5,071	5.3
								4,965	10.5
		21,465	0.8					10,256	0.4
		4,412	7.4					4,089	6.9
								4,571	1.6
								3,014	3.8
								503	9.4
								6,353	7.6
								3,100	2.2
								618	2.4
,219	0.9	97,793	0.8	80,661	0.6	7,298	0.1	152,420	1.2

1980 PRESIDENTIAL GENERAL ELECTION RESULTS

Ronald Reagan

	EV	Ronald Reagan (Republican) Votes	%	Jimmy Carter (Democrat) Votes	%	John B. Anderson (Independent) Votes	%	Ed Clark (Libertarian) Votes	%	Other Votes	%
Alabama	9	654,192	48.8	636,730	47.5	16,481	1.2	13,318	1.0	21,208	1.6
Alaska	3	86,112	54.3	41,842	26.4	11,155	7.0	18,479	11.7	857	0.5
Arizona	6	529,688	60.6	246,843	28.2	76,952	8.8	18,784	2.2	1,678	0.2
Arkansas	6	403,164	48.1	398,041	47.5	22,468	2.7	8,970	1.1	4,939	0.6
California	45	4,524,858	52.7	3,083,661	35.9	739,833	8.6	148,434	1.7	90,277	1.1
Colorado	7	652,264	55.1	367,973	31.1	130,633	11.0	25,744	2.2	7,801	0.7
Connecticut	8	677,210	48.2	541,732	38.5	171,807	12.2	8,570	0.6	6,966	0.5
D.C.	3	23,545	13.4	131,113	74.8	16,337	9.3	1,114	0.6	3,128	1.8
Delaware	3	111,252	47.2	105,754	44.8	16,288	6.9	1,974	0.8	632	0.3
Florida	17	2,046,951	55.5	1,419,475	38.5	189,692	5.1	30,524	0.8	288	0.0
Georgia	12	654,168	41.0	890,733	55.8	36,055	2.3	15,627	1.0	112	0.0
Hawaii	4	130,112	42.9	135,879	44.8	32,021	10.6	3,269	1.1	2,006	0.7
Idaho	4	290,699	66.5	110,192	25.2	27,058	6.2	8,425	1.9	1,057	0.2
Illinois	26	2,358,049	49.6	1,981,413	41.7	346,754	7.3	38,939	0.8	24,566	0.5
Indiana	13	1,255,656	56.0	844,197	37.7	111,639	5.0	19,627	0.9	10,914	0.5
Iowa	8	676,026	51.3	508,672	38.6	115,633	8.8	13,123	1.0	4,207	0.3
Kansas	7	566,812	57.9	326,150	33.3	68,231	7.0	14,470	1.5	4,132	0.4
Kentucky	9	635,274	49.1	616,417	47.6	31,127	2.4	5,531	0.4	6,278	0.5
Louisiana	10	792,853	51.2	708,453	45.7	26,345	1.7	8,240	0.5	12,700	0.8
Maine	4	238,522	45.6	220,974	42.3	53,327	10.2	5,119	1.0	5,069	1.0
Maryland	10	680,606	44.2	726,161	47.1	119,537	7.8	14,192	0.9	—	—
Massachusetts	14	1,057,631	41.9	1,053,802	41.7	382,539	15.2	22,038	0.9	8,288	0.3
Michigan	21	1,915,225	49.0	1,661,532	42.5	275,223	7.0	41,597	1.1	16,148	0.4
Minnesota	10	873,268	42.6	954,174	46.5	174,990	8.5	31,592	1.5	17,956	0.9

Mississippi	7	49.4	441,089	48.1	429,281	1.3	12,036	0.6	5,465	0.5	4,749
Missouri	12	51.2	1,074,181	44.3	931,182	3.7	77,920	0.7	14,422	0.1	2,119
Montana	4	56.8	206,814	32.4	118,032	8.0	29,281	2.7	9,825		
Nebraska	5	65.9	419,937	26.0	166,851	7.0	44,993	1.4	9,073	0.6	4,193
Nevada	3	62.5	155,017	26.9	66,666	7.1	17,651	1.8	4,358		
New Hampshire	4	57.7	221,705	28.4	108,864	12.9	49,693	0.5	2,064	0.4	1,664
New Jersey	17	52.0	1,546,557	38.6	1,147,364	7.9	234,632	0.7	20,652	0.9	26,479
New Mexico	4	54.9	250,779	36.7	167,826	6.5	29,459	1.0	4,365	1.0	4,542
New York	41	46.7	2,893,831	44.0	2,728,372	7.5	467,801	0.8	52,648	1.0	59,307
North Carolina	13	49.3	915,018	47.2	875,635	2.8	52,800	0.5	9,677	0.1	2,703
North Dakota	3	64.2	193,695	26.3	79,189	7.8	23,640	1.2	3,743	0.4	1,278
Ohio	25	51.5	2,206,545	40.9	1,752,414	5.9	254,472	1.1	49,033	0.5	21,139
Oklahoma	8	60.5	695,570	35.0	402,026	3.3	38,284	1.2	13,828		
Oregon	6	48.3	571,044	38.7	456,890	9.5	112,389	2.2	25,838	1.3	15,355
Pennsylvania	27	49.6	2,261,872	42.5	1,937,540	6.4	292,921	0.7	33,263	0.8	35,905
Rhode Island	4	37.2	154,793	47.7	198,342	14.4	59,819	0.6	2,458	0.2	660
South Carolina	8	49.4	441,841	48.1	430,385	1.6	14,153	0.6	5,139	0.3	2,553
South Dakota	4	60.5	198,343	31.7	103,855	6.5	21,431	1.2	3,824	0.1	250
Tennessee	10	48.7	787,761	48.4	783,051	2.2	35,991	0.4	7,116	0.2	3,697
Texas	26	55.3	2,510,705	41.4	1,881,147	2.5	111,613	0.8	37,643	0.0	528
Utah	4	72.8	439,687	20.6	124,266	5.0	30,284	1.2	7,226	0.5	2,759
Vermont	3	44.4	94,628	38.4	81,952	14.9	31,761	0.9	1,900	1.4	3,058
Virginia	12	53.0	989,609	40.3	752,174	5.1	95,418	0.7	12,821	0.9	16,010
Washington	9	49.7	865,244	37.3	650,193	10.6	185,073	1.7	29,213	0.7	12,671
West Virginia	9	45.3	334,206	49.8	367,462	4.3	31,691	0.6	4,356		
Wisconsin	11	47.9	1,088,845	43.2	981,584	7.1	160,657	1.3	29,135	0.6	13,000
Wyoming	3	62.6	110,700	28.0	49,427	6.8	12,072	2.6	4,514		
Totals	**538**	**50.7**	**43,904,153**	**41.0**	**35,483,883**	**6.6**	**5,720,060**	**1.1**	**921,299**	**0.6**	**485,826**

Source: *Congressional Quarterly's Guide to U.S. Elections*, 2d ed. (Washington, D.C.: Congressional Quarterly, 1985), 365.

RONALD REAGAN'S FIRST
INAUGURAL ADDRESS

January 20, 1981

Senator Hatfield, Mr. Chief Justice, Mr. President, Vice President Bush, Vice President Mondale, Senator Baker, Speaker O'Neill, Reverend Moomaw, and my fellow citizens:

To a few of us here today, this is a solemn and most momentous occasion, and yet in the history of our Nation it is a commonplace occurrence. The orderly transfer of authority as called for in the Constitution routinely takes place as it has for almost two centuries and few of us stop to think how unique we really are. In the eyes of many in the world, this every-4-year ceremony we accept as normal is nothing less than a miracle.

Mr. President, I want our fellow citizens to know how much you did to carry on this tradition. By your gracious cooperation in the transition process, you have shown a watching world that we are a united people pledged to maintaining a political system which guarantees individual liberty to a greater degree than any other, and I thank you and your people for all your help in maintaining the continuity which is the bulwark of our Republic.

The business of our nation goes forward. These United States are confronted with an economic affliction of great proportions. We suffer from the longest and one of the worst sustained inflations in our national history. It distorts our economic decisions, penalizes thrift, and crushes the struggling young and the fixed-income elderly alike. It threatens to shatter the lives of millions of our people.

Idle industries have cast workers into unemployment, human misery, and personal indignity. Those who do work are denied a fair return for their labor by a tax system which penalizes successful achievement and keeps us from maintaining full productivity.

But great as our tax burden is, it has not kept pace with public spending. For decades, we have piled deficit upon deficit, mortgaging our future and our children's future for the temporary convenience of the present. To continue this long trend is to guarantee tremendous social, cultural, political, and economic upheavals.

You and I, as individuals, can, by borrowing, live beyond our means, but for only a limited period of time. Why, then, should we think that collectively, as a nation, we are not bound by that same limitation?

We must act today in order to preserve tomorrow. And let there be no misunderstanding. We are going to begin to act, beginning today.

The economic ills we suffer have come upon us over several decades. They will not go away in days, weeks, or months, but they will go away. They will go away because we as Americans have the capacity now, as we have had in the past, to do whatever needs to be done to preserve this last and greatest bastion of freedom.

In this present crisis, government is not the solution to our problem; government is the problem.

From time to time, we have been tempted to believe that society has become too complex to be managed by self-rule, that government by an elite group is superior to government for, by, and of the people. Well, if no one among us is capable of governing himself, then who among us has the capacity to govern someone else? All of us together, in and out of government, must bear the burden. The solutions we seek must be equitable, with no one group singled out to pay a higher price.

We hear much of special interest groups. Well, our concern must be for a special interest group that has been too long neglected. It knows no sectional boundaries or ethnic and racial divisions, and it crosses political party lines. It is made up of men and women who raise our food, patrol our streets, man our mines and factories, teach our children, keep our homes, and heal us when we are sick—professionals, industrialists, shopkeepers, clerks, cabbies, and truckdrivers. They are, in short, "We the people," this breed called Americans.

Well, this administration's objective will be a healthy, vigorous, growing economy that provides equal opportunities for all Americans, with no barriers born of bigotry or discrimination. Putting America back to work means putting all Americans back to work. Ending inflation means freeing all Americans from the terror of runaway living costs. All must share in the productive work of this "new beginning," and all must share in the bounty of a revived economy. With the idealism and fair play which are the core of our system and our strength, we can have a strong and prosperous America at peace with itself and the world.

So, as we begin, let us take inventory. We are a nation that has a government—not the other way around. And this makes us special among the nations of the Earth. Our Government has no power except that granted it by the people. It is time to check and reverse the growth of government which shows signs of having grown beyond the consent of the governed.

It is my intention to curb the size and influence of the Federal establishment and to demand recognition of the distinction between the powers granted to the Federal Government and those reserved to the States or to the people. All of us need to be reminded that the Federal Government did not create the States; the States created the Federal Government.

Now, so there will be no misunderstanding, it is not my intention to do away with government. It is, rather, to make it work—work with us, not over us; to stand by our side, not ride on our back. Government can and must provide opportunity, not smother it; foster productivity, not stifle it.

If we look to the answer as to why for so many years we achieved so much, prospered as no other people on Earth, it was because here in this land we unleashed the energy and individual genius of man to a greater extent than has ever been done before. Freedom and the dignity of the individual have been more available and assured here than in any other place on Earth. The price for this freedom at times has been high, but we have never been unwilling to pay that price.

It is no coincidence that our present troubles parallel and are proportionate to the intervention and intrusion in our lives that result from unnecessary and excessive growth of government. It is time for us to realize that we are too great a nation to limit ourselves to small dreams. We are not, as some would have us believe, doomed to an inevitable decline. I do not believe in a fate that will fall on us no matter what we do. I do believe in a fate that will fall on us if we do nothing. So, with all the creative energy at our command, let us begin an era of national renewal. Let us renew our determination, our courage, and our strength. And let us renew our faith and our hope.

We have every right to dream heroic dreams. Those who say that we are in a time when there are no heroes, they just don't know where to look. You can see heroes every day going in and out of factory gates. Others, a handful in number, produce enough food to feed all of us and then the world beyond. You meet heroes across a counter, and they are on both sides of that counter. There are entrepreneurs with faith in themselves and faith in an idea who create new jobs, new wealth and opportunity. They're individuals and families whose taxes support the Government and whose voluntary gifts support church, charity, culture, art, and education. Their patriotism is quiet but deep. Their values sustain our national life.

Now, I have used the words "they" and "their" in speaking of these heroes. I could say "you" and "your" because I am addressing the heroes of whom I speak—you, the citizens of this blessed land. Your dreams, your hopes, your goals are going to be the dreams, the hopes, and the goals of this administration, so help me God.

We shall reflect the compassion that is so much a part of your make-up. How can we love our country and not love our countrymen; and loving them, reach out a hand when they fall, heal them when they're sick, and provide opportunity to make them self-sufficient so they will be equal in fact and not just in theory?

Can we solve the problems confronting us? Well, the answer is an unequivocal and emphatic "yes." To paraphrase Winston Churchill, I did not take the oath I've just taken with the intention of presiding over the dissolution of the world's strongest economy.

In the days ahead I will propose removing the roadblocks that have slowed our economy and reduced productivity. Steps will be taken aimed at restoring the balance between the various levels of government. Progress may be slow, measured in inches and feet, not miles, but we will progress. Is it time to reawaken this industrial giant, to get government back within its means, and to lighten our punitive tax burden. And these will be our first priorities, and on these principles there will be no compromise.

On the eve of our struggle for independence a man who might have been one of the greatest among the Founding Fathers, Dr. Joseph Warren, President of the Massachusetts Congress, said to his fellow Americans, "Our country is in danger, but not to be despaired of.... On you depend the fortunes of America. You are to decide the important questions upon which rests the happiness and the liberty of millions yet unborn. Act worthy of yourselves."

Well, I believe we, the Americans of today, are ready to act worthy of ourselves, ready to do what must be done to ensure happiness and liberty for ourselves, our children and our children's children.

And as we renew ourselves here in our own land, we will be seen as having greater strength throughout the world. We will again be the exemplar of freedom and a beacon of hope for those who do not now have freedom.

To those neighbors and allies who share our freedom, we will strengthen our historic ties and assure them of our support and firm commitment. We will match loyalty with loyalty. We will strive for mutually beneficial relations. We will not use our friendship to impose on their sovereignty, for our own sovereignty is not for sale.

As for the enemies of freedom, those who are potential adversaries, they will be reminded that peace is the highest aspiration of the American people. We will negotiate for it, sacrifice for it; we will not surrender for it, now or ever.

Our forbearance should never be misunderstood. Our reluctance for conflict should not be misjudged as a failure of will. When action is required to preserve our national security, we will act. We will maintain sufficient strength to prevail if need be, knowing that if we do so we have the best chance of never having to use that strength.

Above all, we must realize that no arsenal or no weapon in the arsenals of the world is so formidable as the will and moral courage of free men and women. It is a weapon our adversaries in today's world do not have. It is a weapon that we as Americans do have. Let that be understood by those who practice terrorism and prey upon their neighbors.

I'm told that tens of thousands of prayer meetings are being held on this day, and for that I am deeply grateful. We are a nation under God, and I believe God intended for us to be free. It would be fitting and good, I think, if on each Inaugural Day in future years it should be declared a day of prayer.

This is the first time in history that this ceremony has been held, as you've been told, on this West Front of the Capitol. Standing here, one faces a magnificent vista, opening up on this city's special beauty and history. At the end of this open mall are those shrines to the giants on whose shoulders we stand.

Directly in front of me, the monument to a monumental man, George Washington, Father of our country. A man of humility who came to greatness reluctantly. He led America out of revolutionary victory into infant nationhood. Off to one side, the stately memorial to Thomas Jefferson. The Declaration of Independence flames with his eloquence.

And then, beyond the Reflecting Pool the dignified columns of the

Lincoln Memorial. Whoever would understand in his heart the meaning of America will find it in the life of Abraham Lincoln.

Beyond those monuments to heroism is the Potomac River, and on the far shore the sloping hills of Arlington National Cemetery, with its row upon row of simple white markers bearing crosses or Stars of David. They add up to only a tiny fraction of the price that has been paid for our freedom.

Each one of those markers is a monument to the kind of hero I spoke of earlier. Their lives ended in places called Belleau Wood, The Argonne, Omaha Beach, Salerno, and halfway around the world on Guadalcanal, Tarawa, Pork Chop Hill, the Chosin Reservoir, and in a hundred rice paddies and jungles of a place called Vietnam.

Under one such marker lies a young man, Martin Treptow, who left his job in a small town barbershop in 1917 to go to France with the famed Rainbow Division. There, on the western front, he was killed trying to carry a message between battalions under heavy artillery fire.

We're told that on his body was found a diary. On the flyleaf under the heading, "My Pledge," he had written these words: "America must win this war. Therefore, I will work, I will save, I will sacrifice, I will endure, I will fight cheerfully and do my utmost, as if the issue of the whole struggle depended on me alone."

The crisis we are facing today does not require of us the kind of sacrifice that Martin Treptow and so many thousands of others were called upon to make. It does require, however, our best effort, and our willingness to believe in ourselves and to believe in our capacity to perform great deeds; to believe that together with God's help we can and will resolve the problems which now confront us.

And, after all, why shouldn't we believe that? We are Americans. God bless you, and thank you.

CHAPTER 1 CRISIS OF CONFIDENCE

1 Gurney Breckenfeld, "The Perilous Prospect of a Low-Growth Economy," *Saturday Review,* July 12, 1975, 40.

2 Robert Heilbroner, "Does Capitalism Have a Future?" *New York Times Magazine,* August 15, 1982, 20–22+.

3 John Lewis Gaddis, "Strategies of Containment: Post-Cold War Reconsiderations," speech delivered during the commencement ceremony of the Elliott School of International Affairs, April 15, 2004, http://www.gwu.edu/~elliott/news/transcripts/gaddis.html.

4 *Soviet Military Power* (Washington, D.C.: Department of Defense, 1981), 9.

5 Paul H. Nitze, "Strategy in the Decade of the 1980s," *Foreign Affairs,* Fall 1980, 86.

6 Ben J. Wattenberg, "It's Time to Stop America's Retreat," *New York Times Magazine,* July 22, 1979, 16.

7 David Frum, *How We Got Here: The Decade That Brought You Modern Life (for Better or Worse)* (New York: Basic Books, 2000), 173.

8 Samuel Beer, "In Search of a New Public Philosophy," in *The New American Political System,* ed. Anthony King (Washington, D.C.: American Enterprise Institute, 1978), 44.

9 Quoted in John Aloysius Farrell, *Tip O'Neill and the Democratic Century* (Boston: Little, Brown, 2001), 598.

10 M. Stanton Evans, *The Future of Conservatism* (New York: Holt, Rinehart, and Winston, 1968), 120.

11 Samuel S. Hill and Dennis E. Owen, *The New Religious Political Right in America* (Nashville, Tenn.: Abingdon, 1982), 69.

12 Joel Kotkin, "Ready on the Right: Christian Soldiers Are on the March," *Washington Post,* August 25, 1979.

13 Kotkin, "Ready on the Right."

14 George H. Nash, *The Conservative Intellectual Movement in America since 1945* (Wilmington, Del.: Intercollegiate Studies Institute, 1996), 331.

15 Michael Barone, *Our Country: The Shaping of America from Roosevelt to Reagan* (New York: Free Press, 1990), 589.

16 "The New Tilt," *Newsweek,* November 20, 1978, 44.

17 Warren Weaver Jr., "Conservatives Find Reason for Elation," *New York Times,* February 10, 1979.

18 "The New Tilt," 44.

19 A partial exception to this generalization could be seen in Wendell Willkie's nomination to head the Republican ticket in 1940. Willkie was a utilities executive with no elective experience and a deliberately cultivated appeal as a "maverick." However, he was also the preferred candidate of the party's

eastern establishment, which used him to block conservative Senator Robert Taft of Ohio.

20 Peter G. Bourne, *Jimmy Carter: A Comprehensive Biography from Plains to Postpresidency* (New York: Scribner, 1997), 443.

CHAPTER 2 THE CANDIDATES

1 Jimmy Carter, *Keeping Faith: Memoirs of a President* (New York: Bantam Books, 1982), 463.

2 Jules Witcover, *Marathon: The Pursuit of the Presidency, 1972–1976* (New York: Viking Press, 1977), 105.

3 Quoted in Witcover, *Marathon*, 107.

4 Stephen Skowronek, *The Politics Presidents Make: Leadership from John Adams to George Bush* (Cambridge, Mass.: Belknap Press, 1993), 362.

5 Quotations from Kenneth E. Morris, *Jimmy Carter: American Moralist* (Athens: University of Georgia Press, 1996), 249–253.

6 Timothy D. Shellhardt, "The Jimmy Carter Legacy," *Wall Street Journal*, November 6, 1980.

7 Quoted in Francis X. Clines, "A Dump Carter Movement?" *New York Times*, February 24, 1979.

8 "The Other Carter's Magazine Interview Creates Waves," *New York Times*, January 3, 1979.

9 Theodore H. White, *America in Search of Itself: The Making of the President, 1956–1980* (New York: Warner Books, 1982), 274–275.

10 Kandy Stroud, *How Jimmy Won: The Victory Campaign from Plains to the White House* (New York: Morrow, 1977), 298.

11 Wallace Turner, "Brown's Political Strengths," *New York Times*, January 11, 1979.

12 Terence Smith, "Reporter's Notebook: Suddenly a New Look for Carter," *New York Times*, May 7, 1979.

13 Adam Clymer, "Like Carter, Brown Profits from Role as Outsider," *New York Times*, September 9, 1979.

14 White, *America in Search of Itself*, 270.

15 John B. Anderson, *Vision and Betrayal in America* (Waco, Tex.: Word Books, 1975), 16.

16 White, *America in Search of Itself*, 238.

17 Peter Schweizer and Rochelle Schweizer, *The Bushes: Portrait of a Dynasty* (New York: Doubleday, 2004), 279.

18 Quoted in Craig Shirley, *Reagan's Revolution: The Untold Story of the Campaign That Started It All* (Nashville, Tenn.: Nelson Current, 2005), 339.

19 Ronald Reagan, *An American Life* (New York: Simon and Schuster, 1991), 129.

20 Reagan, *An American Life*, 141–142.

21 Michael Barone, *Our Country: America from Roosevelt to Reagan* (New York: Free Press, 1990), 416.

22 Kiron K. Skinner, Annelise Anderson, and Martin Anderson, *Reagan in His*

Own Hand: The Writings of Ronald Reagan That Reveal His Revolutionary Vision for America (New York: Touchstone Press, 2001), xv.

23 Quoted by William E. Pemberton, Exit with Honor: The Life and Presidency of Ronald Reagan (Armonk, N.Y.: M. E. Sharpe, 1998), 49.

24 Theodore H. White, The Making of the President 1968 (New York: Pocket Books, 1969), 42.

25 Quoted in Jonathan Moore, ed., The Campaign for President: 1980 in Retrospect (Cambridge, Mass.: Ballinger, 1981), 13.

26 Edwin Meese III, With Reagan: The Inside Story (Washington, D.C.: Regnery Gateway, 1992), 10.

27 Cited by Lou Cannon and William Peterson, "GOP," in The Pursuit of the Presidency 1980, ed. Richard Harwood (New York: Berkley Books, 1980), 125.

28 Charles O. Jones, "Nominating 'Carter's Favorite Opponent': The Republicans in 1980," in The American Elections of 1980, ed. Austin Ranney (Washington, D.C.: American Enterprise Institute, 1981), 63.

29 Gerald R. Ford, A Time to Heal (New York: Harper and Row, 1979), 294.

30 Quoted in Marjorie Hunter, "Ford Isn't Running but Won't Bar Race," New York Times, April 22, 1979.

31 Jones, "Nominating 'Carter's Favorite Opponent,'" 74.

32 White, America in Search of Itself, 241.

33 Barone, Our Country, 588.

CHAPTER 3 THE RACE FOR THE NOMINATIONS

1 Quoted in Theodore H. White, America in Search of Itself: The Making of the President, 1956–1980 (New York: Warner Books, 1982), 276.

2 David Farber, Taken Hostage: The Iran Hostage Crisis and America's First Encounter with Radical Islam (Princeton, N.J.: Princeton University Press, 2005), 152.

3 White, America in Search of Itself, 278.

4 Ronald Reagan, An American Life (New York: Simon and Schuster, 1990), 211.

5 Lou Cannon and William Peterson, "GOP," in The Pursuit of the Presidency 1980, ed. Richard Harwood (New York: Berkley Books, 1980), 137.

6 Quoted in Jonathan Moore, ed., The Campaign for President: 1980 in Retrospect (Cambridge, Mass.: Ballinger, 1981), 99.

7 Reagan, An American Life, 211.

8 Gerald Carmen, telephone interview with the author, February 10, 2005.

9 Reagan, An American Life, 213.

10 Richard Wirthlin, telephone interview with the author, April 12, 2005.

11 Gerald Carmen, telephone interview with the author, February 10, 2005.

12 Quoted in Moore, The Campaign for President, 124.

13 Quoted in ibid., 123.

14 Lou Cannon, Governor Reagan: His Rise to Power (New York: Public Affairs, 2003), 472–473.

15 Michael J. Robinson, "The Media in 1980: Was the Message the Message?" in *The American Elections of 1980*, ed. Austin Ranney (Washington, D.C.: American Enterprise Institute, 1981), 204.

16 Tom Wicker, "Kennedy vs. Anderson," *New York Times*, March 14, 1980; Max Lerner, *Ted and the Kennedy Legend* (New York: St. Martin's Press, 1980), 181.

17 McCarthy's votes exceeded Gerald Ford's plurality by about 39,000 in Oregon, 8,000 in Iowa, 6,000 in Maine, and 1,000 in Oklahoma.

18 Elizabeth Drew, *Portrait of an Election* (New York: Simon and Schuster, 1981), 178.

19 Burton Hersh, *The Shadow President* (South Royalton, Vt.: Steerforth Press, 1997), 51.

20 Quoted in Moore, *The Campaign for President*, 156.

21 Adam Clymer, *Edward M. Kennedy: A Biography* (New York: Morrow, 1999), 315.

22 Drew, *Portrait of an Election*, 223.

23 Clymer, *Edward M. Kennedy*, 315.

24 Quoted in *Congressional Quarterly's Guide to U.S. Elections*, 2nd ed. (Washington, D.C.: Congressional Quarterly, 1985), 141.

25 Quoted in *Congressional Quarterly's Guide to U.S. Elections*, 142.

26 Drew, *Portrait of an Election*, 251–252.

27 Quoted in ibid, 249–251.

28 Jimmy Carter, "Remarks Accepting the Presidential Nomination at the 1980 Democratic National Convention," August 14, 1980, http://www.4president. org/speeches/carter1980convention.htm.

29 Robinson, "The Media in 1980," 205.

30 Delegates received on the decisive ballot was the standard used through 1976 in New York and through 1968 in Pennsylvania. Primary votes have been used since.

CHAPTER 4 THE GENERAL ELECTION

1 Elizabeth Drew, *Portrait of an Election: The 1980 Presidential Campaign* (New York: Simon and Schuster, 1981), 158.

2 Albert R. Hunt, "The Campaign and the Issues," in *The American Elections of 1980*, ed. Austin Ranney (Washington, D.C.: American Enterprise Institute, 1981), 147.

3 Jimmy Carter, *Keeping Faith: Memoirs of a President* (New York: Bantam Books, 1982), 569.

4 Hunt, "The Campaign and the Issues," 161.

5 Quoted in Jonathan Moore, ed., *The Campaign for President: 1980 in Retrospect* (Cambridge, Mass.: Ballinger, 1981), 233.

6 Jack W. Germond and Jules Witcover, *Blue Smoke and Mirrors: How Reagan Won and Why Carter Lost the Election of 1980* (New York: Viking Press, 1981), 238.

7 Carter, *Keeping Faith*, 542.

8 Hunt, "The Campaign and the Issues," 150.

9 Lyn Nofziger, telephone interview with the author, February 8, 2005.

10 Quoted in Drew, *Portrait of an Election*, 178.

11 Debate transcript, Commission on Presidential Debates, http://www.debates.org/pages/trans80a.html.

12 Carter, *Keeping Faith*, 561.

13 Drew, *Portrait of an Election*, 310.

14 Carter, *Keeping Faith*, 555, 564.

15 Ronald Reagan, *An American Life* (New York: Simon and Schuster, 1991), 220–221.

16 Richard Wirthlin, telephone interview with the author, April 12, 2005.

17 Hamilton Jordan, *Crisis: The Last Year of the Carter Presidency* (New York: G. P. Putnam's Sons, 1982), 352.

18 All subsequent debate quotes are from the debate transcript, Commission on Presidential Debates, http://www.debates.org/pages/trans80b.html.

19 Carter, *Keeping Faith*, 565.

20 Jordan, *Crisis*, 358.

21 Richard Wirthlin, telephone interview with the author, April 12, 2005.

22 Reagan, *An American Life*, 222.

23 Carter, *Keeping Faith*, 570.

24 Most of the data that follow are from *New York Times* exit polls and Gallup postelection polls. The data on ethnic voters are drawn from NBC exit polls as discussed in Theodore H. White, *America in Search of Itself: The Making of the President, 1956–1980* (New York: Warner Books, 1982), 414.

25 Seymour Martin Lipset and Earl Raab, "The Election and the Evangelicals," *Commentary*, March 1981, 30.

26 Herbert E. Alexander, *Financing the 1980 Election* (Lexington, Mass.: Lexington Books, 1983), 115.

27 Carter, *Keeping Faith*, 542.

28 Drew, *Portrait of an Election*, 304.

29 White, *America in Search of Itself*, 394.

30 Jody Powell, *The Other Side of the Story* (New York: Morrow, 1984), 275–289, esp. 287.

31 Gerald M. Pomper, "The Presidential Election," in *The Election of 1980*, ed. Gerald M. Pomper (Chatham, N.J.: Chatham House, 1981), 85.

32 Quoted in Hunt, "The Campaign and the Issues," 167.

33 William C. Adams, "Media Power in Presidential Elections: An Exploratory Analysis, 1960–1980," in *Television Coverage of the 1980 Presidential Campaign*, ed. William C. Adams (Norwood, N.J.: Ablex, 1983), 180–181.

34 Jonathan Alter, "Rooting for Reagan," *Washington Monthly*, January 1981, 12–17.

35 Michael J. Robinson, "The Media in 1980: Was the Media the Message?" in Ranney, *The American Elections of 1980*, 177–211; see also Michael J. Robinson and Margaret A. Sheehan, *Over the Wire and on TV: CBS and UPI in Campaign '80* (New York: Russell Sage Foundation, 1983), 100, 129, 135, 138.

36 Patrick H. Caddell, "The Democratic Strategy and Its Electoral Consequences," in *Party Coalitions in the 1980s*, ed. Seymour Martin Lipset (San Francisco: Institute for Contemporary Studies, 1981), 286.

37 Robert G. Kaiser, "Reading Tea Leaves," *Washington Post*, November 9, 1980.

38 Caddell, "The Democratic Strategy," 289–290.

39 William Schneider, "The November 4 Vote for President: What Did It Mean?" in Ranney, *The American Elections of 1980*, 224–225.

40 Drew, *Portrait of an Election*, 345.

41 Quoted in Moore, *The Campaign for President*, 253.

42 Quoted in Germond and Witcover, *Blue Smoke and Mirrors*, 319.

43 See James E. Campbell and James C. Garand, eds., *Before the Vote: Forecasting American National Elections* (Thousand Oaks, Calif.: Sage, 2000).

44 White, *America in Search of Itself*, 391.

45 James L. Sundquist and Richard M. Scammon, "The 1980 Election: Profile and Historical Perspective," in *A Tide of Discontent: The 1980 Elections and Their Meaning*, ed. Ellis Sandoz and Cecil V. Crabb Jr. (Washington, D.C.: Congressional Quarterly Press, 1981), 21.

46 Lyn Nofziger, telephone interview with the author, February 8, 2005.

47 Richard Wirthlin, telephone interview with the author, April 12, 2005.

48 Schneider, "The November 4 Vote," 247.

49 Moore, *The Campaign for President*, 195.

50 Pomper, "The Presidential Election," 91.

51 William G. Mayer, *The Changing American Mind: How and Why American Public Opinion Changed between 1960 and 1988* (Ann Arbor: University of Michigan Press, 1992), 318.

52 Schneider, "The November 4 Vote," 241–248.

53 Paul R. Abramson, John H. Aldrich, and David W. Rohde, *Change and Continuity in the 1980 Elections* (Washington, D.C.: Congressional Quarterly Press, 1982), 155 and, generally, chapters 6 and 7.

54 Everett Carll Ladd, "The Reagan Phenomenon and Public Attitudes toward Government," in *The Reagan Presidency and the Governing of America*, ed. Lester M. Salamon and Michael S. Lund (Washington, D.C.: Urban Institute Press, 1984), 230. See also Daniel Yankelovich, "When Reaganomics Fails, Then What?" in the same volume.

55 Richard Harwood, "October," in *The Pursuit of the Presidency 1980*, ed. Richard Harwood (New York: Berkley Books, 1980), 310.

56 Bill Prochnau, "Epilogue," in Harwood, *The Pursuit of the Presidency 1980*, 327.

CHAPTER 5 CONGRESSIONAL AND STATE ELECTIONS

1 Charles W. Hucker, "Senators Stockpile Campaign Money Early," *Congressional Quarterly Weekly Report*, July 28, 1979, 1539.

2 Elizabeth Drew, *Portrait of an Election: The 1980 Presidential Campaign* (New York: Simon and Schuster, 1981), 18.

3 Irwin B. Arieff, "Reduced Influence in House Seen for GOP's Rep. Bauman," *Congressional Quarterly Weekly Report*, October 11, 1980, 3104.

4 *Congress and the Nation*, vol. 5, *1977–1980* (Washington, D.C.: Congressional Quarterly Press, 1981), 16.

5 David S. Broder, "The Post Survey," *Washington Post*, October 5, 1980.

6 Richard E. Cohen, "A Chairmanship No Longer Guarantees a Lengthy Career in Congress," *National Journal*, October 25, 1980, 1795.

7 Quoted in Jonathan Moore, ed., *The Campaign for President: 1980 in Retrospect* (Cambridge, Mass.: Ballinger, 1981), 196–197.

8 Quoted in Christopher Buchanan, "Convention Unity, Polls Boost GOP's Congressional Hopes," *Congressional Quarterly Weekly Report*, July 19, 1980, 2010.

9 Quoted in Buchanan, "Convention Unity," 2009.

10 Quoted in Martin Tolchin, "Reagan and Others in G.O.P. Vow to Be Unified if They Control Congress," *New York Times*, September 16, 1980.

11 Quoted in Helen Dewar, "Iowa Liberal Culver Rejects Bending to Conservative Winds," *Washington Post*, July 9, 1980.

12 "Californian Reagan, Heading for Sweep, Rounds Up Western States," *Washington Post*, November 5, 1980.

13 Marjorie Hunter, "Democrats Keep Control of the House; 4 Major Committee Chairmen Defeated," *New York Times*, November 6, 1980.

14 See Irwin B. Arieff, "Jenrette Is Second Member of Congress Convicted in Abscam Trial," *Congressional Quarterly Weekly Report*, October 11, 1980, 3103.

15 Thomas E. Mann and Norman J. Ornstein, "The Republican Surge in Congress," in *The American Elections of 1980*, ed. Austin Ranney (Washington, D.C.: American Enterprise Institute, 1981), 296.

16 Albert R. Hunt, "The Campaign and the Issues," in Ranney, *The American Elections of 1980*, 172.

17 Charles E. Jacob, "The Congressional Elections," in *The Election of 1980: Reports and Interpretations*, ed. Gerald M. Pomper (Chatham, N.J.: Chatham House, 1981), 126.

18 Paul R. Abramson, John H. Aldrich, and David W. Rohde, *Change and Continuity in the 1980 Elections*, rev. ed. (Washington, D.C.: Congressional Quarterly Press, 1983), 222.

19 Mann and Ornstein, "The Republican Surge in Congress," 297–298.

20 Abramson, Aldrich, and Rohde, *Change and Continuity in the 1980 Elections*, 221.

21 Jacob, "The Congressional Elections," 120; also Gerald M. Pomper, "The Presidential Election," in Pomper, *The Election of 1980*, 91.

22 Neil MacNeil, "The New Conservative House of Representatives," in *A Tide of Discontent: The 1980 Elections and Their Meaning*, edited by Ellis Sandoz and Cecil V. Crabb Jr. (Washington, D.C.: Congressional Quarterly Press, 1981), 75.

23 Mann and Ornstein, "The Republican Surge in Congress," 294.

24 Abramson, Aldrich, and Rohde, *Change and Continuity in the 1980 Elections*, 204–205.

25 Arthur H. Miller and Martin P. Wattenberg, "Politics from the Pulpit: Religiosity and the 1980 Elections," *Public Opinion Quarterly* 48 (1984): 301–317.

CHAPTER 6 THE RETURN OF CONFIDENCE

1 Roger H. Davidson and Walter J. Oleszek, "Changing the Guard in the U.S. Senate," *Legislative Studies Quarterly* 9, no. 4 (November 1984): 639.

2   Hugh Heclo, "Ronald Reagan and the American Public Philosophy," in *The Reagan Presidency: Pragmatic Conservatism and Its Legacies*, ed. W. Elliott Brownlee and Hugh Davis Graham (Lawrence: University Press of Kansas, 2003), 18.

3   In the same way, Herbert Hoover had anticipated much of the early New Deal with the Reconstruction Finance Corporation and a variety of regulatory schemes. Progressive hagiography aside, Franklin Roosevelt did not so much reverse his predecessor as extend and rationalize him, embracing the progressive Hoover and leaving behind the limited-government Hoover.

4   Richard Reeves, "The Ideological Election," *New York Times Magazine*, February 19, 1984, 29.

5   Richard Nathan, "Institutional Change under Reagan," in *Perspectives on the Reagan Years*, ed. John L. Palmer (Washington, D.C.: Urban Institute Press, 1986), 122–123.

6   Richard Neustadt, *Presidential Power and the Modern Presidents: The Politics of Leadership from Roosevelt to Reagan* (New York: Free Press, 1990), 269.

7   Larry J. Sabato, *The Party's Just Begun: Shaping Political Parties for America's Future* (Glenview, Ill.: Scott Foresman, 1988), 60–61.

8   Earl and Merle Black, *The Rise of Southern Republicans* (Cambridge, Mass.: Belknap Press, 2002).

9   Ronald Brownstein, "GOP Has Lock on South, and Democrats Can't Find Key," *Los Angeles Times*, December 15, 2004.

10 Benjamin Ginsberg and Martin Shefter, "The Presidency, Interest Groups, and Social Forces," in *The Presidency and the Political System*, ed. Michael Nelson (Washington, D.C.: Congressional Quarterly Press, 1990).

11 "America Votes 2004: Election Results," *CNN.com*, http://www.cnn.com/ELECTION/2004/pages/results/states/US/P/00/epolls.0.html (accessed November 2004). This cohort, representing 29 percent of the electorate, gave Bush 53 percent of their votes; voters over age sixty gave Bush a slightly bigger percentage (54 percent) but made up only 24 percent of all voters.

12 William Schneider, "The November 4 Vote for President: What Did It Mean?" in *The American Elections of 1980*, ed. Austin Ranney (Washington, D.C.: American Enterprise Institute, 1981), 261.

13 Bert A. Rockman, "Cutting with the Grain: Is There a Clinton Leadership Legacy?" in *The Clinton Legacy*, ed. Colin Campbell and Bert A. Rockman (Chatham, N.J.: Chatham House, 1999), 293.

14 Bill Keller, "Reagan's Son," *New York Times Magazine*, January 26, 2003, 26–31, 42–44, 62.

15 John W. Sloan, *The Reagan Effect: Economics and Presidential Leadership* (Lawrence: University Press of Kansas, 1999), 20.

16 Walter Williams, *Reaganism and the Death of Representative Democracy* (Washington, D.C.: Georgetown University Press, 2003), 1–2.

17 Ronald Reagan, *An American Life* (New York: Simon and Schuster, 1990), 335.

18 Aaron Wildavsky, *The Beleaguered Presidency* (New Brunswick, N.J.: Transaction Press, 1991), 213.

19 Marc Landy and Sidney M. Milkis, *Presidential Greatness* (Lawrence: University Press of Kansas, 2000), 219.
20 Stephen Skowronek, *The Politics Presidents Make: Leadership from John Adams to George Bush* (Cambridge, Mass.: Belknap Press, 1993).
21 David R. Mayhew, *Electoral Realignment* (New Haven, Conn.: Yale University Press, 2003).

BIBLIOGRAPHIC ESSAY

A story of this sort can only be adequately told by reference to a wide range of sources. Consequently, this book draws on journalism, history, political science, biography, memoirs, and original documentary evidence.

Original journalistic accounts often lack context or perspective, but they are invaluable for coming to grips with both the details of the race and contemporary events and analysis. Easily accessed sources include the *New York Times, Wall Street Journal,* and *Washington Post* newspapers and *Time, Newsweek,* and *U.S. News and World Report* magazines. More-specialized political journals include *Congressional Quarterly Weekly Report,* and the *National Journal.* Books by political reporters are another sort of journalistic source. These are filled with details and analysis that improve on contemporary newspaper and magazine articles in two ways: First, they include many details from inside the campaigns that are given in confidence and so cannot be reported until after election day. Second, because these books are written after an election, they present a more coherent story and better-grounded analysis. Three such books were particularly useful: Elizabeth Drew's *Portrait of an Election: The 1980 Presidential Campaign* (New York: Simon and Schuster, 1981), Theodore H. White's *America in Search of Itself: The Making of the President 1956–1980* (New York: Warner Books, 1982), and a collection of essays by *Washington Post* reporters, edited by Richard Harwood, entitled *The Pursuit of the Presidency 1980* (New York: Berkley Books, 1980). The Harwood volume includes a useful appendix with election data. Jack W. Germond and Jules Witcover also published a journalistic account, *Blue Smoke and Mirrors: How Reagan Won and Why Carter Lost the Election of 1980* (New York: Viking Press, 1981). In a similar vein, *Congressional Quarterly* published a volume of *Congress and the Nation,* volume 5, *1977–80* (Washington, D.C.: Congressional Quarterly Press, 1981), a comprehensive summary of congressional and presidential legislative activity during the Carter administration.

The memoirs of key participants can provide an inside view of the campaign and its context. They can also be highly selective and even self-serving. The two most important memoirs, of course, are those of President Carter (*Keeping Faith: Memoirs of a President* [New York: Bantam Books, 1982]) and Ronald Reagan (*An American Life* [New York: Simon and Schuster, 1991]). Although both contain interesting tidbits, both focus on governing rather than campaigning. Neither treats the 1980 campaign at great length, though Carter's memoirs are more detailed and are also useful for understanding the Carter presidency, which was so much at issue in the election. *Looking Forward* (New York: Doubleday, 1987), published by George H. W. Bush with Vic Gold in 1987, gives Bush's account of his political career to that date, including the 1980 election.

Perhaps the best book featuring inside campaign participants is *The Campaign for President: 1980 in Retrospect* (Cambridge, Mass.: Ballinger, 1981), edited by Jonathon Moore. This book features the transcripts of seven roundtable discussions held in December 1980 among key figures in the primary and general election campaigns, primarily pollsters, consultants, and strategists. It also includes an insightful introduction by the editor and an appendix containing primary and general election statistics and a campaign chronology. *Why Reagan Won: A Narrative History of the Conservative Movement, 1964–1981* (Chicago: Regnery, 1981) by F. Clifton White and William J. Gill traces the rise of both the conservative movement and Reagan himself and contains several chapters on 1980. White directed the "draft Goldwater" effort in 1963–1964 and was active in the Reagan campaign in 1980. Two more Reagan campaign accounts come from Martin Anderson, who devotes part of *Revolution* (New York: Harcourt, 1988) to the formulation of the campaign's economic plan, and Edwin Meese III, whose book *With Reagan: The Inside Story* (Washington, D.C.: Regnery Gateway, 1992) addresses some of the campaign's inside politics. On the Carter side are Hamilton Jordan's *Crisis: The Last Year of the Carter Presidency* (New York: G. P. Putnam's Sons, 1982), written in the form of a diary, and Jody Powell's *The Other Side of the Story* (New York: Morrow, 1984). Both Richard Wirthlin and Patrick Caddell have chapters in *Party Coalitions in the 1980s*, ed. Seymour Martin Lipset (San Francisco: Institute for Contemporary Studies, 1981), discussed further below. Wirthlin also has a book of his own, *The Greatest Communicator: What Ronald Reagan Taught Me about Politics, Leadership, and Life* (Hoboken, N.J.: John Wiley and Sons, 2004), one chapter of which is devoted to the 1980 campaign. In the decade before running for president, John Anderson authored two books that give an insight into his thinking: *Between Two Worlds: A Congressman's Choice* (Grand Rapids, Mich.: Zondervan, 1970) and *Vision and Betrayal in America* (Waco, Tex.: Word Books, 1975).

Only major figures warrant many biographies, but biographies abound for Carter and Reagan and can be found as well for some other figures involved in the 1980 election. The biographies typically feature no more than a chapter or two on the election. Later biographies tend to contain unexpected tidbits, revelations that time finally allowed the participants to disclose.

The official biography for Reagan is *Dutch: A Memoir of Ronald Reagan* (New York: Random House, 1999) by Edmund Morris. If one can get past the unusual presentation, in which Morris constructs a fictional persona for himself as narrator, *Dutch* is an interesting but spare source. There are a number of other biographies of Reagan. Some are generally favorable (*Early Reagan* [New York: William Morrow, 1987] by Anne Edwards, *Reagan: A Political Biography* [San Diego: Viewpoint Books, 1967] by Lee Edwards, and *The Age of Reagan: The Fall of the Old Liberal Order, 1964-1980* [Roseville, Calif.: Forum, 2001] by Steven Hayward, all of which focus on the pre-presidential Reagan, and *When Character Was King: A Story of Ronald Reagan* [New York: Viking, 2001], by Peggy Noonan); some are genuinely neutral (James Pemberton's *Exit with Honor: The Life and Presidency of Ronald Reagan* [Armonk, N.Y.: M. E. Sharpe, 1998], Kenneth Walsh's *Ronald Reagan* [New York: Random House, 1997], and Lou Cannon's *Governor Reagan: His Rise to Power* [New York: Public Affairs, 2003] and *President Reagan: The Role of a Lifetime* [New York: Simon and Schuster, 1991]); some are unfavorable (Ronnie Dugger's *On Reagan: The Man and His Presidency* [New York: McGraw-Hill, 1983] and Gary Wills's *Reagan's America: Innocents at Home* [Garden City, N.Y.: Doubleday, 1987]). Paul Kengor's *God and Ronald Reagan: A Spiritual Life* (New York: Regan Books, 2004) demonstrates the importance of Christian religion to Reagan throughout his life. The most unfavorable biography of Carter was *The Real Jimmy Carter: How Our Worst Ex-President Undermines American Foreign Policy, Coddles Dictators, and Created the Party of Clinton and Kerry* (Chicago: Regnery, 2004) published in 2004 by Steven Hayward. *Jimmy Carter: A Comprehensive Biography from Plains to Postpresidency* (New York: Scribner, 1997) by Carter's long-time confidant Peter G. Bourne is on the other end of the spectrum but contains interesting inside information. Betty Glad wrote a skeptical *Jimmy Carter: In Search of the Great White House* (New York: Norton, 1980) as Carter's reelection effort was coming to a head. In *Jimmy Carter: American Moralist* (Athens: University of Georgia Press, 1996), Kenneth E. Morris looks at his subject from the perspective of the mid-1990s and offers insights into the coalitional and intellectual dilemmas faced by the Carter administration. Dan Ariail and Cheryl Heckler-Feltz assess Carter's "Spiritual Biography," both in and out of the White House, in the highly favorable *The Carpenter's Apprentice The Spiritual Biography of Jimmy Carter* (Grand Rapids, Mich.: Zondarvan, 1996). Other Carter biographies, such as Douglas Brinkley's *The Unfinished Presidency: Jimmy Carter's Journey beyond the White House* (New York: Penguin, 1998) and Rod Troester's *Jimmy Carter as Peacemaker: A Post-Presidential Biography* (Westport, Conn.: Praeger, 1996), focus on Carter's career after his presidency. Not quite a biography, James Fallows's "The Passionless Presidency: The Trouble with Jimmy Carter's Administration" was a scathing close-up portrait of the president that appeared in the *Atlantic Monthly* (May 1979, 33–48, 75–81).

The only other major figures of the 1980 election to warrant a number of biographies were George H. W. Bush and Edward Kennedy. Bush was featured in the campaign biography *George Bush* (New York: Dodd, Mead, 1980) by Nicholas King as well as in Fitzhugh Green's *George Bush* (New York: Hippocrene Books, 1989), Herbert Parmet's *George Bush* (New York: Scribner, 1997), and Tom Wicker's *George Herbert Walker Bush* (New York: Lipper/Viking, 2004). Peter and Rochelle Schweizer's tome *The Bushes: Portrait of a Dynasty* (New York: Doubleday, 2004) weaves the story of George H. W. Bush, his father, and his sons. Kennedy's life has also spawned a number of biographies, including *The Education of Edward Kennedy: A Family Biography* (New York: Morrow, 1972) by Burton Hersh, *Ted and the Kennedy Legend: A Study in Character and Destiny* (New York: St. Martin's Press, 1980) by Max Lerner, *The Last Brother* (New York: Simon and Schuster, 1993) by Joe McGinniss, *The Shadow President: Ted Kennedy in Opposition* (South Royalton, Vt.: Steerforth Press, 1997) by Burton Hersh, and *Edward M. Kennedy: A Biography* (New York: Morrow, 1999) by Adam Clymer. The Clymer version is the least hagiographical and contains the most-interesting details.

Among histories, Michael Barone's *Our Country: The Shaping of America from Roosevelt to Reagan* (New York: Free Press, 1990) contains a short but interesting section on the crisis of 1979 and election of 1980. One favorable history of the Carter administration is *The Carter Presidency: A Re-evaluation* (Manchester, UK: Manchester University Press, 1993), published in 1993 by John Dumbrell. A more neutral scholarly history is Burton I. Kaufman's *The Presidency of James Earl Carter, Jr.* (Lawrence: University Press of Kansas, 1993). For a valuable time line of Jimmy Carter's life and administration, see *James E. Carter, 1924–* (Dobbs Ferry, N.Y.: Oceana, 1981), edited by George J. Lankevich. For a lively review of the generally disastrous 1970s, see David Frum, *How We Got Here: The Decade That Brought You Modern Life (for Better or Worse)* (New York: Basic Books, 2000). Other accounts of the economic distress of the era and of the rise of supply-side economics can be found in *The Seven Fat Years: And How to Do It Again* (New York: Free Press, 1993) by Robert L. Bartley and *The Supply Side Revolution: An Insider's Account of Policymaking in Washington* (Cambridge, Mass.: Harvard University Press, 1984) by Paul Craig Roberts. The Iranian hostage crisis is surveyed by academic historian David Farber in his 2005 book *Taken Hostage: The Iran Hostage Crisis and America's First Encounter with Radical Islam* (Princeton, N.J.: Princeton University Press, 2005) and by journalist David Harris in *The Crisis: The President, the Prophet, and the Shah* (Boston: Little, Brown, 2004). The rise of the conservative movement is surveyed by sources such as William A. Rusher's *The Rise of the Right* (New York: National Review, 1993), George H. Nash's *The Conservative Intellectual Movement in America since 1945* (Wilmington, Del.: Intercollegiate Studies Institute, 1996), and Gilbert Hodgson's *The World Turned Right Side Up: A History of the Conservative Ascendancy in America* (Boston: Houghton Mifflin, 1996). Gary Donaldson's history *Liberalism's Last Hurrah: The Presidential Campaign of 1964* (Armonk, N.Y.: M. E. Sharpe, 2003) focuses on the 1964 election as the apogee of postwar liberalism and the launching pad of Reagan's political career. Rick Perlstein's *Before the Storm: Barry Goldwater and the Unmaking of the American Consensus* (New York: Hill and Wang, 2001) pursues similar themes, while *The Right Nation: Conservative Power in America* (New York: Penguin, 2004), by John Micklethwait and Adrian Woolridge, examines both the rise of conservatism and the tensions among conservatives. The most definitive account of Reagan's 1976 run for the Republican presidential nomination can be found in Craig Shirley's *Reagan's Revolution: The Untold Story of the Campaign That Started It All* (Nashville, Tenn.: Nelson Current, 2005). Matthew Dallek's *The Right Moment: Ronald Reagan's First Victory and the Decisive Turning Point in American Politics* (New York: Free Press, 2000) likewise examines Reagan's pivotal 1966 gubernatorial win.

Political scientists examine a variety of issues that come into play in studying the election of 1980. Some examine Jimmy Carter's relationship to the institution of the presidency. Richard Neustadt's *Presidential Power and the Modern Presidents: The Politics of Leadership from Roosevelt to Reagan* (New York: Free Press, 1990) is something of a classic in political science. Originally published in 1960, it was amended to include presidents through Bill Clinton. The chapter on Carter is enlightening and unflattering. For a comprehensive treatment of the way presidents use their office when running for reelection—a major theme in Carter's renomination drive—see *Presidents as Candidates: Inside the White House for the Presidential Campaign* (New York: Garland, 1997) by Kathryn Dunn Tenpas.

Other political scientists study elections and have much to say about 1980. Austin Ranney edited a collection of essays, entitled *The American Elections of 1980* (Washington, D.C.: American Enterprise Institute, 1981), that included pieces on the nominations, media, the parties, the course of the general election campaign, issues, demographics, and the congressional elections. Similar anthologies include *The Election of 1980: Reports and Interpretations* (Chatham, N.J.: Chatham House, 1981), edited by Gerald Pomper, and *A Tide of Discontent: The 1980 Elections and Their Meaning* (Washington, D.C.: Congressional Quarterly Press, 1981), edited by Ellis Sandoz and Cecil V. Crabb Jr. The former is a bit thin; the latter focuses more than the others on the new political environment brought into being by the election. Another anthology, *The Presidential Election and Transition, 1980–81* (Carbondale: Southern Illinois University Press, 1983), edited by Paul T. David and David H. Everson, covers much of the same ground but includes transition issues. The most thorough examination of voting behavior in 1980 was produced by Paul R. Abramson, John H. Aldrich, and David W. Rohde in *Change and Continuity in the 1980 Election* (Washington, D.C.: Congressional Quarterly Press, 1982). The revised version (Washington, D.C.: Congressional Quarterly Press, 1983) incorporates voting trends from the 1982 midterm elections. The role of ideology in 1980 voting behavior is explored by Douglas A. Hibbs Jr. in "President Reagan's Mandate from the 1980 Elections: A Shift to the Right?" appearing in *American Politics Quarterly* 10, no. 4 (October 1982): 387–420, and Kathleen Knight, "Ideology in the 1980 Election: Ideological Sophistication Does Matter," *Journal of Politics* 47, no. 3 (1985): 828–853. Jane J. Mansbridge argues that it was peace issues, rather than the equal rights amendment, that led to the "gender gap" of 1980 in "Myth and Reality: The ERA and the Gender Gap in the 1980 Election," *Public Opinion Quarterly* 49, no. 2 (1985): 164–178. Other political scientists produced more narrowly focused works, for instance, *Television Coverage of the 1980 Presidential Campaign* (Norwood, N.J.: Ablex, 1983), edited by William C. Adams; *Over the Wire and on TV: CBS and UPI in Campaign '80* (New York: Russell Sage Foundation, 1983), by Michael J. Robinson and Margaret A. Sheehan; and Herbert E. Alexander's *Financing the 1980 Election* (Lexington, Mass.: Lexington Books, 1983), which is by far the most complete compilation of data on that subject.

Yet other political scientists study parties, coalition building, and public opinion. One of the best of these works is Stephen Skowronek's *The Politics Presidents Make: Leadership from John Adams to George Bush* (Cambridge, Mass.: Belknap Press, 1993), which places Carter and Reagan in a framework of coalition politics. Earl and Merle Black, whose work *The Rise of Southern Republicans* (Cambridge, Mass.: Belknap Press, 2002) traces the changing partisan loyalties of the South, include the role of Ronald Reagan in turning the South toward the GOP. Public opinion expert Seymour Martin Lipset edited *Party Coalitions in the 1980s* (San Francisco: Institute for Contemporary Studies, 1981), an early exposition of what the 1980 elections might mean for the parties. An insightful later examination of Ronald Reagan's coalition building can be found in Benjamin Ginsberg and Martin Shefter, "The Presidency, Interest Groups, and Social Forces," in Michael Nelson's volume *The Presidency and the Political System* (Washington, D.C.: Congressional Quarterly Press, 1990). The breakdown of the Democratic coalition is also reviewed by journalists Thomas Byrne Edsall and Mary D. Edsall in their book *Chain Reaction: The Impact of Race, Rights, and Taxes on American Politics* (New York: Norton, 1991) and by political scientists Edward G. Carmines and James A. Stimson in *Issue Evolution: Race and the Transformation of American Politics* (Princeton, N.J.: Princeton University Press, 1989). The 1980 elections spawned considerable literature on the Christian Right and evangelical voters. Robert C. Liebman and Robert Wuthnow edited *The New Christian Right: Mobilization and Legitimation* (Hawthorne, N.Y.: Aldine, 1983), which includes a number of interesting essays. Useful journal articles include Arthur H. Miller and Martin P. Wattenberg, "Politics from the Pulpit: Religiosity and the 1980 Election," *Public Opinion Quarterly* 48 (1984): 301–317; John H. Simpson, "Socio-Moral Issues and Recent Presidential Elections," *Review of Religious Research* 27, no. 2 (December 1985): 115–123; Stephen D. Johnson and Joseph P. Tamney, "The Christian Right and the 1980 Presidential Election," *Journal for the Scientific Study of Religion* 21, no. 2 (1982): 123–131; and Seymour Martin Lipset and Earl Raab, "The Election and the Evangelicals," *Commentary* 71 (March 1981): 25–31. A particularly interesting study of public opinion trends in the 1970s can be found in William G. Mayer's *The Changing American Mind: How and Why American Public Opinion Changed between 1960 and 1988* (Ann Arbor: University of Michigan Press, 1992). Timothy Conlan's *From New Federalism to Devolution: Twenty-Five Years of Intergovernmental Reform* (Washington, D.C.: Brookings Institution, 1998) includes a section tracing shifting public opinion on centralization and federalism. An incisive article examining public attitudes toward government in the 1970s and early 1980s can be found in Robert Y. Shapiro and John M. Gilroy, "The Polls: Regulation—Part I," *Public Opinion Quarterly* 48, no. 2 (Summer 1984): 531–542.

On the so-called October Surprise allegations, see Barbara Honegger's paranoiac *October Surprise* (New York: Tudor, 1989) and Gary Sick's more sober *October Surprise: America's Hostages in Iran and the Election of Ronald Reagan* (New York: Times Books, 1991). See refutations of the allegations in Walter Pincus, "No Proof Found of an 'October Surprise' Plot, House Panel Says," *Washington Post*, January 14, 1993; Neil A. Lewis, "House Inquiry Finds No Evidence of Deal on Hostages in 1980," *New York Times*, January 13, 1993; "October Surprise: Not Guilty," *New York Times*, January 16, 1993; Steven Emerson and Jesse Furman, "The Conspiracy That Wasn't," *New Republic*, November 18, 1991, 164; Steven Emerson, "Gary Sick's Bald-Faced Lies," *American Spectator*, March 1993, 25–28; G. Szamuely, "Desperado Democrats and the Sick Offense," *American Spectator*, July 1991, 15–17; and Michael Ledeen, "Conspiracy Theory," *Commentary* 93 (June 1992): 63–64. More recently, David Farber, *Taken Hostage: The Iran Hostage Crisis and America's First Encounter with Radical Islam* (Princeton, N.J.:

Princeton University Press, 2005), and David Harris, *The Crisis: The President, the Prophet, and the Shah* (New York: Little, Brown, 2004), commented briefly on the allegations but offered nothing new.

A number of sources provided primary data and documentation for this book. These included *Congressional Quarterly's Guide to U.S. Elections*, 2d ed. (Washington, D.C.: Congressional Quarterly Press, 1985), which contained primary and general election statistics; *Official Report of the Proceedings of the Thirty-Second Republican National Convention* (Washington, D.C.: Republican National Committee, 1980); and the *Official Report of the Proceedings of the Democratic National Convention* (Washington, D.C.: Democratic National Committee, 1980). Economic statistics for the era were found in the *Economic Report of the President* published annually by the Council of Economic Advisers. This report can be found in hard copy published by the Government Printing Office or online at http://www.gpoaccess.gov/eop/. Even recent versions contain historical tables with data including the 1970s.

Other useful electronic documentary sources include Web sites where presidential addresses, candidates' acceptance speeches, party platforms, and debate transcripts can be found. These include the Web site of Kenneth Janda, professor of political science at Northwestern University, http://www.janda.org/politxts.html; a Web site devoted to presidential campaigns and candidates at http://www.4president.org; the Web site of the American Presidency Project at the University of California, Santa Barbara, http://www.presidency.ucsb.edu; and the Web site of the Commission on Presidential Debates, http://www.debates.org. The American Museum of the Moving Image offers a view of selected campaign commercials at http://www.ammi.org. The Annenberg Center has compiled a very useful CD-ROM, *The Annenberg/Pew Archive of Presidential Campaign Discourse* (Annenberg School for Communication, University of Pennsylvania, 2000), containing the text of speeches and television advertisements from 1952 to 1996. References to television ads were drawn from this CD-ROM. Finally, appendixes in several books include interesting primary documentation, including internal campaign memos in Elizabeth Drew's *Portrait of an Election: The 1980 Presidential Campaign* (New York: Simon and Schuster, 1981); summary election statistics in Richard Harwood's edited volume *The Pursuit of the Presidency 1980* (New York: Berkley Books, 1980), and Jonathan Moore's edited volume *The Campaign for President: 1980 in Retrospect* (Cambridge, Mass.: Ballinger, 1981); and a time line of campaign events, also in Moore's *Campaign for President*.

Finally, assessments of Ronald Reagan's presidency, and hence of the impact of the 1980 election, are too numerous to list in their entirety. Important academic anthologies coming out during the Reagan presidency included Lester M. Salamon and Michael S. Lund, eds., *The Reagan Presidency and the Governing of America* (Washington, D.C.: Urban Institute Press, 1984); John L. Palmer, ed., *Perspectives on the Reagan Years* (Washington, D.C.: Urban Institute Press, 1986); and Charles O. Jones, ed., *The Reagan Legacy: Promise and Performance* (Chatham, N.J.: Chatham House, 1988). Later works included *The Reagan Pres-*

idency: *Pragmatic Conservatism and Its Legacies* (Lawrence: University Press of Kansas, 2003), a well-done and comprehensive anthology edited by W. Elliott Brownlee and Hugh Davis Graham. Highly critical analyses include Anthony S. Campagna's *The Economy in the Reagan Years: The Economic Consequences of the Reagan Administrations* (Westport, Conn.: Greenwood Press, 1994) and Walter Williams's *Reaganism and the Death of Representative Democracy* (Washington, D.C.: Georgetown University Press, 2003). John W. Sloan's *The Reagan Effect: Economics and Presidential Leadership* (Lawrence: University Press of Kansas, 1999) was a balanced but generally favorable review of Reagan's economic policies. In foreign policy, Peter Schweizer documented the Reagan administration's drive to bring down the Soviet dictatorship in *Victory: The Reagan Administration's Secret Strategy That Hastened the Collapse of the Soviet Union* (New York: Atlantic Monthly Press, 1994) and *Reagan's War: The Epic Story of His Forty-Year Struggle and Final Triumph over Communism* (New York: Doubleday, 2002). Dinesh D'Souza's *Ronald Reagan: How an Ordinary Man Became an Extraordinary Leader* (New York: Free Press, 1997) is a study written by a former White House aide and conservative activist. Much of the policy and political analysis found in chapter 6 was supplied by my *Ronald Reagan and the Politics of Freedom* (Lanham, Md.: Rowman and Littlefield, 2001), and James W. Ceaser's and my *Red over Blue: The 2004 Elections and American Politics* (Lanham, Md.: Rowman and Littlefield, 2005).

Caddell, Patrick, 35, 55, 64, 83, 95,
    100, 115, 120, 121, 124, 132, 134,
    142, 158
California primary, 77, 78, 79
California Proposition 1, 50
California Proposition 13, 25
Calley, William L., Jr., 30
Cambodia, 12, 173
Campaign finance, 92–93, 130–131,
    147–148, 155–156, 158–159, 165
Candidate choice, 138–140
Capitalism, 11
Capitalism and Freedom (Friedman),
    20–21
Capitol Compact, 151
Carey, Hugh, 41, 87
Carmen, Gerald, 66, 68
Carter, Amy, 117
Carter, Billy, 131
Carter, Jimmy, 29–36, 41, 43, 44,
    54–55, 98–100, 175
  abortion issue and, 32–33
  ad campaign of, 99, 101, 114
  American Fighting Man's Day
    and, 30
  on Anderson, 102–103
  vs. Anderson, 75
  "Billygate" and, 86
  call for restraint of, 33
  campaign spending and, 102
  campaign staff of, 100
  campaign strategy of, 92–93, 165
  Carter Doctrine and, 61
  China diplomacy and, 34
  concession call of, 124
  concession speech of, 124–125,
    161–162
  Connally on, 45
  Connecticut primary and, 76
  "crisis of confidence" speech of,
    5–6, 14–15, 56, 164, 178
  "crisis of leadership" and, 37
  Cuba and, 56
  Cuban refugees and, 79
  defeat of, 1–2

  defense spending and, 34
  and Democratic Party, interaction
    with, 178–179
  deregulation and, 34
  disjunction during administration
    of, 32
  early years of, 29
  economic policy of, 173
  Egypt and, 34
  emergency balanced budget
    and, 80
  energy policy of, 8, 33
  equal rights amendment and, 33
  evangelical Christianity and, 33
  federal programs and, 33
  federal regulation and, 33–34
  federal spending and, 10
  Ford, Henry, on, 57
  foreign policy address of, 34
  foreign policy of, 33, 34, 114, 173,
    183, 187
  Georgia Mafia and, 32
  governmental efficiency and, 32
  as governor of Georgia, 29–30
  Habitat for Humanity and, 164
  human rights policy of, 13, 34
  Illinois primary and, 75
  imagination of, failures of, 144
  inaugural address (as governor)
    of, 30
  inflation and, 79
  intraparty challenge to, 35–36, 57
  Iowa debate and, 62
  Iowa primary and, 62, 64–65
  Iran and, 13–14, 34
  Iran hostage crisis and, 58–60,
    78–79, 80, 86, 98, 120–124,
    132, 134
  Israel and, 76
  Israel/Egypt diplomacy and, 34
  Kansas primary and, 77
  "limits to growth" and, 10
  Maine primary and, 69
  vs. McCarthy, 74
  as mean-spirited, 112–113, 132, 133

LaHaye, Beverly, 81
Landy, Marc, 188
Laos, 12
LaRouche, Lyndon, 41
Laxalt, Paul, 48, 82
League of Women Voters, 111–112, 115
Legislative election. *See* Election,
 legislative
Liberalism, 36, 37
 repudiation of philosophical,
 153–154, 169
 in the Supreme Court, and
 disaffection of southerners and
 working-class whites, 17–18
Libya, 185, 187
Limited government, 174–175, 177–
 178, 180
Lincoln, Abraham, 188
Lodge, Henry Cabot, 46
Los Angeles Times, 37
Luce, Clare Booth, 46, 47
Lucey, Patrick, 103
Lugar, Richard, 82

Maddox, Lester, 30
Magnuson, Warren, 149, 151, 153, 155,
 159, 160
Maine primary, 69
Mann, Thomas, 159, 160
Margin of error, 136
Maryland primary, 77
Massachusetts primary, 70, 75
Mathews, Tom, 43, 74
Mayer, William G., 141–142
Mayhew, David R., 189
McCarthy, Eugene, 41, 74, 206n17
McCarthy, Joseph, 21, 72
McGovern, George, 1, 18, 20, 26, 30,
 71, 72, 94, 126, 149, 151, 153,
 159, 161
 as political outsider, 27
McGovern-Fraser Commission, 71
McIntyre, Thomas, 25
Media, 133, 149
 conservatism and, 181–182

Medicaid, 9
Medicare, 9
Meese, Edwin, III, 53, 68
Mengistu Haile Mariam, 12
Men voters, 128. *See also* Voters, in
 election 1980
Meredith, Don, 66
Michigan primary, 70, 73
Middle East, 61
Military spending, 13
Milkis, Sidney, 188
Milliken, William, 73, 97
Minority Rule no. 5, 89
Mises, Ludwig von, 20
Missouri primary, 77
Mondale, Walter, 1, 29, 59, 64, 77, 87,
 92, 102, 114, 125
 postpresidential election (1980)
 career of, 163–164
 resignation of, consideration of,
 2–3, 28
*A Monetary History of the United
 States, 1867–1960* (Friedman), 21
Montana primary, 78
Moral Majority, 23, 106, 115, 151, 153,
 159, 161, 168
Morgan, Robert, 149, 153, 159
Morretti, Bob, 131
Morrison, Susan, 46
Mott, Stewart, 71
Mozambique, 12
Mudd, Roger, 57–58
Muskie, Edmund, 87, 88
Mussolini, Benito, 111

Nashua Telegraph, 66–67
Nathan, Richard, 177
National Conservative Political Action
 Committee (NCPAC), 102, 148,
 151, 153, 160, 161, 168
National Education Association, 88
National health insurance, 89
National Maritime Union, 105
National Organization for Women
 (NOW), 44

Thurmond, Strom, 16, 47, 70, 74, 165
Time magazine, 11
Timmons, William, 101
Tocqueville, Alexis de, 173–174
Truman, Harry S., 57, 126
    civil rights and, 16
    containment of communism
        and, 18
    Fair Deal and, 33

Udall, Morris K., 155
Ullman, Al, 155, 157, 161
Unruh, Jesse, 131
U.S. Department of Education, 88
U.S. Department of Energy, creation
    of, 8
U.S.-Taiwan Mutual Defense Treaty, 34

Vance, Cyrus, 79
Vander Jagt, Guy, 82, 148, 150
Vermont primary, 70, 75
Vietnam War, 18, 30
    antiwar movement and, 18
Viguerie, Richard, 43
Vins, George, 34
Violent crime rate, 14
Volcker, Paul, 170, 173
Voters, in election 1980, 105–108,
    127–128, 179
Voting Rights Act of 1965, 16

Wage and price controls, 6
Walesa, Lech, 106
Wallace, George, 16, 19–20, 30, 31, 74
    as political outsider, 27
Wallace, Henry, 74
Wall Street Journal, 120
Wanniski, Jude, The Way the World
    Works, 21
Washington Post, 54, 149, 189
Wasted vote syndrome, 129

Watergate, 20, 27, 31, 35, 43, 44,
    47, 54
Wattenberg, Ben, 11, 13
    "It's Time to Stop America's
        Retreat," 11
The Way the World Works (Wanniski), 21
Weaver, Richard, 21
Weicker, Lowell, 41
Welfare, 9, 14
Wellstone, Paul, 164
West Virginia primary, 78
Weyrich, Paul, 148, 169
White, John, 159
White, Theodore, 37, 41, 55, 64, 131, 138
White evangelical voters, 106–107,
    179. See also Voters, in election
    1980
Wildavsky, Aaron, 188
Williams, Edward Bennett, 89
Williams, Hosea, 107
Willkie, Wendell, 203–204n19
Wilson, Woodrow, 126
    New Freedom and, 33
    presidency of, pivotal effects of, 188
Wirthlin, Richard, 67–68, 70, 71,
    82, 101, 115, 120, 121, 124, 134,
    139–140, 141
Wisconsin primary, 70, 72, 76–77
Witcover, Jules, 29
Women's issues, 39. See also Abortion
    issue; Equal rights amendment
Women voters, 107, 108, 128. See also
    Voters, in election 1980
Wright, Jim, 155

Yankelovich, Daniel, 143
Yom Kippur War, 6
Young, Andrew, 13
Young Americans for Freedom, 21

Zero-based budgeting, 30